trends
2000

ALSO BY GERALD CELENTE

Trend Tracking

HOW TO PREPARE FOR
AND PROFIT FROM THE CHANGES
OF THE 21ST CENTURY

GERALD CELENTE

WARNER BOOKS

A Time Warner Company

Copyright information continued on page 313.

Warner Books, Inc., 1271 Avenue of the Americas, New York, NY 10020

 A Time Warner Company

Printed in the United States of America

First Printing: January 1997

10   9   8   7   6   5   4   3   2   1

Library of Congress Cataloging-in-Publication Data
Celente, Gerald
    Trends 2000 : how to prepare for and profit from the changes of
the 21st century / Gerald Celente.
        p.   cm.
    Includes index.
    ISBN 0-446-51901-4
    1. Twenty-first century—Forecasts.   I. Title.
CB161.C38   1997
303.49′09′05—dc20   96-20082
                                                            CIP

Text design by Stanley S. Drate/Folio Graphics Co. Inc.

To my loving and wise aunt Phyllis (Zizi).
Thank you Mary Ann for all you gave.

CONTENTS

book three

ACKNOWLEDGMENTS

This book was made possible by the hard work, loyalty, and devotion of the staff and the twenty-five members of the Trends Research Institute. To them my thanks.

Almost from our Institute's inception in 1980, John Anthony West has been a guiding philosophical inspiration. He brought to us a unique combination of skills: literary style, a deep knowledge of ancient wisdom, and a contemporary global awareness. He worked side by side with me writing *Trends 2000*. In addition to his insights, it was his pen that crafted the words and rhythms of this book.

In the spirit of unflagging loyalty and devotion, Gerard Harrington, managing editor of our quarterly *Trends Journal,* Mary Kay Hubert, its graphic designer, and our librarian, Jennifer Krokey, continually give their best so we can produce our best. My thanks also to my hardworking, dedicated, and innovative assistant Julie McKenna, my dear friends and colleagues Dr. Mitchell Skolnick, Gary Abatelli, Bill Hillsman, and my loving friends Nancy Castleman and Marc Eisenson of Good Advice Press who, in keeping with their company's name, always gave good advice—and much, much more when it was most needed. And Tom Milton, who dedicated over a year of his life working with me to write *Trend Tracking,* which helped set the stage for this book.

I am most grateful for the vision and support of Joann Davis, Executive Editor and Vice President of Warner Books. Thanks to her, our vision of the new millennium sees the light of print. Her guidance, insights, and critical analyses were invaluable. And to Harvey-Jane Kowal, Executive Managing Editor, for her highly professional management of the book's production.

And thank you John Perkins, my teacher in close-combat self-defense; my gratitude for his friendship and spiritual support over the years, as well as his true warrior wisdom.

Only connect.

—E. M. FORSTER

book
one

1

MILLENNIUM FEVER

COUNTDOWN 2000

It's January 1, 2000. The world has just celebrated the greatest New Year's Eve party in recorded history. Even cultures that follow a different calendar were reveling in the streets. They were celebrating in Tokyo, Shanghai, Delhi, and Mombasa. But unlike New Year's parties of the past, they didn't wait till December thirty-first to hit the streets. The party had been going full blast since Christmas. The entire world had been psyching itself up for this blowout since 1995—when the symptoms of Millennium Fever were first diagnosed.

Almost no one has escaped the fever (a global anxiety, a mix of dread and hope). But the fever breaks on January 1, 2000. The party's over. The most highly touted predictions have not come to pass.

THE DOOMSDAY SCHOOL

Since 1995, the momentum of religious fanaticism has carried its fears into all kinds of unexpected places. Many people who seemed sober and rational have joined ranks with the prophets of doom preaching the end of the world. No segment of society has escaped. You know them yourself; friends, family, scientists, teachers, business leaders, politicians—all have become fervent Armageddonites.

But the people caught up in this aren't necessarily all religious fanatics. When you look at the events going on in the world around you on January 1, 2000, you can see there is good reason to fear.

The civil war in Russia that began in earnest in 1994 rages throughout the former Soviet Union. Europe has moved from recession to depression, inflaming widespread racism against immigrants. There is saber rattling from Germany as the war in the Balkans spills over its borders. Islamic anti-imperialism has jelled into a mass movement—a holy war, a crusade against the West.

Africa is being decimated by a new plague far more infectious than AIDS, fueling a mass exodus of people with nowhere to go. Inner-city America is at the boiling point and has already exploded into half a dozen wild rampages.

The American educational system is disintegrating, putting millions of unsupervised juveniles on the streets. Within the increasingly hard-pressed university systems, students are again in revolt—this time against a futureless future and an irrelevant curriculum.

The corporate downsizing trend of the nineties has worked its way into government and millions more are jobless.

But even with an increase in nuclear terrorism and nuclear accidents, the world has not come to an end; nor has the great cosmic collision occurred. The world has not gone down in flames or up in smoke.

Armageddon hasn't happened. But neither has the Age of Aquarius.

I SURVIVED 2000

Millennium Fever has not been all gloom and doom. Ever since Woodstock 1969, when the seeds of the New Age trend were sown, eager enthusiasts have been scanning the papers and consulting the stars, convinced that the spiritual New Age of Aquarius, a 2,160-year era of peace, wisdom, and group effort would soon prevail.

The papers on January 1, 2000, make it clear that it hasn't yet.

But just as Armageddonites can justify their fears by events, so Aquarians can justify their hopes by a mood. There is a strange elation threading through the chaos and disruption all over the world. The first signs of the renaissance that will shape the new millennium are unmistakable.

You watch destiny unfold even as society unravels.

The year 2000 marks the end of the Industrial Age— which does not lead to a postindustrial age (business as usual with fancier technology); it leads to the Global Age. The predicted paradigm of new thought has become a reality. The doctrines of the Industrial Age are being replaced by a Globalnomic philosophy. The trend is in its early growth stage.

What has changed are *ideas*. When ideas change, everything changes.

The study and practice of ancient wisdom and values have become a matter of passionate world interest as new discoveries bear out the truth of old legends. Medicine has incorporated alternative therapies on a massive scale, fusing the magic of the past with the science of the present. Forward-thinking businesses are no longer purely profit-driven; they are practicing a new form of compassionate capitalism. The profound search for the spiritual is producing a religious revival. From families to fashion, from food to sex, the flower power of sixties thought is bearing fruit in 2000.

EXTREMISM AT THE CENTER— THE LUNATIC MIDDLE

At both extremes, the "lunatic fringe" presents plausible scenarios. With good reasons to fear and good reasons to hope, there is every reason for confusion. To make matters worse, ever since Millennium Fever was first identified back in 1995, there has been a counter campaign to discredit the diagnosis. Special interests, intent upon preserving the intellectual, political, and economic status quo that shaped the Industrial Age, dismissed Millennium Fever as a figment of inflamed public imagination.

Business leaders, politicians, a corps of academic "experts," and scientists, with astronomers at the forefront, have insisted that the millennium has no meaning. It is just a number applied to a date. Sociologists and psychologists (feverishly) attribute the fever to mass hysteria, or media-induced suggestion. They claim that an unsuspecting and naïve public is being manipulated by irresponsible commercial interests.

On television, in the papers, over the Internet, they advertise a wonder drug to cure the insidious but imaginary virus responsible for the fever. They call it "Reason."

Get Reason shots and immunize yourself. Apply Reason and you will see that underneath the emotional turmoil and obvious change, it is still business as usual. Progress marches on. Sure there is war, poverty, pollution, famine, and crime; there has always been. These are the growing pains of progress. It is a price that has to be paid.

As the world wakes up on January 1, 2000, it is increasingly clear that the call to reason is coming from the lunatic middle. Everything *has* changed. The fever is real.

Both Cassandra and Pollyanna, in their own ways, have been in tune with the times; it was Miss America who was out of sync.

THE TREND TRACKERS GUIDE TO THE MILLENNIUM

This book is intended to guide you through the times to come: out of the twentieth century and into the first decades of the new millennium. Though we are certain the United States, along with the rest of the world, will be going through increasingly troubled times in the immediate future, this is emphatically not a gloom-and-doom book. There is light at the end of the tunnel. Powerful positive countertrends are already surfacing and visible, or more often, still hidden but bubbling beneath the surface. There is a very real global Renaissance in store. It is the unrecognized clash between the disruptive forces of the dying Industrial Age and the subtler constructive forces of the renaissance to come that produce the ferment we call Millennium Fever.

But you don't have to be consumed by the fever. You don't have to feel betrayed and confused. It is possible to understand Millennium Fever for what it is. It is also possible to determine and act upon the trends that are shaping today, and that will shape the new millennium. With this knowledge, you can position yourself to survive the coming chaos intact, to avoid the worst dangers and to take advantage of the many foreseeable opportunities arising.

By taking to heart the picture that will be drawn in these pages, you will be in a position to ride out the tempest, to prosper within it, both materially and spiritually, and finally to participate in the exhilaration of Millennium Fever without succumbing to it.

2

THE MEANING OF
THE MILLENNIUM

A NEW AGE

The turn of a century is a time to celebrate, think back, look
ahead, make predictions, and issue pronouncements.

> The Century is dead; long live the Century! . . . The lights
> flashed, crowds sang, the sirens of craft in the harbor
> screeched and roared, bells pealed, bombs thundered, rock-
> ets blazed skyward, and the new century made its trium-
> phant entry. . . .
>
> Tonight when the clock strikes twelve, the present century
> will have come to an end. We look back upon it as a cycle
> of time within which the achievements in science and in civi-
> lization are not less than marvelous.
>
> The advance of the human race during the past one hun-
> dred years has not been equalled by the progress of man
> within any of the preceding ages.
>
> The possibilities of the future for mankind are the subjects
> of hope and imagination. . . .
>
> On this occasion, which is one of solemnity, I express the
> earnest wish that the rights of the individual man shall con-

tinue to be regarded as sacred, and that the crowning glory of the coming century shall be the lifting up of the burdens of the poor, the annihilation of all misery and wrong, and that the peace and goodwill which the angels proclaimed shall rest on contending nations as the snowflakes upon the land.

Thus, the twentieth century was issued in by the *New York Times:* all advances in learning and achievements in science and possibilities for the future; no World War I, no World War II, no Hiroshima, no gulags, no death camps, no toxic wastes, and the peace and goodwill falling like snowflakes . . . or fallout.

The twenty-first century comes at us with "official" proclamations and visions of the future no less surrealistic.

But this time, there is a difference. There is something special about this year 2000. It is not just the turn of another century, or even ten centuries making up a millennium, three zeros instead of just two. (Actually, the new millennium starts on January 1, 2001. The year 2000 represents the last year of the twentieth century. But the big celebration takes place on New Year's Eve December 31, 1999, and we will be using 2000 as our reference point.)

What is important is not one year rather than the other, but that worldwide fever, that sense of impending change.

Certainly there is nothing in modern science to account for it. On the other hand, it may be that ancient science provides a clue.

THE PRECESSION

To the ancients, a phenomenon called the "precession of the equinoxes" was a matter of gravest concern.

Due to a "wobble" of the Earth on its own axis (like a spinning top that wobbles as it slows down), the Earth very slowly changes its relationship to the great circle of the heavens, the familiar zodiac.

Each morning, the sun rises against the backdrop of a constellation, or astronomical/astrological sign. This backdrop is actually constant, but due to the wobble of the Earth, the zodiac appears to move backward. The zodiacal sign against which the sun rises shifts, or "precesses," very gradually.

Over the course of 25,920 years, the sun at the equinox (about March 22 and September 22) "precesses" or moves backward through the entire cycle of twelve astrological signs.

This is what is responsible for the so-called Ages. It takes one-twelfth of 25,920 years, or 2,160 years, for the sun to precess or move backward through one sign. So, the Age of Taurus is followed by the Age of Aries, and then by the Age of Pisces, and so on.

At the moment, the sun rises against the last degrees of the sign of Pisces. Soon, it will rise against or "in" the sign of Aquarius, signaling the dawn of the Age of Aquarius.

To believers of the "New Age," this is an event of real significance. In fact, the term *New Age* has taken hold because astronomically speaking it will be a new age.

This is an astronomical fact. To astronomers, however, this is a fact without significance. The constellations making up the zodiac are light-years away, and there is no known force or energy or influence that physically distinguishes one age from another.

This raises an interesting question. Since modern science can detect no measurable physical effect from the precession, why should the ancients have ascribed any importance to it at all?

The precession is not like a full eclipse of the sun—a bizarre, dramatic event understandably striking terror in the superstitious heart. There is nothing outwardly dramatic about the precession. Just to discover it means that a very careful observational astronomy has to be in place, extend-

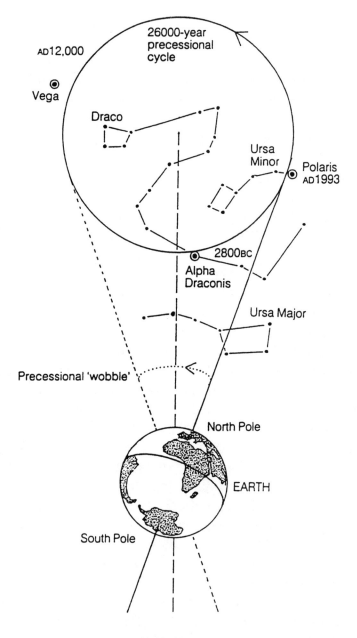

PRECESSION

ing over long periods of time (it takes seventy-two years for the equinox to precess just one degree).

Why should these ancient and careful scientific observers have placed so much importance in this barely detectable phenomenon? Initially, it was believed that the Greek scholar Hipparchus discovered the precession in the second century B.C. But more advanced scholarship demonstrates that the precession was known by civilizations preceding the Greeks by thousands of years. Moreover, knowledge of the precession is written into the mythology and legends of tribal and traditional peoples who have no present knowledge of astronomy at all. How could they have acquired such knowledge?

In this mysterious star lore, handed down over thousands of years, the shift from one age to another was a matter of grave concern, and was attended by miraculous signs (the Star of Bethlehem is the best known, signaling the advent of Pisces—a symbol of early Christianity was the fish). The ancients also believed the precession was accompanied by cataclysmic earth changes (earthquakes, floods, volcanic eruptions), as well as drastic upheavals in human civilization. There is a certain amount of provocative historical support for these beliefs. (*Hamlet's Mill; Fingerprints of the Gods; When the Sky Fell;* and *The Orion Mystery* are just a few of the books devoted to the evidence.)

Did the ancients know something of consequence that modern science has been unable to detect?

We are moving into a new precessional age. That is certain. Maybe it's just a coincidence that we seem to be going through a period of tumult, chaos, and change like that traditionally ascribed to the transition from one age to another. On the other hand, maybe it's not just coincidence. Maybe the ancients knew what they were talking about.

Perhaps that is why Millennium Fever has not been confined to the Western Christian world, reckoning its centuries from the birth of Jesus some two thousand years ago. And maybe it is the precession (or at least belief in the power of the precession) that has provoked the riotous celebrations in Tokyo, Shanghai, Delhi, Mombasa, and the rest of the world, among peoples using different calendars.

THE YEAR 2000

We must leave it to the science of the future to determine whether there is any validity to the power of the precession.

Formally, scientifically, astronomically, the year 2000 means nothing at the moment. But symbolically, emotionally, psychologically, it represents a turning point—the fulcrum upon which the new millennium moves. Emotions and psychology are also real, and the symbol represents and embodies realities.

Here and now, we can say with total certainty that the fever is real; the changes are real.

The year 2000 is not to be taken too literally.

We use the year 2000 as a convenient reference point. Millennium Fever has everyone talking 2000. Nevertheless, as a general rule, short of a sudden global cataclysm, changes, however dramatic, take place over the course of time.

These changes are the trends identified and studied by the Trends Research Institute. Tracking trends is a way of seeing where we are, how we got there, and where we're going. And all trends go through a life cycle. Indeed, everything that lives obeys the same organic process. Galaxies, nebulae, star systems, planets, species, and individuals are all subject to the same organic cycle. Everything is seeded, or fertilized, gestates, is born, grows, matures, ages, and dies. A trend is no different, and like organic life, any given trend is subject to the same vicissitudes, not all of them predictable. It is not always possible to forecast the exact speed at which important trends will pass through their life cycle, or interact with one another.

Some of the trends we forecast will just be born by 2000, others will be already maturing, others may still be in time's womb. But the seeds have all been planted. Most, if not all, will see the light of day and run through their life cycles over the course of the decades to come.

For example, it is certain the trend toward the destruction of the environment is leading to massive national and global health problems. But it is impossible to apply exact numbers to the casualties, or to forecast how long it will take to begin reversing the trend.

Because the economic recovery of the early nineties was politically inspired and artificially engineered, we can forecast the coming financial crash, but we can only approximate a date. We still can't tell when or if they'll come up with some new economic wonder drug that will again suppress the symptoms for a while, and buy another respite.

Crusades 2000 has already begun. It will pit Islamic nations against the West. We can't say how long it will last or how many nations may stumble their way into battle. But we know the consequences will be grim. The Renaissance that will characterize the coming Global Age has already taken root. But how quickly it will grow, spread, and prevail cannot be precisely predicted, since the life of this trend will extend beyond the foreseeable future.

Prodigious changes are taking place.

3

SEEING INTO
THE FUTURE

2020 TREND VISION

You'll be able to anticipate the future. Your vision will be clear. You'll be prepared for what will be happening in the year 2000 and beyond. How?

This has been the business of the Trends Research Institute since 1980. With a long track record and a high degree of accuracy, we have been able to forecast major trends/events months, years, even decades before they become headlines in your daily paper.

We are business consultants specializing in trends, a consortium of scholars, scientists, artists, writers, and businesspeople with wide-ranging experience in a number of fields: "A network of twenty-five experts whose range of specialties . . . would rival many university faculties," according to *The Economist.*

We study and analyze key newspapers, trade publications, and a host of specialized and popular journals—from *Alternative Therapies* to the *Skeptical Inquirer;* from *Infinite Energy* to *Advertising Age.*

Over three hundred separately defined trends are tracked daily. Our files run from abortion, agriculture, art, and astrology to video conferencing, voluntary simplicity, walking, water, zoning, and zoos. No trend exists in isolation. Opportunity misses those who view the world only through the eyes of their own profession. The key to our system is making connections between seemingly unrelated fields.

We are not soothsayers, nor astrologers, nor economic forecasters—all of whom draw their data from restricted fields or sources. The astrologer, for example, uses only configurations of the stars to make predictions; the economic forecaster uses only economic data—as though economics were the single driving force behind civilization. The real world is more complex than their elegant quantitative models.

Nor are we futurists. The futurists of the 1960s predicted that by the 1990s we'd be working only twenty-two and a half hours a week and would have more leisure time than we knew what to do with. They had visions of the technology that would give us PCs, fax machines, and modems. Sure enough, we now have PCs, faxes, and modems. But we work a lot more than twenty-two and a half hours a week and have less leisure time than ever before—that is, if we have jobs at all!

The futurists based their forecasts mainly on technological changes. What the futurists *didn't* see were drastic changes in the family and in the economy. They didn't envision the two-income household, day care, or elder care, drugs or crime. They didn't foresee economic fallback, a complex global post–World War II world where U.S. wages and standards of living actually declined from a pre–Vietnam War peak. They were drawing conclusions from a one-dimensional worldview: the world of scientific and technological progress.

A new generation of futurists has learned nothing from the mistakes of the old. A sales pitch to techno-yuppies from *Wired,* a magazine devoted to the "electronic frontier," states:

> From Wall Street to Hollywood, from Madison Avenue to the White House, from Moscow to Main Street the most powerful force shaping our world today is not ideology or armies, it's the merger of computing, communication, and the media that's come to be known as the Digital Revolution.

Yes, the digital revolution is a major trend. Yes, it's changing the way we live and work. But it is merely the evolution of existing technology. It's not more powerful than ideology or armies. It is a tool. It is a means to an end.

A hundred and fifty years ago, the telegraph was being touted as the technology that would revolutionize the world. But it was only a communications device. All that dot-dot-dashing did little to enrich the lives of people around the world.

The unfulfilled promise of the telegraph was then shunted onto the movies, the radio, and television in turn, with similar results. But the telegraph did not prevent the Civil War. Movies and radio did nothing to prevent two monstrous world wars; television has not helped to prevent violence on American streets or the dissolution of the American family. The new, highly touted "virtual life" digital revolution will do nothing to replace real life. It won't think for us. Artificial intelligence won't solve life's real problems.

To futurists, advances in technology are equated with advances in civilization. Intellectually sophisticated, philosophically naïve, the futurists live in a world where new equals better.

Actually, today's technophiliacs busily touting cyberspace, multimedia, and virtual reality are overlooking the one relatively simple invention whose universal acceptance *will* make a difference—though industry giants were slow to recognize its potential. It is a replay of the seventies, when IBM and Digital totally misread the future of PCs.

"There is no reason for any individual to have a computer in their home," declared Ken Olson, chairman of Digital Equipment, addressing the World Future Society in Boston in 1977.

▶**TRENDPOST** *The next dramatic shift in the momentum of the digital revolution will take place with the perfection of . . . the videophone!* ◀

TRUMPETS, DRUMS, FANFARE . . .

The videophone (or whatever name it may eventually go by—remember, the automobile started out as the "horseless carriage") will reshape the way we communicate more than any other single device or invention. The psychological and social connections—the intensely personal, intimate feelings people will experience when looking at someone in the eye—the face behind the voice, will transform human interaction at a distance. The telephone, invented in the 1870s, was a technological extension of the ear and voice; the video will add the all-important visual dimension.

When we use the telephone today, we are still communicating by radio. With the videophone, we will step up to television. In an increasingly decentralized world, people everywhere will be able to communicate and exchange ideas with something approaching the intimacy and certainty that comes with face-to-face personal communication. When you can see who you are talking to, body language—nonverbal communication—comes into play; another human being is not just a disembodied voice at a distance or a still-more-depersonalized stranger on the Internet.

As the trends of self-employment, downsizing, and work decentralization keep more people in their homes, face-to-face, interactive communication will become increasingly important. It will in many ways replace the familiar social context of the office.

Yet despite the potential of the videophone, industry "experts" resist it, relying upon data collected by market researchers and pollsters who report that people would rather preserve the comparative anonymity of the telephone.

Similar objections attended the telephone answering machine back in the late seventies. Analysts said that people felt intimidated by the new devices and would not leave messages. In the beginning, people *did* feel intimidated, and often they did not leave messages, but in the mid-1990s if you call and don't get an answering machine to pick up a call, you are probably annoyed. You will have to call back. It's an inconvenience.

Modern technology is sufficiently sophisticated to solve the pressing privacy problem. Just as the mute button preserves us from listening to unwanted television commercials, so a "blind" button will preserve us from unsolicited Peeping Toms. Still, the tele-videophony trend is in its infancy.

Intel's ProShare, turning a PC into a videophone, sold only 31,750 systems in 1994. Sales are expected to reach the half-million mark by 1997. "If we're successful by 2000 every PC will be a communication tool," says Intel's Patrick Gelsinger.

Once everyone has a videophone, there will be other spin-off benefits: Many business meetings and on-site product demonstrations will no longer be necessary. This will result in less business travel and commuting, which will ease air traffic and highway congestion and, coincidentally, decrease air pollution.

For investors, money invested in tele-videophony should repay handsomely sometime early in the millennium. But singling out a major future technological success is no automatic guarantee of profits. Back in 1912, did you go with Stanley Steamer or Ford; in the 1970s, did you back Beta or VCR?

By keeping abreast of advances in the industry, the skillful trend tracker should be able to determine which of the competing systems to buy into.

While we can with assurance forecast the development and universal spread of tele-videophony, we do not share the naïve technophiliac vision.

Of course, before very long, computer literacy will be as universal as knowing how to drive. Only under special circumstances will people *not* know how to use a computer. But in and of itself, the digital revolution will revolutionize nothing. Ease of communication means nothing in itself.

Only what is being communicated counts, and what human beings do with that communication.

Some futurists wrongly believe that technology alone will determine the future. It is people who determine the future.

THE "WHAT-IF'S"

Other futurists are scenario builders. They work with a predetermined set of socioeconomic "characters" whose interaction produces a variety of possible "plots"—they play "what-if" games, "rehearsing" for a variety of possible outcomes. The problem with scenario building is that the future is invariably more complex than their "middle-case, worst-case, best-case" scenarios.

There is no way to rehearse effectively for the future, any more than it is possible to rehearse for a blind date. As everybody knows, no matter how much you have been told about him/her, no matter how many possible scenarios you may have elaborately constructed for the occasion, the reality is invariably different.

Or put another way, scenarios are like studying the formal katas in karate—a set of ritualized, predetermined moves, strikes, and blocks. They look great in the movies, but, as close-combat experts will testify, they do not usually work in real life because the mugger jumping out at you from a dark alleyway does not know or follow the ritual.

The future is that mugger. There is no middle-case, best-case, or worst-case mugger. However, it is possible to prepare yourself against muggers—to actually anticipate the unexpected. It is a question of knowing which combat art to practice and of not being fooled by the ones that work in the dojo (training school) but not on the streets.

MARKET RESEARCH AND THE POLLS

Apart from the economic forecasters, futurists, astrologers, and soothsayers, trend forecasting is also attempted by market researchers and pollsters. They perform useful functions. They take the public pulse at a specific moment in time on a specific issue, event, or mood. We make use of their findings in our own research analysis. But the narrow focus of subject matter and snapshot-in-time approach of the market researcher's or pollster's inquiry does not provide the broad base of information needed to make trend forecasts. It is like the skilled, well-trained hospital technician who takes your pulse and blood pressure. You do not expect him/her to give you an expert medical diagnosis of your condition.

GLOBALNOMIC FORECASTING

Our system of forecasting goes beyond the limits of any single discipline. At the Trends Research Institute, we use many sets of data, drawing not only from socioeconomic and political sources but also from the arts, sciences, and currents in philosophy, fashion, and pop culture.

In this book, we make use of quotes culled mainly from a handful of mainstream newspapers and magazines. Many of the headlines and quotes will ring memory bells. Our purpose in using familiar rather than arcane material from the specialized journals and newsletters in our files is to show that the trend information is public, not inside information.

The Globalnomic® method does not rely on content analysis, in which volume of coverage often determines the existence and strength of a trend. Nor is evidence selected that happens to fit in with predetermined conclusions, while contrary evidence is excluded. Our trends and our forecasts are based upon a synthesis of all the available information. The secret lies in putting together the relevant evidence and coming up with the correct big picture. With the interlocking constituent elements in place, we are able to provide a trends consultancy service on specifics as the situation demands.

The Trends Research Institute's proven success in identifying, forecasting, and tracking trends shows the soundness of our Globalnomic methodology. Since 1980, we have compiled a record that makes us the world leader in trend forecasting. Our approach is equally valid when applied to sweeping global change or the specific needs of individual businesses or industries.

We forecast the great stock market crash of 1987 eleven months before it happened. In 1988 we zeroed in on Ross Perot as a political maverick and forecast the emergence of a new third political party in the 1990s. We warned of a civil war in the Balkans and in the former Soviet Union, the collapse of the Mexican economy, the downsizing of the great American middle class, and the growing and shocking disparity between the incomes of the rich and poor, along with many other world and national events and trends that others either did not see or misread. We were among the first to forecast the "green" marketing revolution—its ups and downs; home offices, home-health-care market growth; new trends in health, fitness, and nutrition as the baby boom generation came of age and began implementing the New Age ideas that had fired its imagination two decades earlier.

We forecast the boom in gourmet coffees, the surge in microbrews, the changing trends and fads in fashion, music, and advertising. We coined the words *clean food* and *dumbsizing* (subsequently picked up by the *New York Times,* the *Wall Street Journal, Time* magazine, and others), describing, respectively, the new trend in food quality and the implications of excessive corporate staff reductions normally euphemistically termed "downsizing."

Needless to say, we do not get it right every time. We did not forecast the economic "recovery" following Clinton's election, since there was no way to know the Federal Reserve would take out an unredeemable second mortgage on the country's future by flooding the world with cheap dollars. We thought gold would go up in the 1980s, not seeing that the Reagan/Bush administrations would take out the first mortgage with an orgy of deficit spending. We also forecast a loss for Clinton in 1992, since there was no way to know Ross Perot would sabotage and discredit himself by pulling out of the race and then jumping back in at the last minute. Unforeseeable and arbitrary events like these are wild cards and may spoil the hand; they do not spoil the game.

On a consistent, long-term basis, our method allows us to spot and isolate important trends from out of the fads and the noise and then to monitor them closely to see if they are viable and if they take hold and grow. With this method, we can forecast with considerable accuracy the direction these trends will be taking in the immediate and foreseeable future. By projecting those trends forward, we can forecast how the events of today will affect your life and the life of society tomorrow. And we then fit the separate pieces into an ever-changing larger picture. We call this the Globalnomic method (from *globus,* meaning "globe" or "sphere"—that is, the earth—and *nemein,* meaning "to manage").

By taking advantage of this method, you will be able to *pro*act. You don't have to just watch things happen. You can take positions, and influence positive trends or try to reverse negative trends.

Trends can be *managed*—on the personal level and also, when critical mass is achieved, on the wider scale. Globalnomic forecasting is more than an analytical tool. It is a management system. By implementing Globalnomic forecasting, *you* will be able to act positively and intelligently instead of just reacting blindly and automatically.

The millennium is upon us. It is January 1, 2000. The party is over.

4

THE MORNING AFTER

THE RESOLUTION

Even though the world wakes up with the granddaddy of all hangovers, through the headache you vow to keep your resolutions for this unique New Year.

There can be no doubt about it: The world is out of control.

But your resolution is: No matter what the state of the world, I will take control of my own life. It can be done. You know it can be done. Your concerns are about your family, your business, your profession—your life, inner and outer. You're determined to get "on-trend," to be prepared.

How did you, and the rest of the world with you, get so "off-trend" in the first place? Looking back, you can see how easy it was—almost inescapable.

Life in the nineties made it very difficult to look ahead. *Stress* and *time* were the buzzwords. "I have no life," was the common refrain. You got up in the morning. Day care, elder care, the forty-minute commute in traffic. The job you once took pride in had become a burden. You worked too long for too little. Benefits were evaporating. The office was physically hostile, a faceless, soulless rabbit warren of offices. The windows didn't even open. Between the stress and the overwork and the toxic-building syndrome, your health was suffering. By the time you got home, you were exhausted. No time to cook. You put something processed and frozen into the microwave. You paid some bills; you did some laundry. No time or energy to read. By 1993, workplace stress levels were double their 1985 levels. One in three said job stress was the single-greatest stress in their life. But still you were terrified of losing your job. New jobs were hard to find, and most jobs paid less.

Stress related problems account for 60 percent to 90 percent of U.S. doctors visits. Fifty-two percent of Americans suffered from stress on the job.

There was a strange uneasiness running through America. A sense of depression prevailed; a weird mood, both feverish and anxious, had taken hold of the entire country. That feeling was reflected in the figures: Poll after poll showed that Americans had lost confidence in the present and lost hope for the future. This loss of faith extended beyond economics to our political, educational, medical, legal, and religious institutions.

Nearly three quarters of Americans tell pollsters they are "dissatisfied with the way things are going." Some 32%, the highest in two decades, say their financial situation is worsening. Fully 80% say government favors the rich and powerful, vs only 29% in 1964. And 48% say their kids will be worse off. . . . Fortune 500 layoffs, more than 4 million since 1980, continue. (*USA Today*, 11/4/93)

This marked a departure, a new trend for Americans, renowned for their unshakable optimism.

Depression was in the air. But it wasn't in the numbers—yet.

Because it wasn't in the numbers, the "experts" whose job it was to see it coming didn't see it coming. The whole of the corporate world was in a state of high anxiety. Widespread reengineering and downsizing policies hit the corporate faithful like the Inquisition; and like the Inquisition, no one was safe, from CEOs to secretaries. Outside the corporate world, no one was safe, either. As major local employers pulled up stakes and moved to Mexico or Indonesia, local economies withered.

Americans were being told that as the most advanced nation on Earth, the United States was the first to move from an industrial-based economy to a service economy. An underlying mutually-agreed-upon deception was: Let the Third World take care of those nasty, boring factory jobs. We can do better. But it wasn't only the factory jobs that were being exported.

With trade barriers falling and multinational corporations growing, corporations swiftly moved to acquire both their hardware and their software from the most inexpensive sources.

U.S. companies typically pay software writers in the former Soviet Bloc countries from $10,000 to $20,000 a year, or about one fifth what U.S.-based programmers usually earn. (*Wall Street Journal*, hereafter, *WSJ*, 2/2/95)

High-tech corporations (IBM, Hewlett-Packard, and so on) were charged with hiring foreign-national professionals (brought into the United States on special H-1B visas) at less-than-market salaries. This was a violation of the immigration laws and an upscale application of the sweatshop principle.

Life was an emotional roller coaster. Like practically everyone else, your personal story was one of increasing stress and decreasing time. You could see that easily enough.

JUNK NEWS

But it wasn't so easy to see the big picture. Most people didn't see it. How could they have? In the 1990s, 70 percent of Americans were relying on television for their news. And what was TV calling news in the nineties? O.J. Simpson, the Bobbitts, and Joey Buttafuoco.

In one week in January 1995, television devoted 400 percent more time to O.J. Simpson than to the second-most-covered story, Clinton's State of the Union address (106 minutes compared to 28 minutes, according to the *Tyndall Report*). Never before in the history of television had so much time been spent on a murder case. Was O.J. guilty? What about the DNA tests? Would a jury with eight black women on it acquit O.J.? And what about the feuding lawyers?

From *Day Break* to *Nightline,* it was anchors aweigh! Media spokesmen, for the most part, were unapologetic, even defiant.

Speaking to TV critics as if they were schoolchildren, he [Ted Koppel] said: "This [O.J.] is a terrific story. We are in the news business as are you, as are the people you work for. We live in a commercial competitive world. What was it that the public lost? What were they deprived of? Soaps? Is that what we're in this righteous snit about?" (*USA Today,* 7/19/94)

Actually, the public was being deprived of more than soaps. It was being deprived of news about the breakdown and dissolution of the entire society.

"Broadcast journalism has gone from Edward R. Murrow to P. T. Barnum," said Dr. Ronald Villane, professor of communications at the State University of New York. "Newscasters are not journalists; they pitch stories like barkers luring people to circus side shows." (*Trends in the News,* 7/15/94).

60 Minutes correspondent Lesley Stahl told *America's Talk-*
ing Straight Forward Tuesday the secret to success in TV
journalism these days: "a little violence, a little sex and a
little peek under the skirt, so to speak." (*USA Today*,
10/27/94)

Or a "little peek" under the circus tent, "so to speak." On
rare occasions, media spokesmen had an inkling of reality.
In 1993, Dan Rather took his own colleagues to task at a
meeting of the Radio and Television Directors Association.
He complained that news programs were put in competition with entertainment programs, leading to an emphasis
on "dead bodies, mayhem and lurid tales." Rather scolded
news media managers for believing that:

Americans won't put up with news from other countries.
Americans won't put up with economic news. Americans
won't put up with serious, substantive news of any kind.

The new motto is kiss ass, move with the mass, and for
heaven's and the rating's sake, don't make anybody mad—
especially not the mayor, the governor, the senator, the
president or vice-president, or anybody in a position of
power. Make nice, not news.

We all should be ashamed of what we have and have not
done, measured against what we could do, ashamed of
many of the things we have allowed our craft, our profession, our life's work to become.

That was Dan Rather in 1993. In 1995, he was doing
"O.J. Minutes" for CBS.

The O.J. Simpson story, like a hundred barely remembered sensational stories that preceded it, is junk news.
Sex, crime, disaster, more sex, more crime, more disaster,
and all those babies lost, kidnapped, falling off a building
and surviving, or not surviving—all make for junk news.
Nothing is learned, nothing solved, nothing gained.

Even as people submitted to the bombardment, they

knew better. (The *Wall Street Journal* reported that just 13 percent of the people picked the O.J. trial as the most significant story of the year.) But since 70 percent of the people were relying on television for their news, they learned little or nothing of what they themselves acknowledged was significant. Like junk food, junk news fills us up and leaves no room for anything else.

TOWER OF BABBLE

DONNELLY

Source: *The Trends Journal*, Summer 1992.

Just two months before defending the attention paid by TV to O.J., Ted Koppel was sounding rather Rather-like. "We now communicate with everyone and say absolutely nothing. We have reconstructed the Tower of Babel and it is a television antenna" (*New York Times*—hereafter, *NYT*, 5/21/94).

Junk news is to food for thought what junk food is to real food. It has no nutritional value, but it is addictive. Our nation of junk-news junkies paid a terrible price for its habit. Lost in its reverie, the public did not notice that on every issue of real consequence, it was being disinformed, misinformed, and uninformed.

MIDDLE MUDDLE

But if it's obvious why 70 percent of the people didn't see it coming, what about the other 30 percent? Thirty percent! That amounts to millions of people—more than 50 million. Most of them didn't see it, either.

Even though you read the papers consistently, kept abreast of current events, debated and discussed the issues, the chances are you still couldn't see what was coming.

Only now, on January 1, 2000, looking back, can you see why. Your vision of the future was being obscured by the smoke screen sent up by the lunatic middle. Any time a major issue had to be confronted, government officials and panels of "experts" were assembled. But since invariably both government officials and the "experts" had by definition a vested interest in perpetuating the status quo, they could neither recognize nor handle dramatic change. Always sounding authoritative and knowledgable, never really facing up to a reality the entire country felt and expressed in poll after poll, the result was a muddle, a recipe for disaster.

(From *The Status Quo Cookbook*)
A RECIPE FOR DISASTER
Middle Muddle

INGREDIENTS:
6 red herrings
1 gallon fudge
1 trial balloon
1 bottle liquid smoke
1 tablespoon political solution
wishful thinking according to taste
mirrors
basket of statistics
6 to 12 experts
silver spoons
rose-colored glasses

Place ingredients in statistic basket. Sprinkle with political solution. Have experts stir with silver spoons. Cook over moderate heat. Observe through rose-colored glasses until smoke rises. Reflect smoke in mirrors. Televise. Serve to public. Feeds millions.

People were sensing loss, pain, and uncertainty. Middle Muddle magic was losing its potency; yet even as the public expressed its distrust, it could not see through the smoke screen. All that could be seen was that actions taken by "experts" did not produce the desired results. These experts were no longer in control. Actually, they had never been in control. But the economic and political situation prior to the nineties had fostered that illusion. As long as people prospered and felt optimistic about the future, there was no pressing need to try to see through the smoke screen.

The nation was sleepwalking into the future.

5

QUACKENOMICS

ECONOMIC FALLBACK

A new economic trend was developing in the United States. But it did not fit into any of the standard economic categories; nor could it be handily labeled. People were no longer prospering, and optimism was rare, yet the government and Wall Street could see only recovery, growth, gain.

Remember back in 1995 and 1996? Economists and the U.S. Labor Department were bragging about all the great new jobs that were being created to fill the void left by the loss of old jobs. This was cited as proof of the nation's economic strength.

What was not making headlines was the Census Bureau report confirming (what the Trends Research Institute had reported for years) that most of the new jobs paid significantly less than the former jobs. Between 1990 and 1992, when people who lost jobs found new ones, they saw their incomes drop by 23 percent on average.

The decline wasn't felt just by people who took new, lower-paying jobs. Real wages for 75 percent of U.S. workers fell every year from 1987 to 1993. Between 1989 and 1993, median income adjusted for inflation dropped more than fifteen hundred dollars.

Department of Labor reports showed that 80 percent of American households were losing ground. But both Wall Street and the White House were calling the economy "robust"; "best growth since Reagan era," enthused the National Association of Business Economists. The Commerce Department reported that "the economy headed into 1995 with strong momentum and only scattered signs of slowing." SPENDING AND INCOME BOTH UP IN DECEMBER read the headline.

But when you looked behind the headlines and beyond the numbers, it was a different story. Rarely mentioned was *where* the new growth was going.

MOST AMERICANS SEE THEIR INCOME SLIP EVEN THOUGH ECONOMY IS BOOMING

And while the total income expanded last year, the gains went largely to the wealthiest 20%. (WSJ, 10/26/94)

WEALTH: STATIC WAGES, EXCEPT FOR RICH

According to Ed Wolff, an N.Y.U. economist who tracks wealth, the very rich have improved their lot in life by getting richer. Half a million U.S. households (½ of 1% of the population) now owns 39.3% of all assets (stocks, bonds, cash, life insurance policies, paintings, jewelry, etc.). This makes the U.S. No.1 among prosperous nations in the inequality of income. (*Time*, 1/30/95)

This was not part of the ongoing Washington/Wall Street pep talk. However, suddenly, in mid-1995, flat wages and the income gap were finally recognized as issues.

The gains were being fed back to the already-prosperous

top 20 percent of the population. (No doubt, this was the 20 percent who did *not* think government favored the rich and powerful in the *USA Today* story cited on page 28.)

Everybody else was losing ground. This was an affront to American idealism. Americans fervently believed that the standard of living of hardworking people would continue to rise as inevitably as the sun in the morning. But by 1995, "economic fallback" was a fact of life as masses of Americans were dropping out of prosperity. The haves had more than ever, but the have-nots were recruiting big numbers from the middle class. According to studies issued by Northwestern and Syracuse universities, 70 percent of American households were middle class.

However, the middle-class line itself (1993 statistics) was set at $23,042 per year for a family of three, or double the poverty line. Obviously, this absurd standard had been set by a panel of government experts, none of whom had ever tried to live a middle-class family life for three on $23,042 a year. It can't be done, as more and more Americans were learning.

By using this fantasy middle-class line, experts could solemnly reassure Americans that fully 70 percent of the nation was middle class. However, when a genuine middle-class line is set, the figures produce a very different economic picture. In the real world, a middle-class lifestyle for a family of three in 1995 began somewhere around forty thousand dollars a year—as anyone who has tried to lead a middle-class life knows full well.

When Department of Labor statistics are analyzed, it turns out that less than 40 percent—not 70 percent—of Americans are truly middle class. Six percent are in the upper class (over $100,000 per year). The other 55 percent of Americans are essentially the working poor, and the percentage of poor is growing yearly.

STEROID GROWTH

The economy was getting stronger! Yes, like an athlete on steroids.

Anabolic steroids increase the appearance and metabolism of muscle; on the surface, everything looks great. The pumped-up economy had more glistening muscle than Arnold Schwarzenegger. Steroids work. Not only is handsome muscle added but short-term performance is also significantly enhanced.

But the long-term use of steroids results ultimately in impotence, liver cancer, and behavioral problems. The strength is real but fleeting; the damage is lasting and disastrous. The United States was busy grooming its external appearance; inside, it was diseased, and the longer it stayed on steroids, the worse it would become.

As every athlete knows, you can't quit steroids and continue to perform at the steroid-enhanced level—not without a drastic retraining program and a whole new way of life.

QUACKENOMICS

Yet throughout the 1990s, even as wages were dropping, the Federal Reserve Board feared future "wage inflation." Pointing to the gross domestic product figures (the highest since 1984) as proof the economy was overheating and that inflation was at hand, it raised interest rates seven times in just one year!

There were numerous signs of impending economic crisis throughout that year and around the world. Virtually every time the Fed raised interest rates, major tremors shook the world's stock markets. And so they should have. Raising interest rates was the equivalent of cutting back on the steroid dosage. Tremors and convulsions are the customary reactions experienced by addicts trying to kick their habits.

But to Wall Street and Washington, the tremors and convulsions were to be expected—proof that the medicine was working. The *Wall Street Journal* crooned that "many of the forces that have pushed stocks higher over the past three years remain intact. The economic recovery that took so long to begin is well entrenched." Laura Tyson, chief White House economist, took up the refrain, saying, "Since we believe the fundamentals are strong, and markets are known to overreact on occasion, we are satisfied that the economy is in a sound position."

Ignoring everything that did not spell out *recovery*, experts dipped into the basket of statistics to prove the economy was so robust that it needed checking.

"The administration has conducted an exhaustive review of all the evidence we have and the opinions of everybody we can talk to around the country. No one believes that there is a serious problem with the underlying American economy. It is healthy and it is sound," declared President Clinton. (AP, 4/1/94)

Middle Muddle was still working its magic. Two days later, an Associated Press poll showed that Americans had swallowed the recipe for disaster. Most agreed with President Clinton that the economy remained sound. William Dunkelberg, president of the National Association of Business Economists, and dean of the Business School at Temple University, said that "the current recovery, which began in the Spring of 1991, but has taken a long time to gain momentum, is finally flexing its muscles. It's a lovely way to grow."

PAYING THE PIPER—THE CURRENCY CRISIS

It was more than fears of inflation or wage increases that were driving interest rates up, however. Even the government's numbers verified that inflation was low and wages were actually declining.

To see why interest rates were rising, you had to look globally, to the currency crisis that would soon shake the world economy. This was foreseeable, to those tracking trends. In 1992, in our *Trends Journal,* we forecast that the steroid injections in the form of low interest rates (which were needed to pump up the recessionary Bush presidency) would put downward pressure on the dollar, leading to a world currency crisis.

Meanwhile, low interest rates had pushed the stock markets to historic highs, and these low rates also allowed corporations and consumers to borrow more and refinance. These low rates made for cheap dollars overseas as well as at home.

Again, in the Spring 1994 issue of *The Trends Journal,* we warned that high-flying Pacific Rim and Latin American stock markets would unravel and that the prospects for an international currency crisis were at hand. Every time interest rates were raised, shock waves ran through the highly speculative but popular "emerging markets" (aka Third World countries in the days before speculators found out they could make money on them by exploiting their labor after they had finished exploiting all their natural resources).

NOT-SO-FUNNY MONEY

Artificially low interest rates in the early 1990s created a glut of artificially underpriced dollars. Countries and speculators were able to borrow dollars cheaply to fuel their economies and build their portfolios.

Never before had so many countries had easy access to cheap greenbacks. Even China, Russia, and other formerly closed countries now freely traded dollars. And with inflation soaring and political instability growing in these newly opened markets, investors there put their money into our underpriced dollars rather than in their own shaky inflationary currencies.

The once-mighty and irreproachable dollar was now available to all comers. World currency traders reacting to the glut of dollars flooding the marketplace pushed it further downward. To prevent still further erosion of its value, Washington repeatedly raised interest rates.

Meanwhile, the undervalued dollar made U.S. products cheaper to buy—stimulating exports. However, it also made many imports more expensive to buy. (You needed more underpriced dollars to pay for your Toyota or Sony or Panasonic.)

Also, with American manufacturing factored out to Third World countries in order to take advantage of cheap labor, the United States was sucking in huge quantities of imports. Much of what we needed or wanted no longer had a MADE IN USA label, even if the rest of the label said LEVI STRAUSS or CALVIN KLEIN or NIKE.

Eventually, the profits came back home to roost all right—as Washington and Wall Street said—but most of those profits went to the 20 percent of the population that was still getting richer. The net result of these combined policies widened the U.S. trade deficit to historic highs in 1995—in goods alone it surged to $174.47 billion.

Deficit spending abroad was then added to deficit spending at home. Gradually over the years, servicing interest on our $5 trillion national debt was closing in on defense spending and Social Security as the single-largest chunk taken out of the U.S. tax dollar. And it wasn't buying anything, building anything, producing anything, or curing anything. It was going back to the investors at home and abroad who held the debt.

What applies to the individual applies to society—a concept belittled by economists. They have deluded themselves into believing that what would be universally regarded as irresponsible behavior in an individual becomes "sound policy" when the government does it.

Try borrowing more money when your house is already second-mortgaged to the hilt and you're already paying more in interest than you can afford. You wouldn't even try. And if you did, they'd laugh you out of the bank. But when the government allows itself to go ever deeper into debt, they call this policy "manageable."

But it's only "manageable" because the government cuts other programs that serve public needs in order to service the ever-increasing interest on the national debt. On the individual level, that's like not seeing your doctor when you're sick so that you can keep up your membership in the country club.

You do not need a Ph.D. in quackenomics to know that you can't spend more than you earn forever, even if you're the biggest, richest government in the world. "A Gannett News Service analysis shows that in the Reagan-Bush years of 1981–93 government spent 23% more than it took in." Clinton administration projections hoped to reduce this gap to 12 percent.

Sooner or later, the United States would have to pay for all those steroids. The symptoms of their use were becoming increasingly obvious.

What was happening in the United States was happening everywhere.

Countries that have been running substantial current-account deficits in trade and services—and therefore extremely reliant on foreign capital—were quickly identified as possibly vulnerable. So were countries with relatively low reserves of foreign currency. Mexico had faced both problems before it devalued the peso, but most analysts had been unconcerned. (*NYT*, 2/1/95)

Suddenly, they were concerned! This is how the Middle Muddle smoke screen operates and perpetuates itself. Only after the storm blows the smoke away can the public see the carnage underneath. By then, it is too late to act effectively.

From Mexico to Canada to Russia, the currency markets were in turmoil. In just a few weeks in 1994, the peso lost over 50 percent of its value. The Canadian dollar was trading near an all-time low against the U.S. dollar, and the Russian ruble was effectively worthless.

SOUTH OF THE BORDER

In the case of Mexico, a good dollop of collusion was added to the customary fudge, smoke, and red-herring recipe. It was reported that Washington knew about the impending Mexican calamity months, even years, before it happened. "Everybody was caught off guard. Wall Street had been promised that this was not going to happen," moaned Paul Sachs, president of Multinational Strategies, a financial advisory firm.

Actually, not everybody was caught off guard. Professor Rudi Dornbusch of the Massachusetts Institute of Technology says that "shortly before the devaluation, big investors moved $15 billion from peso-based investments into peso bonds whose value was linked to the dollar and thus protected."

It was subsequently revealed that the U.S. and Mexican governments were conspiring to conceal the true state of affairs. They wanted to ensure the passage of NAFTA (the

North American Free Trade Agreement) and to make sure the ruling party in Mexico would win the upcoming elections.

Mexico had been called "the Rolls-Royce of developing nations." Wall Street invested heavily, and it held up Mexico as a model for other emerging markets to follow. Both governments knew the Mexican economy was on a collision course. When it happened, the proud Rolls was magically transformed into the *Titanic*.

With the Mexican economy sinking fast, governments and investors panicked and sent out a desperate SOS. The financial world put up an $18 billion bailout fund to plug the hole, then pleaded for $40 billion more to keep Mexico afloat.

> Wall Street's market strategists enthusiastically endorse the U.S. Government's proposed $40 billion loan package for Mexico despite charges by critics that it amounts to a bailout for the Wall Street firms themselves and yield-hungry investors.
>
> "If they don't do this rescue, they run the risk of a real global meltdown," says Barton Biggs, chairman of Morgan Stanley Asset Management. (WSJ, 1/26/95)

"A 'catalytic impact around the world' warned Treasury Secretary Robert Rubin, a former co-chairman of Goldman Sachs & Co." Goldman Sachs ranked as the number-one underwriter of Mexican stocks and bonds in the United States and became the first American investment firm licensed to trade in the Mexican market.

According to a report published by the Center for Public Integrity, a nonpartisan research group in Washington, it was Rubin who spearheaded the Goldman Sachs move into the Mexican market, and Rubin and his wife, through their personal foundation, also contributed $275,000 to the 1992 Democratic convention.

Mexico was the first major visible symptom of the global disease. Nine other Latin American nations were also unraveling financially, along with several Asian nations. Even First World countries such as Sweden, Spain, and Italy were facing severe financial crises.

Now, the rising interest rates applied the brakes to global economic growth, putting further downward pressure on wages and income. The steroid world economy, pumped up by the lowest interest rates in twenty years, was turning malignant.

The early warning rumblings that had been going on for years were getting louder but still were not heard over the din of junk-news noise—by at least 70 percent of the people. Those trying to follow the real news were enveloped in the rosy billows of Middle Muddle.

"Once the financial crisis is over—the Mexican economy should be ready for even higher growth," said Nora Lustig, an economist with the Brookings Institute.

Despite such reassurances, this time Americans were angry and suspicious. Polls showed that 80 percent of the public opposed the bailout scheme. "I know no one in the financial community who is against this," said Senator Diane Feinstein, a California Democrat. "I know no one in my constituency who is for it. There is no support."

With the budget ax falling at home, how could the government suddenly find billions of dollars (the eventual bailout package was $50 billion, the lion's share from the United States) to rescue Mexico and Wall Street? The American public had been told there was no money—no money for our inner cities, no money for health care, no money for food stamps, and none for the environment, infrastructure, or education. But now, *presto,* suddenly Washington scared up billions for Mexico.

You may remember wondering where all of those billions came from, and if it really was going to do any good at all.

Would it save the Mexican economy, would it create jobs in America as they promised, or was it just a bailout for Wall Street?

> Today's accord also included new language that specifically permits Mexico's central bank to use American funds to support Mexico's banking system and keep its depositors— including many wealthy Americans—from losing billions of pesos.
> "The depositors will be protected," Mr. Rubin (U.S. Treasury Secretary) said. (*NYT*, 2/22/95)

The depositors were protected! But who were the depositors?

"So we have done the right thing by the American taxpayers and the American people as well," said President Clinton. But the American taxpayers and the American people who funded the bailout were not the depositors the bailout protected. The depositors were members of an exclusive country club.

When the Middle Muddle was blown away, doing the "right thing" meant making sure the country club didn't go broke. After all, if the club members can't pay their dues, all the waiters, groundkeepers, locker room attendants, valets, lifeguards, bartenders, busboys, janitors, and dishwashers lose their jobs. The government had to make sure this didn't happen. Indeed, by bringing the country club to new heights of prosperity, more of these prized "service sector" jobs would be created.

This was called "doing the right thing by the American taxpayers." Lost in the sales pitch was the fact that most of the money used to keep the country club afloat had been provided by the waiters, groundkeepers, locker room attendants, valets, lifeguards, bartenders, busboys, janitors, and dishwashers. Maybe that's why 80 percent of the American people opposed the bailout—which Washington and Wall

Street, in their quaint quackenomic jargon, insisted upon calling a "rescue plan."

"With the signing of this agreement, we are bringing this crisis to a close," said Secretary of State Warren Christopher.

THE RECOVERY THAT WASN'T

By January 1, 2000, the Mexican economy had long since collapsed, taking much of Central and South America with it. Even Asia, the jewel of "emerging markets," is being torn by labor unrest and depression.

Western capital and industry had set up business in Third World countries for two chief reasons: to take advantage of cheap labor and to avoid regulatory interference. Just as workers in the West rebelled against inhumane working conditions and poor wages during the middle years of the Industrial Revolution, so similar conditions provoked a similar and foreseeable response in these so-called emerging markets.

Steeply decreased demand for goods and services by the consumer nations provoked widespread unemployment, which contributed to the mounting unrest throughout the Philippines, Malaysia, Thailand, Sri Lanka, India, Pakistan, Brazil, and Indonesia. And Hong Kong, the financial capital of the East, has not been able to survive the long-planned 1997 takeover by China.

All over the world, house-of-cards economies built on a foundation of low interest rates and glued together with derivatives, hedge funds, and other high-risk financial instruments have collapsed. As the economies went down, so did the currencies.

So out of control was the speculation, so huge were the amounts of money being gambled, that the world's central bank intervention could no longer influence or support imperiled financial markets by quick fixes. By 1995, over a trillion dollars a day was being bet by foreign-exchange traders. The world's central banks had only billions at their disposal to salvage sinking currencies. Adroitly coordinated intervention into the money market could provide short-term relief but could not cure the diease.

The currency crisis that blew Mexico apart would eventually rampage across the globe, sparing nobody. The yen, lira, pound, kroner, dong, yuan, escudo, guilder, riyal, rupee, peseta, shekel, dollar—all succumbed before the blast. It wasn't just inflation; it wasn't just depression; it wasn't just stagflation plus recession. It was a combination of all these factors, with each country producing its own mix. The conventional old labels no longer applied.

A new trend, a long-term descending economy, had settled over the world.

PROACTION

Still, if you were one of those few who did not rely upon junk news for information, and if you saw through the Middle Muddle, you could have seen it coming. You could have taken protective, proactive action. Perhaps you've positioned yourself in a job or profession, ideally with growth potential, but at least with survival value; you take measures not to get caught up in the imminent real estate slump; your children are being educated to prepare them for the new society that can be seen taking root in the midst of the chaos; your retirement is secured, not by under-funded or otherwise-shaky pension programs but by long-term, low-risk, and/or visionary investment strategies. From foreign investment to high tech, from health care to home-based businesses, these opportunities exist.

With the currency crisis both chronic and acute, your immediate concern was to protect the value of your battered dollars. Only the Deutsche mark and the Swiss franc retained a major portion of their former value.

> Swiss francs and Deutsche marks will be the investment in-struments of choice.
> The stability of the Swiss banking system, coupled with the nation's treasured neutrality, will appeal to risk averse investors. Much of the rest of Western Europe will be hit hard by recession, with Eastern Europe beginning to sink into full scale depression.
> Germany is still emerging as the continent's Europower, even though it is supporting its ailing Eastern half.
> The combined nation will fare better in the Great Reces-sion than other EC countries. And to keep inflation from ratcheting upward, Germany will resist lowering interest rates to the extent of the U.S. and Japan, thus preserving the value of the mark. (*The Trends Journal*, Winter 1992)

By 1995, the validity of this forecast was already appar-ent, as day after day, the dollar took a beating. Apart from investing in marks or Swiss francs, you recognized the im-portance of ensuring your financial position against cur-rency chaos.

▶ **TRENDPOST** *Risk insurance meant putting at least 10 percent of your savings into gold. To diversify your portfolio, you bought gold stocks, coins, or bullion.* ◀

People thought you were crazy or an Armageddonite. But you weren't.

The deficit spending steroids of the eighties and the lower interest rate steroids of the nineties disguised the real value of gold. By 2000, as the impotence, liver cancer, and behavioral problems set in, gold had reasserted its value. You didn't bet the ranch on it, and you didn't invest beyond your means. But you were tracking trends and you could see that, apart from the currency turmoil, there were other world situations that made gold look like a safe haven to put your money into.

BROKEN CHINA

The transformation of the great Chinese economic miracle into the great Chinese debacle was the most spectacular event of the Asian collapse. Their experiment with the "socialist market economy" has failed. Dangerous double-digit inflation of the early nineties escalated into uncontrollable hyperinflation by the end of the decade, with its customary by-products of massive unemployment and civil and social disorder.

BY RAISING ITS FLAG BEIJING RAISES FEARS

The sight of a Chinese flag fluttering over a coral reef 135 miles from the Philippines has alarmed China's Southeast Asian neighbors and raised fears that Beijing is prepared to use force in staking claim to shipping lanes and a chain of potentially oil-rich islands in the South China Seas. (*NYT*, 2/19/95)

CHINA SAID TO SEEK TO REIN IN TAIWAN WITH WAR GAMES

China is preparing an escalating series of naval, air and missile force maneuvers intended to bring Taiwan's political leadership to heel, American military officials and foreign diplomats say. (*NYT*, 8/19/95)

By 2000, China is no longer courted as an open-market trading partner. The world now fears the flash point that could send China's billion people and million problems spilling over her borders—with none of her neighbors strong enough to stop her, especially Russia.

According to a 1993 study by Swedish military intelligence, the Russian armed forces were already in such disarray that Russia would not have been able to mount a successful campaign against even a small nation such as Sweden. By 2000, Russia could no longer be depended upon to forestall Chinese territorial expansion.

6

BACK IN THE USSR

BAD ACID

The Berlin Wall came tumbling down in 1989, taking the Kremlin with it. An ecstatic world watched through rose-colored glasses. But anyone not seeing a rosy vision saw the inevitability of civil war that would rage from Vladivostok to Sarajevo.

In October 1993, the starting guns went off. Russian president Boris Yeltsin launched a military attack on the parliamentary White House. It was the bloodiest clash in Moscow since the 1917 revolution. This was a historical crisis with global implications. If you were depending on television for your news, you may only vaguely remember this incident. Two days after it happened, the story disappeared from the screen, preempted by news of basketball star Michael Jordan's retirement.

For those who stayed on the story, the overwhelming official spin was that Yeltsin was in control, the crisis was over, and "market democracy" had been born.

Though bloody, with more than 140 deaths, the uprising

was described as no more than a temporary setback. Quackenomic experts were undismayed. Their prescribed economic shock therapy designed to jolt Russia out of its long Communist torpor and into Western-style capitalism was doing the job, according to them.

The shock worked; the therapy didn't. Imaginary capitalism was accompanied by equally imaginary democracy.

The patient was suffering from a host of chronic, acute, malignant, and terminal illnesses brought on by seventy years of dictatorial abuse. No amount of economic shock therapy or any other kind of therapy would jolt Russia out of depression and into recovery, or into democracy, or out of civil war. Tracking trends according to our Globalnomic method, we at the Trends Research Institute could see this coming well in advance. On March 11, 1991, five months before the coup that unseated Mikhail Gorbachev, we warned that "the Soviet Union was on the eve of a civil war."

In January 1992, before the shootout at the Russian White House, *The Trends Journal* reported:

> Civil war will spread across the post-Soviet Commonwealth of Independent States. The divisive issues that spawned the civil war in Yugoslavia are fermenting similar violence in the newly independent republics. . . . We don't need official confirmation to see that the demise of the Soviet Union created power vacuums . . . aggravating pre-existing ethnic tensions.

In the Spring 1993 issue, *The Trends Journal* published a story headlined POST-SOVIET POWDER KEG TO IGNITE GLOBAL CRISIS. The foreseeable spark took another year and a half to burn its way to the keg.

"I think Yeltsin faces some challenging times," Clinton said. "He's a very tough guy. He believes in democracy. He's on the right side of history."

On December 11, 1994, the right side of history invaded

the Chechen Republic, setting the stage for the civil war chain reaction that would soon lead to horrific consequences. Still unwilling to acknowledge the realities of Russia and the delusions of Washington, President Clinton urged continued support for Yeltsin: "Russia is still a democracy. Russia is still pursuing economic reform which is critical to the kind of political stability that will lead to a responsible partnership."

This was the latest version of a familiar refrain. Earlier, Clinton had said, "As Russia's only democratically elected leader he [Yeltsin] has our support, as do his reform government, and all reformers throughout the Russian federation."

This constituted a significant foreign policy evolution. The United States had always been willing to do business with dictators. But we did not customarily confuse them with democrats. As Harry Truman bluntly said of the notorious Dominican Republic dictator Rafael Trujillo, "He's an S.O.B., but he's *our* S.O.B."

But now, the definition of democracy itself proved pliable. Any government—totalitarian, dictatorial, Communist—could be labeled "democratic" as long as it embraced open-market policies. "Our aim has been nurturing the transformation to democracy, undergoing a rather painful internal controversy now," understated State Department spokesman Mike McCurry.

The Russians themselves did not share Washington's illusions about ongoing events, or about their new leader. To silent dissent, Yeltsin had banned public rallies, instituted curfews, ordered police to arrest and search—even strip-search—citizens at random. Russian newspapers compared Moscow to a police state. YELTSIN LEADING RUSSIA INTO CHAOS—AGAIN read the headline in *Izvestia*. Throughout Russia, Yeltsin was widely regarded as a drunk, a czar, and a tyrant. "Yeltsin as a democrat was invented abroad, not

here in Russia," said Viktor Kremenyuk of the Russian
Academy of Science.

SOAKED IN BLOOD

Amid the wreckage of the Chechen city of Grozny, only
death and destruction prevail. The capital of the separatist
Russian region has been bombed into empty ruins. After
more than seven weeks of war, its roads are pocked by
bomb craters, its buildings are aflame, and those who
emerge from its shelters risk death from sniper fire. (*Time*,
2/13/95)

"This is a time for the United States to be steady and cau-
tious," said Secretary of State Warren Christopher. "We
need to not rush to judgment or rush to conclusions. It is
worth remembering that he [Yeltsin] is the first elected president of Russia. He has been the exponent of reform. And
we are in favor of reform. . . . Russia is operating in a democratic context." (*NYT*, 1/7/95)

In the standard language of Middle Muddle, the ghastly
and futile carnage was tolerable. The context was democratic. Yeltsin stood for economic reform.

With atrocities mounting and the carnage escalating, the
lunatic middle muddled on. Republican majority leader
Bob Dole said the Chechnya invasion "makes it very difficult for President Clinton or many of us in the Congress
who've been strong supporters of President Yeltsin. This is
a no win situation for Yeltsin and an indication that democracy *may* [emphasis added] be on the brink."

These calls for support continued over the rest of the
decade, even as Russia was visibly disintegrating. As everyone knows, on January 1, 2000, there was no responsible
partnership. There was no political stability. There was no
democracy. There was no open market.

What there was, was civil war, chaos, misery, a Communist Reformation . . . and . . .

THE GREAT FORESEEABLE, INEVITABLE UNTHINKABLE

Suppose you owned a fleet of sixty aging trucks. And suppose these trucks had been designed by second-rate, indifferent engineers, shoddily built by morose, underpaid workers, and serviced only in emergencies by ill-trained, alcoholic mechanics. Your sixty trucks have been running nonstop since they were first built more than thirty years ago. For the last five years, business has been so terrible, you haven't been able to pay the mechanics, who've refused to continue working.

As the owner of this proud fleet, would you expect every one of these trucks to keep on getting to its destination in 1997, or 1998, or 1999, and into perpetuity without a major breakdown? Probably not. If you were determined to stay in the trucking business, you'd try to get new trucks, or at least insure yourself heavily against the inevitable accident. If these options turned out to be impractical, you might consider getting out of the trucking business before it was too late.

If you substitute real-life aging Russian nuclear reactors for those hypothetical aging trucks, you will realize that the options mentioned above are unrealistic luxuries.

There are no options. Knowing this, you would be taking steps to immunize yourself in every way possible against the effects of the inevitable.

RISING PERIL SEEN AT EUROPE A-SITES. U.S. REPORTS SAFETY RISKS IN FORMER EAST BLOC STATES AND THE SOVIET UNION.

New safety problems are piling on top of old ones at the nuclear reactors in Eastern Europe and the Soviet Union because of the economic and political upheavals there, the chairman of the Nuclear Regulatory Commission said today. . . . Plants lack the resources to make needed improvements and because of overreliance on nuclear power there is no chance to shut unsafe reactors. (*NYT,* 10/8/91)

RUSSIANS PLANNING TO CONTINUE USING
FAULTED REACTORS

Senior Russian nuclear officials have told a watchdog group of Western experts that Russia's notorious graphite-core nuclear reactors—the kind that blew up at Chernobyl in 1986—will go on operating indefinitely. (*NYT,* 11/8/92)

UNSAFE REACTORS AND NEED FOR ENERGY
A RISKY COMBINATION

Today's leak of radioactive gas from a Russian reactor underscores the need to help Eastern Europe modernize its old—and potentially hazardous—reactors, experts say. . . .

German experts say the 16 RMBK reactors—all in Russia, Ukraine and Lithuania—should be shut along with 10 others.

"We remain convinced that the RMBK reactors cannot be brought up to standards and that they must be shut down as fast as possible," Klaus Topler, Germany's environmental minister, said Tuesday. (*USA Today,* 3/25/92)

A NUCLEAR TIME BOMB TICKING TOWARD CATASTROPHE

The former Soviet Union's aging nuclear reactors, increasingly short of spare parts and staffed by demoralized workers, pose a grave threat . . . according to officials and experts recently interviewed. . . .

"We cannot buy spare parts," says Yevgeny Ignatenko, a spokesman for the . . . ministry of atomic energy. "We lack fuel. At the Kalinin power station, workers for three months received only 50 percent of their salaries. How can we work like that when prices are soaring?" (*Washington Post*, 4/6–12/92)

---

40 CHERNOBYLS WAITING TO HAPPEN

. . . up to 40 potential Chernobyls are waiting to happen in the former Soviet Union and Central Europe. By the time this nuclear nightmare catches the world's attention it may be too late to prevent a catastrophe that could do irreparable human, economic and environmental damage.

Warnings about this danger come not from anti-nuclear activists but from leaders of the nuclear industry, which would be a primary victim of new Chernobyls. Percy Barnevik president of ABB Brown Boveri, one of the world's principal nuclear contractors, says many plants are so unsafe they should be shut immediately. (Maurice Strong, secretary general of the United Nations Conference on Environment and Development, Op-Ed page, *NYT*, 3/22/92)

REPORT: RUSSIAN NUKES UNSAFE

A secret survey of Russian nuclear safety ordered by President Boris Yeltsin reveals covered-up accidents. . . .

From 1992 to May 1995, Russian nuclear power plants reported 25 serious incidents and 7,673 minor ones. (AP, 8/6/95)

U.S. LISTS 10 SOVIET-BUILT NUCLEAR REACTORS AS HIGH RISKS

A Federal intelligence report says 10 reactors in Slovakia, Lithuania, Russia, Bulgaria and Ukraine face an abnormally high risk of failure.

". . . these reactors continue to experience serious incidents, raising the specter of another accident akin to Chernobyl." (*NYT*, 7/23/95)

FIVE WILL GET YOU TEN

It wasn't just the decrepit power plants, badly designed to begin with, badly maintained, barely supervised, rusting and rotting away over there in what used to be the Soviet Union, that made it inevitable.

Back in the good old Cold War days, the world feared nuclear annihilation at the hands of one or another of the superpowers. But there were only a handful to have to worry about. In the 1990s, the "Evil Empire" decentralized, and metastasized into nuclear guerilla terrorism.

RUSSIAN MOBSTERS LINKED TO
NUCLEAR ARMS ACQUISITION

Russian mobsters see the country's 15,000 nuclear warheads as a new profit-making possibility. . . . The Russian government is unable to account for all its bombs and weapons-grade uranium and plutonium. (*USA Today*, 5/16/94)

GERMANY IN A FUROR OVER
PLUTONIUM SMUGGLING ARRESTS

Germany charges that weapons-grade nuclear material is slipping past Russian security. . . . In the largest confiscation of weapons-grade material police seized a suitcase of plutonium from a Colombian . . . as he disembarked in Munich from a flight from Moscow. Two Spanish businessmen were also arrested. (AP, 7/17/94)

CLEAR DANGER OF PLUTONIUM THEFT

More than 100 tons of plutonium from dismantled U.S. and Russian nuclear missiles pose "a clear danger" because there is no sure way to keep stockpiles from terrorists, says the National Academy of Sciences. (A 13 pound ball of plutonium is enough for a nuclear bomb.) (*USA Today*, 1/25/94)

RISE OF NUCLEAR ARMS BAZAAR FEARED

Iran's massive new arms build-up, a Libyan attempt to hire Russian nuclear experts and reports that Iran purchased three nuclear weapons have heightened fears that the Soviet Union's break-up will spur nuclear proliferation and enable terrorists to acquire weapons of mass destruction. (*Los Angeles Times*, 1/11/92)

BOMB FUEL KEEPS VANISHING AS THE CASES OF PEDDLING RISE ALL OVER EUROPE

German federal police had four cases of nuclear peddling in 1990. The number rose to 41 the next year, 158 the year after that. In 1993 it hit 241. (*WSJ*, 5/11/94)

MORE SMUGGLED NUKES

The number of cases of smuggling radioactive materials more than doubled in the past two years, the news magazine Der Spiegel reported Saturday, quoting an intelligence report. (AP, 2/18/95)

Fears of nuclear terrorism had been voiced many times prior to 1995. It was speculated that Iran, India, Pakistan, Israel, North Korea, and several other nations had nuclear weapons. But those who knew were not telling. The fears had been largely theoretical and abstract.

"Dressed in combat fatigues, the former air force general [Dzhokar Dudayev] Chechen President also claimed he had contacted several heads of state, including President Clinton, and warned them of 'the danger of nuclear weapons in Chechnya.' " This time, a former commander of the Soviet military forces, someone who knew the ins and outs of the Russian nuclear complex, was issuing the alert. The fears were no longer theoretical and abstract.

Even though the Chechen revolt was not among the top ten television stories of the month (January 1995), it was a watershed event.

New military alliances were forming along ethnic and religious lines. "We are ready to fight anywhere, not only in the mountains, but even in Moscow," said the Chechen vice president, Zelimkhan Yanderbiev. "This is a jihad, a holy war." If you were following the real news closely, you knew that further disintegration of the Russian states was at hand.

Assistant Defense Secretary Ashton Carter attacked moves in Congress to end U.S. military aid to Russia and three other former Soviet republics to help reduce and protect thousands of warheads and tons of chemical arms left over from the cold war.

"If there is one lesson that I draw from Chechnya, it is that revolutionary change in the former Soviet Union is far from over," he told reporters in an interview.

Carter, a key figure in U.S. nuclear policy, said he was not worried so much about nuclear weapons being fired in anger by young democracies such as the Ukraine, but by "accident or by an unauthorized terrorist party of some kind."

"For years and years and years there is going to be economic and political change of a very rapid sort throughout the former Soviet Union. . . . And all the while, those 30,000 nuclear weapons and hundreds of tons of fissile materials and tens of thousands of tons of chemical weapons are still there amidst all that," he said. (Reuters, 2/24/95)

Middle Muddle connoisseurs will appreciate the distinction made by Ashton Carter between nuclear weapons fired in anger by young democracies and those set off by irresponsible "unauthorized" terrorists.

The United States economically and militarily supported "authorized" terrorism by governments we favored (Russia, Indonesia, China) and also supported "unauthorized" terrorism by groups opposed to governments we disapproved of (Iran, Libya, Cuba). As long as we took sides, the wrath of whichever faction we opposed was automatically assured.

NUCLEAR PLANTS WARNED ABOUT BOMBS

Nuclear power plants must install barriers to guard against truck bombs like the one that exploded under the World Trade Center, the Nuclear Regulatory Commission has ruled.

The NRC had refused for years to require the anti-terrorist barriers at nuclear plants. . . .

A man driving a station wagon crashed through a fence and a metal garage door at the Three Mile Island Nuclear plant in Pennsylvania. (AP, 8/4/94)

Terrorism was eminently exportable software. The prospect of nuclear terrorism could not just be added to the threat of a meltdown of those decrepit, rusting, unmaintained nuclear reactors. The two had to be multiplied. The formula came out to reactors times terrorism equals inevitability squared.

7

FROM MELTDOWN TO MAYHEM

ATOMIC CAFE

The handwriting on the wall was not only in Cyrillic letters.

While terrorism (authorized or unauthorized) and the scores of decrepit potential Chernobyls were the most obvious candidates for disaster, the threat of meltdown was not reserved for the former Communist world.

New trucks develop faults, as well. From Ford to Intel to NASA, there has never been a manufacturer of *anything* who did not produce a lemon. Whether it's Ford recalling 8.7 million vehicles, or Intel manufacturing 5.5 million defective Pentium computer chips, or the dozens of failed or exploding space launches, there has never been a fault-free technology. In 1995, there were 432 nuclear reactors worldwide and 48 under construction.

NEW DELHI CLOSES 8 NUCLEAR PLANTS

The government has ordered the temporary shutdown and inspection of India's eight nuclear power stations after learning that safety violations caused a fire at one plant. (AP, 7/10/93)

CANADIAN NUKE PLANT CLOSED

Part of Canada's oldest nuclear plant will remain switched off until officials can determine what caused the first emergency shutdown of a commercial reactor in the country. . . .

"We're glad the system worked as it was designed to," said Hugh Spence, a spokesman for the Atomic Energy Control Board. "If it hadn't, you would have a major event." (AP, 13/12/94)

REACTOR CRACKS

Seven U.S. nuclear reactors have developed cracks and three others appear they could crack, according to a group of utilities that use the reactors. The Nuclear Regulatory Commission said the cracks could lead to a meltdown if earthquakes or other disasters strike. Two reactors in Europe and China also were cited for cracks. (*USA Today*, 7/1/94)

But unless it is catastrophic, nuclear news doesn't make the junk-news circuit. It is duly reported in deceptively dispassionate journalese on the inner pages of the major national newspapers.

You read an article here, another three weeks later, still another in two months, a few more over the course of the year. Ditto for the following year, and the year after that. There is enough time between incidents to keep them separate from one another. In between, there is the customary barrage of war, crime, earthquakes, hurricanes, floods, famines, epidemics, congressional scandals, environmental disasters, and baseball strikes to diffuse the effect.

VITAL GAUGE IN REACTOR FOUND PRONE TO ERROR

Federal regulators said today that nuclear plants around the country were using instruments to measure the depth of cooling water in reactors that were prone to error and could lead to operator error in the event of an accident. (*NYT*, 7/30/92)

NUCLEAR PLANT IS CRITICIZED ON PROCEDURES

The failure of employees to follow established work-control procedures led to last month's shutdown of Nine Mile Point 1 nuclear plant, Federal Nuclear Regulatory Commission officials said today. (*NYT*, 3/5/92)

SHUTDOWNS

Three nuclear power plants went through emergency shutdowns Saturday—but for different reasons. (*USA Today*, 8/24/92)

URANIUM LEAK AT TENNESSEE LABORATORY BRINGS FEARS OF ACCIDENTAL CHAIN REACTION

Uranium leaking from an old experimental reactor at the Oak Ridge National Laboratory in Tennessee has lodged in a pipe outside the reactor building, raising fears of an accidental nuclear chain reaction. (*NYT*, 11/25/94)

NUCLEAR SAFETY

Turkey Point nuclear plant operators almost shut down the reactors too late during Hurricane Andrew, couldn't tell if radiation was being released and wouldn't have been able to warn the outside world anyway, a federal report says. (AP, 4/2/93)

If you were digging out the real news from under the junk news back in the nineties, forecasting nuclear disaster was like betting on the favorite in a one-horse race.

PLUTONIUM POSES THREAT REPORT SAYS

As much as 26 metric tons of highly radioactive plutonium is being stored in conditions that could endanger workers and "potentially threaten the public and surrounding environment," says an internal Energy Department report. . . .

The report identified 299 potential risks to either workers or the public at the 35 sites examined. Investigators found welded steel pipes that had ruptured . . . bulging cans of incinerator ash containing plutonium; and hundreds of plastic containers of plutonium solution, many of them cracking. (AP, 12/11/94)

URANIUM RUSTING IN STORAGE POOLS IS TROUBLING U.S.

Millions of pounds of highly radioactive reactor fuel have been sitting in Energy Department storage pools for so long they are rusting and spreading radioactivity, the Energy Department said today. (*NYT*, 12/8/94)

MISHAP CASTS PALL OVER BIG ATOMIC WASTE SITE

Hanford is the nation's largest nuclear waste site, with 177 underground tanks containing 61 million gallons of radioactive wastes left over from four decades of plutonium production for nuclear weapons. Many have leaked and others are considered to be at risk of explosion. More than 17,000 people work at the site. (*NYT*, 7/15/93)

DEADLY NUCLEAR WASTE SEEMS TO HAVE LEAKED IN WASHINGTON STATE

About 75,000 gallons of deadly radioactive waste have apparently leaked from a tank at the government's Hanford Reservation in Washington State. (*NYT*, 12/28/93)

REPORT QUESTIONS SAFETY

An internal Energy Department report maintains that inept management, internal friction and worker sabotage has created conditions that undermine safety at nuclear weapons factories, according to a published report. (AP, 4/18/93)

ON THE DOWN SIDE, DAMAGE AND DISPOSAL

Despite its many benefits nuclear technology carries human and environmental risks:

- Reactors at aging nuclear power plants can crack . . . releasing deadly radioactivity.
- Malfunctioning equipment or mismanagement can cause dangerous situations, such as what happened at . . . Three Mile Island in 1979.
- Plutonium production at nuclear weapons plants can cause lasting damage to the environment—polluting the air, land and water.

At the power plants, the problem is waste disposal. . . . For now, most of the waste is stored in pools of water at the plants themselves, and the amount of waste nationwide has more than tripled since 1980 to 21,760 tons.

"The destructive things about nuclear technology are not only bombs . . . but the disposal of waste," says nuclear physicist Leo Seren. (*USA Today*, 12/2/92)

In 1992, it was still possible to begin an article on lurking nuclear disaster with "Despite its many benefits, nuclear technology carries human and environmental risks." This was like saying, "Despite its wonderful almond taste, eating cyanide is usually followed by death."

The world had already lived through Three Mile Island, Chernobyl, nuclear testing in Utah, and a wide variety of other local nuclear mishaps with major consequences.

UKRAINE: CHERNOBYL KILLED 125K

An estimated 125 thousand people in Ukraine have died because of the Chernobyl nuclear disaster and disease rates have soared. (AP, 4/25/94)

These figures were compiled nine years after the notorious accident. Health officials expected them to get much worse over time. Over 2 million people had been subjected to high doses of radiation.

Nevertheless, as long as people were not living just down-range, or in the affected immediate vicinity following some major breakdown, they did not make a fuss. *If* something happened in the future, well, it would happen elsewhere.

Governments and the utility industry actively encouraged this optimism.

Dairy farmer Louise Ihlenfeldt values NUCLEAR ENERGY as a way to keep the *air* clean. (And the milk fresh.)

The nuclear power plant a mile up the road has been generating electricity for 19 years. The Ihlenfeldt family has been working their Wisconsin farm for 125.

Nowadays, modern electrical equipment keeps the cows milked and the milk cold. And the nuclear plant keeps creating electricity without creating air pollution. "We've never had a problem with the plant," Louise says. "It's a clean, safe power source."

There are over 100 nuclear plants in the U.S. Because they don't burn anything to make electricity, they help protect our environment and preserve our natural resources for future generations. All while providing enough electricity for 65 million homes.

No single source is the whole answer to America's energy needs. But, as Louise Ihlenfeldt will tell you, nuclear energy is part of the answer.

NUCLEAR ENERGY MEANS CLEANER AIR

Clean air! Safe plants! Nonpolluting! A protector of the environment! Preserver of natural resources and future generations! Fresh, cold milk! Wow! Nuclear expert and dairy farmer Louise Ihlenfeldt assures us, "We've never had a problem with the plant. . . ."

What, me worry? And until the earthquake struck, there'd been no trouble with the Kobe Hotel or the Santa Monica Freeway.

The mighty quakes in Los Angeles and Kobe made a shambles of the best our modern engineers could do to make structures earthquakeproof. Indeed, in the wake of these events, the nomenclature had taken a beating. Buildings and structures once described as "earthquakeproof" are now called "earthquake-resistant." We now see what happens when a big tremor hits an "earthquake-resistant" hotel or office building or highway.

But what does happen when one of our "safe" nuclear plants takes a direct hit from a 7.5 quake? Ask the U.S. Council for Energy Awareness. Ask Louise.

But even as Louise was milking Elsie, the glowing cow, and Madison Avenue was trying to distract us from absorbing what we already knew, the press was revealing some things we had been prevented from knowing for the last forty years.

NUCLEAR NAZIS

It took until 1993 to learn that the U.S. government, from 1944 until 1974, was systematically using the nation as nuclear guinea pigs.

SECRET NUCLEAR RESEARCH ON PEOPLE COMES TO LIGHT

For three decades after World War II, top medical scientists in the nation's nuclear weapons industry undertook an extensive program of experiments in which civilians were exposed to radiation in concentrations far above what is considered safe today.

The experiments, at government laboratories and prominent medical research institutions, involved injecting patients with dangerous radioactive substances like plutonium or exposing them to powerful beams of radiation. (*NYT*, 12/17/93)

U.S. SPREAD RADIOACTIVE FALLOUT IN SECRET COLD WAR WEAPONS TESTS (NYT, 12/6/93)

RADIATED KIDS CALLED COLD WAR'S INFANTRY (*USA Today*, 1/14/94)

---

200 INFANTS FED RADIATION IN 50'S, 60'S (*USA Today*, 12/23/94)

PANEL SAYS U.S. MAY HAVE DONE THOUSANDS OF HUMAN RADIATION EXPERIMENTS (*NYT*, 10/22/94)

---

204 SECRET NUCLEAR TESTS ARE MADE PUBLIC (*NYT*, 12/8/93)

These grotesque experiments included feeding pregnant women radioactive pills without their knowledge, injecting radioactive plutonium into people's bodies, marching troops onto ground zero after a nuclear explosion, lacing milk with radioactive iodine, feeding children radioactive food, and releasing radioactive substances into the air to track their progress and effects on humans.

Some may find it difficult distinguishing between these scientific experiments carried out on a nation of unsuspecting victims in the name of American democracy and those carried out on prisoners in Nazi concentration camps.

The disclosure of this deliberate testing was only made public in 1993, and then only through the relentless four-year efforts of a daughter of one of the victims. The disclosures made it absolutely clear that what was finally, grudgingly revealed was but a portion of more widespread experimental programs.

Since the first revelations were made public, others have come to light.

OFFICIALS CITE MORE U.S. TESTS WITH RADIATION

About 9,000 Americans, including children and newborns, were used in 154 human radiation tests sponsored by the Atomic Energy Commission . . . government officials said today.

The figures released by the Office of Human Radiation Experiments at the Department indicate that the scope of the experimentation is greater than had been previously known. It does not include tests done by the Pentagon and other federal agencies. (*NYT*, 2/10/95)

However repellent the story, the scare factor is reduced to a minimum. Stories like these are typically reported in bland language in the journalistic boondocks. The story above appeared in the thin Saturday *New York Times*. The Saturday paper, with its diminished circulation, is a good place to find unsettling items of this nature. Unpopular or embarrassing disclosures are often made on a Friday afternoon, ensuring minimum media coverage.

With the readership of Saturday's newspapers the lowest of any day of the week, the Associated Press wrote, and the viewership of weekend television newscasts below that of any weekday, Friday is the first choice for state and federal officials who'd just as soon have no one notice some announcements. (*Trend Tracking*, Warner Books, 1990)

Six months after the February announcement, the Energy Department nearly doubled its estimate of radiation experiments on people to sixteen thousand. This announcement was boondocked onto page 27 of the *New York Times* in the heat of the summer (August 20, 1995).

The typically drawn-out process of disclosure conformed to a standard pattern for breaking bad or embarrassing news to the public. First, the government denies the charges. Then the charges are admitted but minimized. The initial public outrage is given time to die down. Then, over time, in stages, the greater extent of the damage is acknowledged. But by this time, crucial documents have been shredded or have disappeared, and the issue is obscured in a morass of charges, countercharges, congressional investigations, and politicizing.

Will we *ever* know about those tests run by the Pentagon and other federal agencies? According to the polls, not many Americans would be willing to bet on it.

A 1994 Harris poll revealed that 80 percent of Americans did not feel the government "can generally be trusted to look after our interests."

There is nothing comparable in our history to the deceit and the lying that took place as a matter of official government policy in order to protect this [the nuclear] industry. . . . Nothing was going to stop them. And they were willing to kill our own people. [Former Congressman and Secretary of the Interior Stewart Udall] (*NYT*, 6/9/93)

Victims of the experiments paid with their lives; the rest of Americans just paid—a total of $4 trillion to finance our nuclear weapons, according to the Federation of American Scientists.

The foregoing stories represent a tiny fraction of the volume of similar items appearing in mainstream news sources.

Whether we ever find out about other tests is actually immaterial. Even with the government and industry's proven and unrelenting policy of secrecy, what was out there in the open for all to see was more than enough to know that home-based nuclear bad times were in store—*if* you put the pieces together. Most people didn't. They did not see that all these nuclear incidents came together, thus revealing a trend—a trend with an inescapable, definite, foreseeable conclusion: foreseeable long ago.

8

THE FALLOUT FROM FALLOUT

BLASTERS

The only things not foreseeable were the actual extent of the nuclear crisis and its eventual provocation.

With the end of the Cold War, it was unlikely that it would be caused by someone pressing the Doomsday button—the final battle fervently predicted by the Armageddonites. But you could say with certainty that it would be brought about by some combination of mega Chernobyls, nuclear terrorism, spills, mishaps, whoopses, and all those sinister little secrets we were never told about for security reasons.

The result? Loss of life, radiation poisoning, the air, the soil, the water contaminated, everything alive on earth affected to a greater or lesser degree—nuclear disaster.

The unthinkable—for decades legitimately feared by the informed, and persistently ignored by the lunatic middle—happened.

On January 1, 2000, it's still hard to believe. That's human nature. Most people don't believe a catastrophe, any catastrophe, will happen. Then they believe that even if it does happen, it won't hit them. And then they believe that even if it does hit them, they'll survive it.

In one sense, this attitude is healthy and necessary for survival. If you follow the news and take into account every possible life-endangering threat in the air, you become paralyzed with fear and you barricade yourself into your house. On the other hand, to go through modern life blithely ignoring visible hazards with predictable ominous outcomes is folly. Somewhere in between the hyperparanoid ant and the kamikaze grasshopper, there is a proactive lifestyle. It's possible to prepare without getting paranoid.

The continental United States and the whole Western Hemisphere did not take any direct hits. The brunt of the fallout affected the former Soviet Union, Europe, Asia, the Middle East. While worldwide radiation levels increased dramatically, here at home the more immediate fears centered around swiftly proliferating local disasters.

Stores of spent weapons-grade and commercial nuclear fuels have leaked out of their inadequately designed storage containers or containment pools and have found their way into aquifers, groundwater, and, finally, the mainstream bloodstream.

The major nuclear calamities abroad and the proliferation of leaks, spills, transport mishaps, and other localized accidents (man-made and natural) at home have blown away the Middle Muddle.

By the year 2000, life—and attitudes—are going through a period of dizzying, accelerated change. An aroused and incensed public has turned vehemently antinuke. Activists have initiated class-action lawsuits against the nuclear industry and criminal lawsuits against individuals within the industry who are guilty for deliberately suppressing information and willfully endangering life. The entire nuclear-power industry is in the process of dismantling.

The planetary camel was already staggering under its load of toxins, pesticides, chemicals, and pollutants. The nuclear crisis was the last straw. Fallout was more than a figure of speech, a kind of radioactive dandruff; it was a deadly fact of life. It was taking its toll.

PRESERVE AND PREVENT

The cancer rate had been soaring for a decade. In 1995, cancer ranked second as the cause of death in the United States after heart disease. By 2000, it had become the number-one killer.

Zooming radiation levels have made it a statistical certainty that the cancer death rate will go up still more dramatically within decades.

The nuclear events finally galvanized the floundering environmental movement, demoralized and dispersed over the course of five successive hostile administrations.

A combination of socioeconomic, health, and philosophical factors created a radical and cresting shift in spirit and consciousness. One major consequence of that shift was that people were either voluntarily giving up or being forced out of their urban and suburban professions and occupations. Many were returning to the land. At first they were a mere trickle, then a stream, then a powerful, statistically significant river—a trend.

This movement did not go unnoticed by the media, but was mostly downplayed. Instead, the junk-news networks concentrated on the flight of the Armageddonites into the wilderness, and chortled over the boom in bunkers, fallout shelters, assault rifles, MREs (meals ready to eat), and pork and beans.

But this parallel diaspora did not translate easily into news bites, or lend itself to labels. These people pulling up stakes and moving out could no longer be crammed into the New Age pigeonhole that had been devised twenty-five years earlier to contain and trivialize them: a world of flakes, preyed on by charlatans, following weird diets and healing themselves with therapies unapproved by the American Medical Association.

That quarter century of negative publicity slowed down the trend but did not prevent these now-grown-up visionaries from being prepared. However, it lulled the lunatic middle into believing its own press: They were still in control; their actions were based upon "reason," and they reasonably stayed put as their world crumbled around them.

But to those moving out, the nuclear calamity was just a part, the most terrifying part, of a larger crisis, the logical culmination of a set of trends that had been gathering strength and direction for decades.

Who were these people who saw the impending situation so clearly? Where did they come from?

They first surfaced publicly and spectacularly in the 1960s, riding the wave of the protest movement. They marched for civil rights, for women's liberation, for the environment, and against the Vietnam War. In the sixties, there was a sense that they could really make things change. They were visionaries—but prepared to act, not just dream. Even if much of the action amounted to no more than growing hair, wearing beads or beards, burning bras or draft cards, attending love-ins and happenings, it was a time of high expectations. They saw very clearly that life on Earth was threatened, not only by nuclear war but also by damage to the environment. They raised the issues that led to some major legislation in the 1970s, including the creation of the Environmental Protection Agency.

But the vision was not sufficiently clear, the time not yet ripe. The movement waned as the World War II mentality reasserted itself with Ronald Reagan as its champion. Much that was gained in the seventies was lost in the eighties. Reviving the economy and building up the military became priorities—indeed, obsessions.

The disappearance of beads and beards and the reappearance of bras did not matter much, but the willful disregard of the environment had serious repercussions.

The EPA budget was cut, its staff reduced, and career officers were replaced by political hacks. Like other agencies, the EPA was co-opted by special interests and its positions reflected their views. The agency relaxed its standards on air and water quality, permitted the dumping of toxic waste in landfills, approved the use of known carcinogens in pesticides, and ignored the evidence of global problems such as acid rain and damage to the ozone layer.

The media sometimes wondered what had happened to all those baby boomers who had once marched for peace under a flower-power banner. They concluded that most had become Yuppies.

But most never became Yuppies. They outgrew their bell-bottoms and their tie-dyes, but they never abandoned their values. For them, the do-nothing nineties were even more disappointing than the give-'em-hell eighties. The positions of Reagan and Bush on environmental issues were clear. They promised little and gave less. "Americans did not fight and win the wars of the 20th century to make the world safe for green vegetables," said Bush's budget director, Richard Darman.

The baby boomers hoped for better from their own classmates Bill Clinton (even though he didn't inhale) and especially Al Gore, with his best-selling book on the environment. Ignoring campaign promises, both quickly sold out to special interests. Even with an all-Democratic Congress in power, every major environmental initiative was defeated during the first two years of the Clinton presidency.

It came as no surprise when betrayal by supposed friends

was followed by retribution by avowed enemies. The 1994 election brought Republicans back into control of the Senate and House of Representatives. This was widely trumpeted by the winners, interpreted by the losers, and labeled by the media as a "mandate." The people had spoken. With mandate in hand, Congress went to work.

In 1996, Congress cut spending for the Environmental Protection Agency to $6.5 billion from $7.2 billion in 1995. Meanwhile we were spending $100 billion a year to keep NATO running, and another $35 billion for military research and development.

But there was no mandate. In the "landslide" victory, only 38.8 percent of eligible voters turned out, according to the Committee for the Study of the American Electorate; 19 percent voted Republican; 16.6 percent voted Democratic.

In the infinitely flexible language of Middle Muddle, however, the meaning of the word *mandate* was changed. According to *Webster's New Twentieth Century Dictionary Unabridged, mandate* means: "The wishes of constituents expressed to a representative, legislature, etc. as an order, or regarded as an order."

But in the Dictionary of Middle Muddle, *mandate* was redefined as "the prerogative of a representative or the legislature to willfully ignore the wishes of constituents and to act upon the orders of special interests."

THE NEXT ENVIRONMENTAL THREAT

The Democrats who ran Congress in President Clinton's first two years routinely massacred good environmental legislation. They defied Interior Secretary Bruce Babbitt's efforts to reform grazing and mining laws. They blocked efforts to rewrite demonstrably bad law like Superfund, the toxic waste cleanup program.

Could things get worse? Under Newt Gingrich, they already are. The Democrats never set out to destroy 25 years of legislative history aimed at making America's air breathable and America's waters drinkable, swimmable and fishable. But that is what the House Republicans seem bent on doing. (editorial, *NYT*, 2/12/95)

Mandate or no mandate, the press in general was outraged.

The *San Francisco Chronicle* accurately characterized the Republican contract as "a wholesale assault on the entire body of environmental protections achieved over the last 25 years—a virtual clear-cutting of laws and regulations designed to conserve environmental resources and protect human health and safety." (*In These Times*, 2/6/95)

Government had been taken out of the hands of the inept—and handed over to the insane.

A February 1995 poll showed that 88 percent of the public believed environmental protection to be one of the most important problems facing our country. (Eighty-three percent of those who voted in the November 1994 elections described themselves as "an environmentalist.")

In the sixties and seventies, the baby boomers were too young to bring about change; in the eighties, they were building careers and raising their families. By the nineties, they were in their fifties. Seasoned and established, their vision had become clear. And what they saw as the nineties wore on was an increasingly flagrant disparity between what the government did and what the people wanted.

Wherever you looked, government officials at every level were ignoring the will of the people who had put them into office in the first place. While some environmental issues were complex and involved conflicting points of view, others were simple and had unanimous voter support.

The people made it absolutely clear to the government at the local, state, and federal levels that they did not want nuclear waste stored anywhere near them. With the possible exception of Louise and her glowing cow, when it came to the storage of nuclear waste, everyone became a fervent NIMBY (not in my backyard).

Unable to get an uncomprehending public to understand that what was good for Three Mile Island was good for the country, and unable to do what was good for Three Mile Island via democracy, the government redefined democracy.

BY DEFAULT AND WITHOUT DEBATE, UTILITIES READY LONG-TERM STORAGE OF NUCLEAR WASTE

For the foreseeable future, more than 70 communities near nuclear generating plants will become repositories for spent nuclear fuel, the most radioactive of all atomic wastes, without any public hearings or environmental studies of the sites. (*NYT*, 2/15/95)

What distinguishes a democracy from every other form of government is that elected representatives are supposed to carry out the will of the majority of the people.

And the will of Americans is not to have nuclear waste, the most radioactive substance in the world, stored in their backyards, particularly when there is no known safe storage method.

While there have always been abuses of the democratic method of government, in the late nineties this became brazen and systematic; it was the rule rather than the exception—on practically every issue of substance.

Just as environmental protection was scuttled against the will of 73 percent of the people, so the Mexican bailout was paid for by the American public, even though 80 percent of the people opposed it.

" 'It's clear from the polling data that there's just no base of popular support out there,' he [Newt Gingrich] told reporters at a news conference. 'Until it's explained and until people understand it, it's very hard to move something like that in a free society.' "

Actually, it was very easily explained. And Americans understood. They understood that more than $20 billion of their money had been taken directly out of supposedly empty coffers to bail out a handful of Wall Street billionaires and bankers. And a substantial percentage of the remaining $30 billion of "international" money was also provided by U.S. taxpayers. Nor did it prove "hard to move in a free society." It was easily moved. Gingrich, Dole, Clinton, and their fellow politicians, acting upon the new meaning of *mandate,* simply ignored the will of the people and moved it.

The only thing that was hard to explain was that America was a "free society."

The polls were showing that the percentage of people who could be fooled all of the time was shrinking. Even before the Mexican bailout, 80 percent of the people "did not think the government has the best interests of the public in mind." Ninety-one percent said that they had "little or no confidence in Washington to solve problems."

Never before in polling history had there been figures reflecting this level of disgust and distrust. The lunatic middle talked about change, followed its own set of directives, and did not notice change was happening all around them, without them, and in spite of them.

THE SEARCH FOR A SOLUTION

Though feeling helpless to alter the downhill course of events, well before the millennium clock struck, many were acting individually. The voices crying out in the wilderness began sounding louder and clearer as the wilderness disappeared. When many join hands, hearts, and voices, they become a force. When the force begins to move, it becomes a trend.

Who were these "many"? They came from across the board and spanned the generations. Mostly, they were children of the sixties. And *their* children, now in their teens and twenties (Generation X)—angry and distrustful of government, respecting the environment, ambivalent about big science, suspicious of corporate culture, thinking for themselves and looking for a meaning to their lives that was never a part of their formal education—white-collar, blue-collar, no-collar.

The New Age had come of age.

But to act—individually or collectively—it was first necessary to survive. This was no longer just a question of keeping the tigers at bay, or having a roof over your head. It wasn't a political issue; it wasn't about economic growth; it wasn't about foreign policy. It was quite literally about survival—a matter of life and death.

One in every three Americans will get cancer and one in five will die of the disease. The overall mortality rate is 8% higher than in 1971, and cancer is destined to surpass heart disease as the No 1. killer. (AP, 9/29/94)

NO MORE PESTICIDES FOR DINNER

A price is paid when society relies so heavily on toxic chemicals: 68 pesticide ingredients have been determined to cause cancer. One out of every 10 community drinking-water wells contains pesticides. . . .

Because of improved detection methods, we now know we are being exposed daily to dozens of carcinogenic toxic agents in many different foods, with no attempt made to calculate the aggregate risk to health. At the same time, the incidence of many forms of cancer, including breast cancer and childhood cancer, is on the rise. (Al Meyerhoff, a lawyer with the Natural Resources Defense Council, Op-Ed page, *NYT*, 3/9/93)

In 1995, cancer had become the number-one killer of children between the ages of one and fourteen. By age five, millions of youngsters have received up to 35 percent of their safe lifetime doses of some pesticides known to cause cancer, according to a study by the Environmental Working Group.

By the time the average child is a year old he will have received the acceptable lifetime doses of 8 pesticides from 20 commonly eaten foods. Compared to late in life exposure, exposure to pesticides early in life can lead to a greater risk of chronic effects that are expressed only after long latency periods have elapsed, the National Academy of Sciences report concludes.

Such effects include cancer, neuro-development impairment and immune dysfunction. Much more study is needed to test how pesticides affect children the author emphasizes.

"The likely significant health risk to children is exceedingly remote," insists John McClung of the United Fresh Fruit and Vegetable Association. "Just because there's not enough data to confirm or debunk the notion there's a health risk, that doesn't mean there is one." (USA Today, 6/28/93)

In 1987, a National Academy of Sciences report said that the nation's food supply was inadequately protected from cancer-causing pesticides. . . . In 1989, a Natural Resources Defense Council released its report, "Intolerable Risk: Pesticide in Our Children's Food." But the Federal government . . . did nothing significant to change the regulations. (NYT, 6/27/93)

KIDS IN A TOXIC WORLD

According to the Natural Resources Defense Council, cancer rates rose 19% among all children between 1973 and 1990. (USA Today, 8/24/94)

POLLUTANTS BREED DEADLY SYNTHETIC

Scientists say the evidence is starting to resemble a gigantic biological puzzle. But how can they connect the dots when the clues seem so unrelated?

Florida alligators with undeveloped sex organs. Great Lakes babies with learning disabilities. Adult women with breast cancer. For all the apparent differences scientists think they found a common link, and that link is estrogen—not the natural hormone, but a synthetic version that researchers have traced to pollutants in the environment. . . .

Despite the mounting evidence, the chemical industry says more studies are needed to verify the environmental estrogen theory. (*USA Today*, 4/21/94)

To the chemical industry, and just about any other industry destroying life on the planet, evidence can never mount so high that "more studies" are not needed. The campaign to divert, deny, and obscure the evidence was combined with the incessant lobbying efforts in Washington by powerful special-interest groups, who financed the "mandate." (Ironically, these special-interest groups were financed in part by the American taxpayer. Agribusiness, chemical, mining, oil, and other polluting industries were the recipients of an estimated $4.5 billion a year in special tax breaks and privileges, according to a consortium of environmental groups.)

The mullahs of the Mandate were making sure that Washington would achieve victory in the one war it was indisputably winning: The war on the environment.

Surviving into the new millennium took planning, intelligence . . . being in the right place at the right time.

9

SURVIVAL KIT FOR THE MILLENNIUM

THE SURVIVORS

This kit contains no assault rifles, no cans of pork and beans, not that much high tech at all. The kit is mainly software: attitudes and ideas, programs, disciplines. Some of its elements are nutritional and health awareness, pioneering, voluntary simplicity, "right livelihood," transformational martial arts, self-responsibility, and the quest for higher consciousness. These are things to be done, actions to be taken, programs for living, not just ideas to be talked about, or legislated for or against.

To begin with, on the most primary level of self-defense, savvy people were taking measures to safeguard their health.

If you were one of those who saw through and beyond the junk news, you knew time was running out. You couldn't wait. The problems were real. You have to build up your own immune system to survive in a poisoned world; no one can do it for you. This was the overall strategy. Millions heard that call and heeded it—though many more millions never heard it, or never heeded it, and paid the consequences.

THE HEALTH CRISIS

Appearances were deceptive regarding the health-conscious eighties and nineties.

If you read magazines or watched television, it looked like the whole country was running, pumping iron, doing aerobics, or was otherwise strenuously physically preoccupied. It appeared that a fitness trend had swept the nation.

On the other hand, if you conducted supermarket trends research, you logged battalions of Twinkies-fed out-of-shape people with shopping baskets filled with soft drinks, salty snacks, cookies, cigarettes, candy, frozen entrées, most everything processed, very little fresh. For those who considered themselves diet-conscious, the frozen, processed, preprepared meals would be low-fat or fat-free or salt-free.

To the majority of supermarket shoppers, nutrition in the nineties meant Healthy Choice or Lean Cuisine. But with 71 percent of Americans overweight, not many in this multitude looked like those lithe and glamorous people in television ads who were peddling these very same products.

Nevertheless, the health trend, hyped by fitness-gear manufacturers and ballyhooed by the media throughout the seventies and eighties *was* real, and it was something new. (Who, over the age of forty now, ever saw an adult running when they were children?)

But however real the trend, it had only just been born, and it was in the early years of its life cycle. Its high-profile popularity was a craze—a fad, more fashion than fitness. Millions in the eighties bought rowing machines and signed up at gyms, but according to the Centers for Disease Control and Prevention, 55 percent of Americans eighteen to thirty-four and 59 percent ages thirty-five to fifty-four were leading sedentary lives. "It's a myth that Americans are becoming more active," said Dr. Paul Siegel, director of the Centers' Adult Behavioral Risk Factor Surveillance Surveys.

What about all those sales of running shoes, walking shoes, tennis shoes, hiking shoes, cross-training shoes, and aerobic shoes that retailers were ringing up? According to *Footwear News*, 90 percent of the people weren't buying them for running, walking, tennis, hiking, cross-training, or aerobics at all. They were fashionable, comfortable, too . . . and they were here to stay.

Many dressed the part; only a hard core played it—like all those suburban Sunday ranchers suddenly buying four-wheel-drive Jeeps and Explorers and using them to take the kids to the supermarket.

Actually, the percentage of people getting fit was deceptively small. In the eighties and nineties, only a dedicated small minority (largely confined to the educated and the upscale, according to the Centers for Disease Control) jogged or swam or hiked to health and fitness and monitored their diets.

This was reflected in health and longevity statistics. The wealthy and educated lived longer, healthier lives than the poor and the uneducated, who for the most part ate badly, too much, and rarely exercised, according to studies published in *The New England Journal of Medicine*.

The majority actually lost ground, and gained weight. A study by the National Center for Health Statistics found that about a third of all adult Americans were obese (defined as being 20 percent or more above a person's desirable weight). These figures were 31 percent above those from a similar study carried out in 1980. The average weight of young American adults had risen ten pounds in the last seven years. Even American kids were overweight:

21 percent in 1991, up from 15 percent in 1980. In 1994, only 37 percent of high school students got regular vigorous exercise, a precipitous drop from the 62 percent recorded by a similar federal survey done six years earlier. Former Surgeon General C. Everett Koop claimed obesity was costing the United States $100 billion and causing 300,000 deaths a year.

The majority exercised too little and ate too much—of the wrong foods. Even as they became more conscious of fruits, grains, and vegetables, and cut down their cholesterol intake, Americans on average consumed twenty-three pounds more sugar, twelve more pounds of fat, and drank twenty-two gallons more soft drinks per person in 1995 than in 1970. The U.S. Department of Agriculture, which compiled the data, also estimated that 40 percent of Americans did not watch their diets.

▶ **TRENDPOST** *The $24 billion spent by Americans on weight control in 1995 would become $30 billion by the year 2000 and accelerating. Well-positioned weight control businesses will grow fat as their clients grow lean.* ◀

For that heedless majority, the consequences piled up over the years. Bad diet was just one factor in an overall assault on the nation's health. By the year 2000, rising medical costs attested to the reality of mounting disease and debility. Even the slowly but steadily rising longevity statistics did not necessarily mean better health. They meant that advances in modern medicine were saving lives that might otherwise have been lost in crisis situations and that new drugs and procedures were keeping sick people alive longer—driving up medical costs in the process.

STAYING HEALTHY

Of course, we've all heard it since we were children: "If you don't have your health, you don't have anything." But the old cliché took on a strange urgency as the twentieth century wound through its last years. Staying healthy wasn't what it used to be. Eating three square meals a day, exercising, not smoking, and drinking in moderation no longer sufficed. A multiplicity of factors conspired to break down people's immune systems.

It was difficult to assign blame precisely or proportionately, but researchers were in overall agreement on many of the agents. Apart from an intrinsically bad diet and all that acknowledged junk food, there were the hidden culprits: food additives and chemicals, food with all the nutrition processed out of it, pesticide residues and preservatives on fresh foods, intensively raised meat and poultry doctored with antibiotics and growth hormones, polluted air, depleted and poisoned land, and contaminated water. In 1993, American industries released 2.8 billion pounds of toxic pollution into air, water, and land, including 180 million pounds of known cancer-causing substances.

But every study claiming that pesticides or other chemicals caused cancers in laboratory animals or that hormones caused genetic defects was typically answered by industry spokesmen claiming that the amounts used by *their* industry were negligible and therefore safe. The typical government response was that the evidence was insufficient to justify banning or controlling the suspected drug or chemical.

"NO SAFE" EXPOSURE TO DIOXIN

Dioxin, even in trace amounts, likely causes cancer and can harm human and reproductive systems the Environmental Protection Agency says today. . . .

The report, a result of 3½ years of research, finds people can be exposed by eating meat, fish, eggs and dairy products.

"There is no safe threshold," says Environmental Defense Fund scientist Ellen Silbergeld.

But EPA scientists recommend against dietary changes, saying the benefits of a balanced diet outweigh the risks.

The National Cattlemen's Association agrees, accusing the EPA of using "incomplete, limited, or outdated" data.

"There is no reason to believe that current levels of dioxin in our bodies and in our diet pose a risk to our health," says Stephen Safe, a professor working for the association. (*USA Today,* 10/12/94)

Despite the assurances of Professor Safe (and his industry co-mercenaries, Professors Harmless, Risk-Free, Beneficial, and Unproven), the accumulating evidence from hundreds of independent studies was indicating that it was not safe at all. It was just impossible to know how much damage, precisely, dioxin was doing, in conjunction with all the additives, preservatives, pesticides, hormones, effluents, runoffs, spills—and by January 1, 2000, the radiation—that people's immune systems were absorbing.

A new and mysterious toxic soup had mounting numbers of people falling prey to new or hitherto rare illnesses, some of them strange, debilitating, chronic, and resistant to treatment, even fatal. The new black plagues forecast in the eighties by the Trends Research Institute (*Trend Tracking*) were starting to surface in the nineties.

INFECTIOUS DISEASES ON THE REBOUND IN THE U.S., A REPORT SAYS

Not so long ago, Government officials and medical leaders all but pronounced the end of infectious diseases as a major health problem. These striking examples (new virulent and fatal viruses, parasites and toxins) of new and emerging diseases prove that prediction wrong. They join a list that includes, among others, AIDS, Legionnaire's disease, Lyme disease, Lassa fever, and bleeding and fever from the Ebola and Marburg viruses. Some were unknown or minor hazards only a decade or two ago. Others increased significantly in incidence over the last 20 years. Still others threaten to become bigger hazards in the near future. (*NYT*, 2/10/94)

TB CASES SPREADING RAPIDLY AMONG CHILDREN, REPORT SAYS (*NYT*, 9/19/93)

RESEARCHER WARNS OF "MEDICAL DISASTER" AS BACTERIA EVOLVE

Common bacteria that cause pneumonia . . . and many other diseases are evolving into forms untreatable by all known medicines, threatening a chilling post-antibiotic era that would be "nothing short of a medical disaster," a researcher said. . . .

"In the post-antibiotic world, the simplest infections could quickly escalate into fatal illnesses," said Alander Tomasz of Rockefeller University in New York City.

"Most people think it will happen," he said. "It's unpredictable when." And the consequences? "No one knows. The mortality is quite high." (AP, 2/20/94)

"FLESH-EATERS," OTHER VIRAL MYSTERIES ARE ON THE RISE (*USA Today*, 9/8/94)

By January 1, 2000, getting healthy and staying healthy was no longer a hobby, something to occupy spare time. It was central to survival. The new black plagues were upon us all.

Scientists have known for years that pollution can magnify the vulnerability of plants and animals to natural threats, but proving the pollution is the main culprit in specific cases is notoriously tricky. Recently, however, examples that may reflect a kind of environmental AIDS, in which the weakening effects of pollution have opened the door for sudden massive damage and other problems, are appearing with disturbing frequency. . . . This year a virus wiped out more than half of the harbor seals along the North Sea coast. A still spreading plague, many researchers speculate, is killing animals whose immune systems have been weakened by toxic chemicals. (WSJ, 10/25/88)

Nobody has ever confused the *Wall Street Journal* with Greenpeace.

When an article talking about an impending epidemic of "environmental AIDS" finds its way into a major *Wall Street Journal* story, maybe it's time to sit up and take notice. Few noticed. Professors Safe, Harmless, Risk-Free, Beneficial, and Unproven prevailed.

The rise and spread of AIDS made the public aware of what happens when the immune system breaks down. But the number of people at risk for AIDS is small compared with the numbers of people at risk for the new black plagues. Unlike AIDS, which is caused by a virus and transmitted under certain conditions by bodily fluids, the new black plagues were caused by pollution of the environment and transmitted by the air we breathe, the water we drink, and the food we eat.

However horrific and scary, AIDS never escalated into worldwide epidemic proportions—as the headlines had threatened throughout most of the eighties. By 1996 the headlines had changed. "AIDS Fight Is Skewed by Federal Campaign Exaggerating Risks. Most Heterosexuals Face Scant Peril but Receive Large Portion of Funds. Less Goes to Gays, Addicts." A May 1, 1996, front page *Wall Street Journal* article reported on a deliberate media campaign launched by the U.S. government to frighten the public unnecessarily, which it did. Contrary to the government's multimillion-dollar media blitz, the overwhelming heterosexual public was not at risk—a fact already well known to many AIDS researchers in 1987, when the campaign was launched, But the insidious and cumulative effects of what was being called "Environmental AIDS" mounted throughout the nineties, eventually driving AIDS off the front pages. With the new black plagues, everyone is at risk. Everyone has been exposed—with the young, the poor, the out-of-shape, and the elderly most at risk, and most afflicted.

By January 1, 2000, it was no longer possible to summon up the wonder drugs of the past half century to combat any and every health problem. The world was awash in wonder drugs. Bacteria had become resistant to treatment, and worldwide misuse of antibiotics was in the process of destroying their effectiveness on a massive scale. Medical authorities around the world were acknowledging a frightening scenario: The wonder bugs were winning the battle with the wonder drugs. "Environmental AIDS" was a fact of life.

DRUG PROOF DISEASE SPREADING

Misuse of antibiotics is producing drug-resistant bacteria fueling the resurgence of cholera, tuberculosis and other diseases, the World Health Organization said.

About one million bacterial infections occur every day worldwide in hospitals alone, most of them drug-resistant, said Professor Jacques Acar of the Pierre and Marie Curie University in Paris.

Antibiotics . . . are losing their effectiveness. Once a new drug has become widely used resistance to it is already emerging somewhere in the world.

"Resistance is epidemic in many countries and multidrug resistance leaves doctors with virtually no room for maneuver in an increasing number of diseases," said Acar.

"The pharmaceutical industry is unlikely to manufacture any new classes of antibiotics in the next five to ten years." (AP, 12/6/94)

Immune system breakdown extended to all of organic life on Earth.

MANY RESOLVING TO IMPROVE THEIR IMMUNE SYSTEM

"The immune system is the most complicated system in the body, along with the neurological system," says Dr. Kenneth A. Bock, director of the Rhinebeck Health Center, one of the world's foremost clinics for immune system treatment.

"But you can picture how the system works if you think of it as a kettle with many different kinds of 'liquids' in it," he says. "The liquids range from environmental toxins to viruses to allergies, to foods. These are on top of the liquid you're born with—your genetic blueprint."

"The more liquids in the kettle, the greater the burden on your immune system," he says. "When the liquids overflow, your immune system malfunctions and you get sick or have other symptoms."

The goal of an immune-system strengthening program is therefore to keep the total volume of immune-system "liquids" as low as possible so the kettle can contain unexpected toxic surges without overflowing. ("Trends in the News," 1/6/95)

IMMUNE SYSTEM EMPOWERMENT

By 2000, the kettle was overflowing. To survive, individually and collectively, concerted, intelligent action had to be taken, and it was being taken by the aware and the unbuffaloed.

This made up a growing and sizable minority. Throughout the eighties and nineties, as awareness of global immune system breakdown spread, knowledge of the antidote spread along with it. The problem posed was twofold. No individual action seemed effective in preventing or mitigating the assault on health from a dozen directions simultaneously. At the same time, it was next to impossible to tap into a practical remedial regime. The information was all out there, but it was not easy to distinguish between the gold and the dross.

As the New Age went mainstream, Madison Avenue appropriated some of its lingo, and suddenly the supermarkets were filled with products calling themselves "pure," "fresh," "wholesome," and "natural." Taking their cue from enterprising Asian greengrocers, who had proved the demand, supermarkets installed salad bars, sandwiched in between the fresh-produce section and the shelves of Twinkies. Did pure and natural mean organic? And if not, what was the difference? And how much difference did it make? Were vitamin supplements really essential? And if so, which vitamins for what reason? Was there a difference between the chemically synthesized vitamins in the major drug chains, compared with vitamins extracted from organic foods (available in so-called health-food stores)?

What about enzymes, blue-green algae, acidophilus, zinc picolinate, magnesium, bee pollen, Mexican wild yam, aloe vera, ginseng, antioxidants? A thousand vying diets were touted on the pages of everything from the *National Enquirer* to its jet-set equivalent, *Vanity Fair*.

Eventually, even the colonialists of the greatest junk-food empire in the world got into the act.

NUTRITION CAMPAIGN DRAWS A COMPLAINT

McDonald's Corporation said that it had joined with the American Dietetic Association to introduce a nutrition education program. A physicians group, however, asked the Government . . . to investigate a portion of the campaign that tells children that meat "can make it easier to do things like climb higher and ride your bike farther." . . . Dr. Neal D. Barnard, President of the Physicians Committee for Responsible Medicine, has asked the Federal Trade Commission to investigate the campaign's claim for meat, which he called "false." (*NYT*, 3/3/93)

A spokeswoman for McDonald's defended the campaign. She said the company was "very comfortable with our program" because it was developed in conjunction with the American Dietetic Association.

Here was junk nutrition justifying junk food. As long as the product could be sold, human ingenuity could invent a rationale that made it sound nutritious.

At the same time, vitamins and food supplements had become a substantial industry. But how much of the health barrage was commercial hype? If you were getting your information only from the American Medical Association and the American Dietetic Association, you might have thought most of it was bogus. Just how much was valid?

And what, specifically, was important for you? Out of the hundreds of books published on every aspect of the health-awareness movement, which ones, in what combination, actually provided answers and a practical regimen? To be vegetarian or not to be vegetarian? That was the question—or one of the questions, anyway. Vegan? Macrobiotic? Biodynamic? Low-calorie, fat-free, low on carbohydrates or high on carbohydrates, Scarsdale, Pritikin, Atkins . . . ?

Aware and unbuffaloed did not necessarily mean clear and unconfused.

LONGEVITY CENTERS

If that's you on January 1, 2000, aware and unbuffaloed but unclear and confused, you could begin to implement your new millennium resolution by checking into one of the new longevity centers. They are springing up around the country in response to the demand.

▶ **TRENDPOST** *Longevity centers represent the cutting edge of the new health trend. Nobody has seen anything quite like them before. Those who implement foresight first will benefit first.* ◀

Longevity centers are not modern versions of the nineteenth-century spa, frequented by the idle but ailing rich. Nor are they modern "fat farms" whose sole objective is weight loss in a congenial, supportive atmosphere. They are not upgraded sixties hippie communes, nor yet Club Med with a slant on health, nor upscale R&R resorts or "ranches" at five thousand dollars a week, nor detox centers, nor sanatoriums, nor hospitals.

They are a bit of all these, catering to the income spectrum but sharing certain guidelines. You don't go to them for a pampered healthy holiday. They are places you go to for clean food, clean water, and clean air—requirements that severely restrict their locations in the year 2000, especially the water requirement.

REPORT: U.S. TAP WATER IS DIRTY

More than 1 in 5 Americans unknowingly drink tap water polluted with feces, lead, radiation, or other contaminants. . . . 53 million Americans drank water that violated EPA safety standards. . . . Nearly 1000 deaths each year and at least 400,000 cases of water-borne illness may be attributed to contaminated water, according to the National Resources Defense Council and the Environmental Working Group. (AP, 1/6/95)

UNDER-TREATED WATER FLOWS TO 50 MILLION
(USA Today, 7/28/94)

EPA: 40% OF FRESHWATER IS UNUSABLE
(USA Today, 4/21/94)

LEAD IN WATER RISK IN 819 CITIES
(USA Today, 5/12/93)

MIDWESTERNERS GETTING PESTICIDES IN DRINKING WATER, STUDY SAYS

Millions of Americans swallow five widely used farm pesticides in their drinking water, said a study by the Environmental Working Group, a private organization that seeks stricter regulations of pesticides. . . .

George Rolofson, spokesman for the Ciba-Geigy Company, the makers of atrazine, said he had not seen the report but questioned the group's use of the narrowest risk standard.

"I think they're misusing it here," he said.

Ciba-Geigy has been asking the E.P.A. to allow higher levels of exposure to atrazine because the company says studies showing its cancerous potential were flawed. The agency denied that request. (*NYT*, 10/19/94)

Also responding to the study's findings, Jay Vroom, of the American Crop Protection Association, a chemical trade group, said the report was an "unnecessary attempt to scare the public. Farmers and ranchers . . . handle [chemicals] carefully and as required by law."

It couldn't have been the farmers and ranchers. It wasn't the chemical industry, or the pesticide manufacturers, or the nuclear power stations, or the defense industry, or the oil companies. Probably it was one of those acts of God the insurance companies won't insure against, but it was an undisputable fact that by 2000, very little clean water flowed from American taps.

Crumbling municipal infrastructures, an emasculated Safe Drinking Water Act, hundreds of thousands of rotting fuel-storage tanks, ruptured pipelines, and the heightened ongoing environmental onslaught of spills, runoffs, and effluents made it difficult even to obtain safe water from public supplies. In the U.S. a record 2.7 billion gallons of bottled water were consumed in 1995, up 1,025 percent from 1975.

The problem was global. The world will spend an estimated $600 billion over the next decade to augment water reserves, according to the World Bank.

And "safe" water does not in any sense mean pure, clean, or healthy. It just means water that has had the contaminants filtered out, otherwise removed, or neutralized by high doses of chlorine. "Safe" water is dead water. All that can be said for it is that it doesn't make you sick—anyway, not often.

CHLORINATED WATER FOUND TO POSE SLIGHT CANCER RISK, announced one headline. "A new Finnish study says the by-products found in some chlorinated drinking water may nudge up the risk of bladder and kidney cancer."

"Safe" water also tasted lousy. "Clean" water came only in bottles from springs far from the cities. But to get clean, *living* water fresh out of Mother Earth meant traveling far and choosing sites carefully.

Indeed, in many American cities, very little water of any kind flowed from the taps; serious water shortages had become endemic in many parts of the nation, in particular the West and Southwest, as a result of population growth and the insatiable needs of agriculture.

► **TRENDPOST** *Any water supply–related business represents a sound investment for the foreseeable future—water sources, purification systems and supplies, distribution, and marketing.* ◄

Longevity centers with the best water got extra stars in the ratings. For many people, clean, living water was a major draw of such centers. But it was the stress, strain, and danger of the *fin de millennium* lifestyle that turned longevity centers into a trend and big business.

book
two

10

NEW MILLENNIUM
MEDICINE

HEALTHY U.

What was troubling you was troubling a lot of people. It wasn't one big thing; it was more one thing after another, a kind of chronic frazzle.

The allergies wouldn't go away. You couldn't sustain your energy level, even though you'd become diet-conscious. You were exercising, but you didn't feel stronger. There were head pains, back pains, stomach pains, and your job was a pain in the neck. Your relationships weren't working out, and the whole world around you seemed to be on a downhill pell-mell course: radiation, environmental poisoning, paramilitary conspiracies, national and international terrorism, economic fallback. Of course, all of this had been going on for years, but by 2000, you couldn't pretend that it was happening to everybody else and that you were okay in the middle of it.

Without quite buying into Armageddon, you could see much more was going wrong than going right, and an awful lot of people were blaming everyone else for the debacle.

Others, in the words of the old Rolling Stones song, waited for the knight in shining armor to come to their emotional rescue. At your age, you didn't believe in knights in shining armor, and you knew that blaming everyone else—even if they were responsible—didn't do *you* any good.

What would do you some good? Years back, you'd found yourself a holistic doctor, and now it was on the doctor's advice that you checked into the longevity center. It was your whole life that you had to put together: body, mind, spirit.

You've barely checked in and already you wish you could stay longer, but you can't. The time crunch and the money crunch restrict you to a month's visit. Aware that restoring abused health was a process as exacting and time consuming as restoring an abused work of art, many of the center's long-term residents were there on sabbatical, committing a precious six months' or year's leave from their industry, office, institution, or practice to recouping their lives. Others will be staying even longer.

You've traveled a long way to get here and you had to book way in advance. You cannot quite put your finger on it, but the center has already put you at ease.

The grounds have been orchestrated by some kind of virtuoso landscape composer. There is nothing showy about it; everything somehow just feels right, in place and where it belongs. Only later will you learn that this was the work of an inspired modern master of ancient Feng Shui, the Chinese art of siting buildings and harmonizing landscapes.

The architects have designed buildings that implement that first impression of effortlessness and relaxation. Back in the twentieth century, if you wanted the best, you had to go still further back into the past, to the nineteenth or early twentieth century, and pay through the nose for it: the Plaza, the Savoy, the Ritz, the Broadmoor, rather than the later Hilton, Marriott, or Sheraton.

Now, some of the high-end centers have taken over stately homes, ex–luxury resorts, and defunct colleges. But in the world of longevity centers, it is often the new that draws the rave notices. Just as the new medicine has integrated the best of the old and the cutting-edge new, so an emergent breed of architect has studied the principles commanding the great sacred architecture of the past and applied them to modern high-tech materials. They have rediscovered the lost secrets of the temples, mosques, and cathedrals that people travel around the world to visit. But they have used them to create visionary twenty-first-century forms—light-filled, spacious, unmistakably modern low-maintenance, high-efficiency buildings that nevertheless produce the kind of emotional effect normally associated only with the work of the very distant past.

You respond to the whole but are specifically aware only of certain striking details—good original paintings and sculpture, fountains, aquariums, ergonomic furniture, full-spectrum lighting . . . and the gardens. Gardens unlike any you've ever seen before. Flowers, flowers in profusion, but not just in ornamental beds; flowers interspersed with berry bushes, fruit trees, and magnificent beds of vegetables.

When you get to your room, you don't even have to check to see if the windows open; you know they will. Over years of travel, you've learned to check into hotels with misgivings, even when you've paid top dollar. A uniformed doorman may have spun the revolving door for you, but once inside, there it was: hotel air—stale, stuffy, lifeless, diseased—permeated with a hundred hidden toxic chemicals lurking in the carpets, plastics, insulation, wall coverings, curtains, furniture, and stirred up daily with cleaning machines and a noxious brew of housekeeping materials: detergents, polishes, disinfectants, sanitizers, and deodorizers. "Sick building syndrome," they called it. According to the American Lung Association, the American Medical

Association, and government agencies, it had been proven to provoke nasal congestion, sore throats, wheezing, asthma, eye irritation, nausea, coughs, rhinitis, headaches, lethargy, rashes, fever, and even cognitive impairment—personality changes. In the workplace alone, it was costing $50 billion a year in lost work time and increased health-care costs.

Here, it smells of wood, beeswax, and a trace of burning sage, the sacred incense of Native Americans.

MENTAL-PROCESS REENGINEERING

The center has an upbeat, unpretentious air about it. It's booked solid, yet the atmosphere is quiet and respectful. The people you've run into seem to have a sense of purpose. How long did it take them to acquire that?

How long will it take you? Over the years, you've read the New Age best-sellers, the ones everyone was talking about. They made sense, or seemed to make sense. Most of them said that whatever you were supposed to do was easy. All you had to do was change your attitude, think more positively, visualize creatively, accept life, move on, let go, think "right brain," return to innocence and choice, use your body as a map, and undergo transformational change. You thought you were doing it. But still, here you are, a classic case of chronic frazzle, checking into a longevity center.

After an intensive day of evaluation, your provisional program has been outlined. In one day, you've learned two things: "Transformational change" doesn't come out of a book, and those who say it's easy don't know what they're talking about. You now see that much of what you thought you were doing was really self-indulgent, the New Age mysticism ridiculed by the lunatic middle. But however indulgent, it put you on the path. You're here, and they're there.

After a week, you've learned a few more things. It's not

easy, but it can be done. You are beginning to come to a different understanding about some of those New Age platitudes that sounded so good but accomplished so little. You are thinking differently about misused but loaded words such as *values, spiritual, consciousness,* and *meaning.*

Now you're ready to work, to heal, to move on. Tomorrow, you start your water fast. Among the chief functions of these centers are controlled, supervised fasting and water-based detoxification programs.

Even in the 1990s, the perception of fasting had mostly negative connotations. Wild-eyed monks fasting in the desert were long out of style; their modern counterparts mainly fasted to register a political or other protest. Only an informed minority knew that controlled fasting was a quick and dramatic method for restoring damaged bodily functions, which in turn produce pronounced emotional and psychospiritual benefits.

> Fasting is a time to relax. A time when all your senses are heightened. A time of reflection. A time to think about changes. During a fast, none of the energy in your body has to go into digestion. It's all channeled into healing. Fasting cleanses the body and detoxifies it of medications, drugs, pollutants and junk foods. When you fast your body repairs and regenerates diseased or injured organs. Your body strives to achieve balance. (*Fairy Tale at Forty,* 1995)

Water fasts often involve one—or several—days of nothing but pure water under the supervision of a doctor. By the year 2000, water and other fasting regimes had become widely accepted as practical therapy. Fasting had always played an important role in the spiritual traditions of the world. As the concept of spirituality itself gained widespread acceptance (even scientific credibility), fasting went mainstream. Nobody ever promoted fasting as fun. But fasts undertaken in the comfortable and supportive surroundings of a longevity center make the ordeal endurable.

Fasting is just one aspect of the revolutionary changes that have taken place in the world of health.

COME THE REVOLUTION

Bowing to both the weight of accumulated incontrovertible evidence and the power of public opinion, the AMA and other august, traditional medical organizations have backed off the hard-line position they held throughout most of the past century. Alternative medicine and therapy have gone mainstream.

Alternative does not mean replacement or substitution. Alternative was a name loosely applied to a spectrum of healing modalities based upon a different fundamental approach to health and healing than established twentieth-century medicine.

Certainly, in recorded history there has never been an emergency medical technology as effective as twentieth-century Western medicine, a surgery as sophisticated, and a science of diagnosis as highly developed. Countless people today are routinely saved who would have died a few decades ago.

Twentieth-century medicine also relieves symptoms—often swiftly and spectacularly. But it is not really designed to cure. It treats the disease rather than the patient. In a civilization obsessed with fast food, instant gratification, and the quick fix, people routinely became prescription-drug junkies, endlessly popping pills just to keep the symptoms at bay or under control. Thirty-seven percent of people over sixty took more than five prescription drugs in 1995 and 19 percent seven or more, according to the Public Citizen Health Research Group.

As for life-threatening or chronic degenerative diseases, Western medicine treated most through a permanent regime of powerful, industrial-strength drugs (often with serious or even fatal side effects) and/or through always dangerous, always expensive, and sometimes maiming surgery (there is no such thing as a risk-free operation).

REDUCE THE RISKS IN PRESCRIPTION DRUGS

The side effects of prescription drugs are the downside of the medical miracles developed by the pharmaceutical industry.

A Boston study group has estimated that 30,000 Americans die each year from reactions to prescription drugs.

Recent estimates indicate that 5% of medical admissions to hospitals are due to unwanted reactions to medications. The Food and Drug Administration acknowledges that it receives notice of only a small fraction of these reactions. Few are reported. Fewer are studied.

From the work of Harvard researchers, we know that one in four prescriptions for the elderly is inappropriate. Prescribing errors are common, the second most common cause of patient injury and malpractice claims. (Drs. Raymond L. Woosley and David A. Flockhart, Op-Ed page, *USA Today*, 9/1/94)

Western medicine was particularly helpless in the face of stress-induced disease. By definition, the root cause defies a scientific or quantitative approach. Nobody has ever been able to weigh stress or measure it under the microscope. Throughout the latter decades of the twentieth century, stress-induced disease was increasingly prevalent and traditional Western medicine had no answers. The answers lay outside its self-limited domain.

Regardless of the cause of any given degenerative or stress-induced disease or ailment, ultimately what is involved in a real and lasting cure was often a lifestyle change.

Twentieth-century medical schools did not teach students about lifestyles—including their own.

Incredible as it now sounds in the year 2000, until the 1980s the role of diet was not officially considered a factor in disease. Since food is the fuel that drives the organism, discounting its significance is like imagining that it doesn't matter what you pour into the gas tank of your car. Chocolate syrup, kerosene, lighter fluid, Coke—as long it's liquid, it will fire the engine:

> Lobbyists for the soft drink industry told a Senate Committee today that it should not restrict the sale of Coca-Cola and similar beverages in schools because soft drinks had a place in a well-balanced diet.
> "To suggest that there are good foods and bad foods—we reject that entirely," said Drew M. Davis, Vice President of the National Soft Drink Association. (*NYT*, 5/17/94)

Only gradually, as the evidence mounted, did the medical establishment concede that there are "good" foods and "bad" foods, and that food plays a major role in health and in ill health. Correct diet reduces high blood pressure, prevents strokes and heart disease, and reduces the threat of certain kinds of cancers. Even so, only a small percentage of medical schools included a few hours (2.5 on average) of basic nutrition in the four-year standard curriculum. The rest provided none at all.

Meanwhile, hospitals, the showcases of establishment medical practice, routinely served food that rivaled the worst that institutional cafeterias could produce. This was food that would make a healthy person sick, but sick people were expected to get well on it.

Diet/nutrition was just one aspect of the holistic approach that was being ignored by conventional medical wisdom. But people were ignoring conventional wisdom and were finding their way to the new therapies in droves.

Where the traditional approach failed or provided only

stopgap solutions, alternatives often produced cures. Alternative medicines and therapies tended to work more slowly and less dramatically, but when intelligently applied and diligently followed, the root cause of the disease was addressed. Many degenerative diseases were stopped in their tracks, operations were avoided, and addictive habits were kicked.

By 1995, one-third of all Americans were making use of alternative treatments, spending over $14 billion of their own money in the process—since most insurance plans refused to pay for anything lacking an AMA imprimatur.

Always sensitive to the voice of the people, the government boldly responded. It allocated $2 million of the National Institutes of Health's $10 billion budget to explore the scientific worthiness of nonconventional therapies. This broke down to $2/100$ of 1 percent, or two cents on every one hundred dollars spent by the NIH. "You heard of the tail wagging the dog," said Dr. Joseph J. Jacobs, the director of the new Office of Alternative Medicine. "Well I feel like the flea wagging the elephant. They must spend more on pens and pencils than they do on us."

Despite the media's emphasis on junk news, they are by definition much more responsive to public opinion than the government. They have to be, since their economic lives depend upon public interest. A phenomenon that in 1995 alone had provoked 500 million visits to alternative practitioners could not be ignored. From PBS to NBC, from the *New York Times* to *Time* magazine, *alternative* was big news.

By 2000, medical research was no longer conducted by lone enthusiasts in makeshift low-budget labs. Massive studies were now being undertaken by credentialed mainstream professionals; finally, with the blessings of the pharmaceutical industry—once it was demonstrated that alternative or natural medicines could make money, not just heal patients.

Younger baby-boom doctors, with their roots in the sixties and seventies, had often been open to the new ideas from the onset. As the positive evidence mounted, they came out of their New Age closets. Many old-school practitioners were also forced to face up to the legions of patients whom they could not help but who were cured through homeopathy, or herbs, or diet, or some other alternative until recently regarded as blatant witchcraft by establishment medicine, and officially witch-hunted by the AMA until it was forced by the courts to desist.

THE AMERICAN MEDICAL ASSOCIATION FOUND GUILTY OF CONSPIRACY

United States Court of Appeals—February 7, 1990
United States District Court—August 27, 1987

AMA FOUND GUILTY

SUMMARY

THE AMA HAS BEEN FOUND GUILTY OF AN ILLEGAL CONSPIRACY TO DESTROY THE COMPETITIVE PROFESSION OF CHIROPRACTIC, THE MEMBERS OF WHICH WERE FOUND TO "OUTPERFORM" MEDICAL PHYSICIANS IN CERTAIN SEGMENTS OF THE HEALTH CARE MARKET. THE QUOTATIONS HEREIN ARE FROM THE OPINION OF THE UNITED STATES COURT OF APPEALS FOR THE SEVENTH CIRCUIT WHICH WAS ISSUED ON FEBRUARY 7, 1990.

The enlightened health care of the future took shape, integrating the best of the various schools old and new. But even as the trend grew and accelerated, a powerful countertrend polarized the world of health care.

HEALTH 'R' US

In response to medical costs escalating out of all proportion to the rest of the economy, the medical/pharmaceutical/insurance industrial complex applied time-honored business principles to the problem: health care equals business; people equal products.

The solution to rising costs were HMOs (health maintenance organizations) and a tiny group of giant companies controlling the national health-care system.

The principle underlying the solution was the tried and trusted economy of scale: The bigger you are, the more you buy. The more you buy, the cheaper it gets. The cheaper it gets, the more you make. (The more you make, the happier you are.) Health care became a matter of dollars, and very little sense.

IN HEALTH CARE, LOW COST BEATS HIGH QUALITY

A new survey shows that corporate buyers of health care plans are more concerned with low prices than high quality.

Peter Brumleve of Group Health Cooperative . . . said he recently showed a longtime customer data on the improved quality of his health maintenance organization. . . . After ten minutes, the customer, a chief financial officer . . . interrupted and said: "This is all fine and good, but what I want to know is when are our premium rates going to go down?" (WSJ, 1/18/94)

Among the largest publicly traded health-care companies, HMOs had the highest overall profit gains.

A vertically integrated medical oligopoly was created to cash in on the trillion-dollar health industry (15 percent of the nation's total output of goods and services, projected to rise to 20 percent by 2000). A handful of giant companies grabbed control of everything from visits to an HMO or doctor and stays in hospitals, nursing homes, and rehabilitation centers to drug prescriptions and insurance claims. In 1994, the five leading insurers—Aetna, Prudential, Met Life, Cigna, and the Travelers—along with Blue Cross, Humana, and United Health Care, already owned 45 percent of the nation's HMOs.

The new trend toward standardized medicine produced a voracious hybrid monster, one-third nineteenth-century robber baron, one-third twentieth-century chain store, and one-third timeless Kafkaesque bureaucracy.

These corporate giants quantified quality and peddled health as if it were tacos and hamburgers. Financier Richard Rainwater, one of Columbia Health Care's founders, proudly envisioned his 190-hospital company becoming the "Wal-Mart of health care."

Financially, this standardized, mass-produced health-care system was a success and CEOs awarded themselves healthy salaries (on average, $7 million in 1994 at the seven largest HMOs).

Investors rejoiced. But growing numbers of disgruntled noninvestors found they couldn't buy health the way they bought tacos, hamburgers, Fruit of the Loom, chain saws, or patio furniture.

Corporate profits rolled in. The quality of mass health care deteriorated. And the rush to cost cutting and standardization spurred the countertrend to individual attention and alternative methods.

Horrified at the prospect of factory-farmed medicine, even people who couldn't afford it found ways to take their health problems elsewhere.

► **TRENDPOST** *HealthGate Data Corp., Health Responsibility Systems, Healtheon, and other on-line health service providers will continue to proliferate as public disenchantment with standard health delivery services spurs entrepreneurs to find ways to make health information easily and cheaply accessible. HMOs providing coverage for alternative therapies will also prove attractive to both member patients and investors.* ◄

THE PLAGUES OF 2000

A whole new approach to health and well-being attracted a growing and substantial minority—and not a minute too soon. What began decades back as a kind of trendy common sense has now become an issue of survival.

The poor have gotten steadily poorer. The minimal health care formerly available to them is no longer available. Declining government services in the nineties have swelled the ranks of the homeless and the hard-pressed. Their immune systems are ravaged by lifetimes of junk food, emotional depression and despair, and the environmental onslaught that affects us all. Poverty in the United States, always regarded as somewhere between a crime and a sin, has now taken on a new medical context.

The poor and homeless have become the lepers of the twenty-first century—and not without reason. Mortality rates among the poor have risen sharply, facilitating the general spread of a spectrum of infectious diseases, some reaching epidemic proportions.

The devastating plagues of a despotic past were entirely democratic. Rich, poor, kings, and beggars were equally at risk. But in the democratic twenty-first century, plagues went elitist. They hit the well-to-do and middle-class, especially the overweight, out of shape, and sedentary. But a strong element of discrimination was involved.

Income/status was not the critical factor. Awareness was

the critical factor—and by and large, it was the educated and better off who were aware. Well before the plagues struck, the informed and the knowledgeable understood the options and alternatives available to them. They were putting in the necessary effort to build up their immune systems. The uninformed, still following their Industrial-Age diets and lifestyles, paid with their health, often their lives.

PREVIEWING

Beyond the issues of clean food, pure water, and fresh air—and without even taking looming catastrophe into account—a significant percentage of baby boomers had already come to a vivid realization of the importance of health. This was the single-largest segment of the American population, the 76 million children born between 1946 and 1964. When this generation set its collective mind upon anything, a trend was born.

America was growing gray.

Middle-aged people were the fastest-growing segment of the population, while young adults were in decline, according to the U.S. Census Bureau. The vanguard of the baby boomers, turning fifty, were finding it emotionally, financially, and physically draining to deal with their parents aging. They were witnessing the suffering and complications of their parents old age, much of it unnecessary. Old age is an unavoidable fact of long life; but sick old age is not.

According to the National Institute on Aging, fully 80 percent of older people's health problems are not due to aging at all. They're due to improper care of the body over a lifetime.

With that heedless sense of immortality common to youth, baby boomers once counseled their generation:

"Don't trust anyone over thirty." But the youngest of the boomers passed that watershed age in 1994. The oldest were touching fifty. What was abstract, remote, and irrelevant in the sixties was now a poignant fact of daily life. Now boomers were *previewing:* seeing in their parents aging what lay in store for them—unless measures were taken to prevent it.

A fifth of all boomers would never have a child, according to the Census Bureau. One-fourth would have only a single child. Couples without children made up nearly a third of all adults; by the year 2005, single adults would account for nearly a half of the adult population. Even adults with children feared they would have no one to care for them when they grew old. After all, they were unable to take proper care of their own parents. Worst of all, they dreaded the prospect of languishing years away as inmates in nursing homes.

Who was going to take care of them when their time came? A robust and healthy old age was the only possible solution to the problem—short of suicide.

► **TRENDPOST** *The health/fitness/nutrition trend, in its infancy and early childhood in the eighties and nineties, will go into an accelerated growth stage at the turn of the century. Driven by an aging baby-boom population, health will become a priority concern.* ◄

DR. WHO?

The consequences of ignoring health grew increasingly obvious and scary. If you were one of that big minority unwilling to shop for your health at Wal-Mart, you took your business elsewhere. But it was difficult to know whom to trust or what to trust.

Throughout the sixties, seventies, and eighties, alternatives to establishment medicine were available, but you had to know where to look. Often the practice was quasi-clandestine, sometimes actually illegal. You had to brave the derision of friends and family, and you did not tell your doctor until after you were cured that you were trying something new. Many never found their way through the obstacle course and thus suffered needlessly.

By 2000, it is more a question of choice, of knowing just when an alternative is preferable to the standard Western modality, whether or not an alternative is to be used in conjunction with the standard modality, and which alternative to choose.

A forty-seven-year-old woman just entering menopause who is working at a high-stress, basically sedentary job needs a very different program than a mid-life-crisis male manager with early prostate problems. Arthritic seniors need different regimes than hyperactive children. Factory workers, bored stiff and suffering from repetitive stress injuries, have different needs than idle or entry-level Generation Xers (born 1965–1977), who have different needs again from lumberjacks and professional tennis players.

Longevity centers provide answers and solutions to these and related questions. They are to health what colleges were to education in the century before. Longevity centers are health universities.

The staffs at longevity centers include qualified medical doctors schooled in alternative therapies and state-of-the-art modalities, as well as nutritionists, acupuncturists, homeopathists, herbalists, chiropractors, Ayurveda and Jin Shin Jyutsu practitioners, vitamin counselors, and a spectrum of physical, emotional, and spiritual therapists and healers. Among them, they have the expertise to teach you how to live in health in a poisoned and stressed-out world—in other words, how to take care of yourself whatever your personal situation.

What you learn at Healthy U. is self-responsibility. Body maintenance, keeping the only machine you've been given running and in good shape, is one aspect of the program. The mind, the heart, and the soul need equal and simultaneous attention. At longevity centers, you learn how to heal yourself and to direct your antennae with assurance to the programs, practitioners, and products that will keep you healthy.

▶ **TRENDPOST** *Longevity centers will provide health professionals with a gamut of new business opportunities. Ranging from family-size clinics staffed by a few specialists to resort-size luxury retreats, longevity centers will quickly become a multi-billion-dollar industry.* ◀

THE FOUNTAIN OF AGE

At longevity centers, you learn how to get healthy and stay healthy as long as possible.

In the twentieth century, a popular slogan was, "Life begins at forty." But the unspoken popular understanding was that it was no fun to get old; it was all downhill from forty on.

In the twenty-first century, the terminology and the standards of aging have changed radically. The slogan now is, "You're as young as you feel." There is no longer the obsessive twentieth-century quest to stay young forever; the emphasis now is on feeling young no matter how old you grow. Many people not only believe it; they live it.

There is a wildfire gold-rush quality to the search. It is trend, fad, and craze simultaneously.

▶ **TRENDPOST** *Ardent life-extension seekers will travel the globe searching for anti-aging therapies and modalities: drugs, herbs, minerals, elixirs, therapies, magic spells, and magic potions to stave off the consequences of old age.* ◀

For those content with cosmetic quick fixes, rejuvenation means hair transplants, state-of-the-art body-lifts, and plastic surgery. For those looking beyond the skin-deep level, there are solidly researched, proven life-extension therapies—treating impotence with herbs, live-cell therapy, phytochemicals, and magical mystery medicinal-mushroom tours. And furiously working in the wings, researchers offer the future promise of a genetic fix: finding the genes responsible for aging and replacing them.

The quest for longevity is no longer deferred to middle or old age. From Generation Xers to centenarians, all those who *previewed* saw that the actions of today influence the quality of their lives tomorrow.

People are learning to live intensely in the present while keeping a visionary eye fixed on the future.

11

LIVING LONGEVITY

VITAMIN COUNSELING

When you wake up on January 1, 2000, you may be forgoing your cup of coffee altogether (or if succumbing, then making sure the coffee is organically grown, sun-dried). You reach for your acidophilus laced with blue-green algae; your antioxidant enzyme nutrition; your liquid chlorophyll, Citricidal; your basic synergistic multiple; and, last but not least, your fructo-oligosaccharides. Then you're ready to start the new millennium.

But how did you know what to take, how much to take, and when to take it?

Among the many lessons you learn at the longevity center is to listen to your vitamin counselor.

▶ TRENDPOST *The new focus on health will become a powerful trend, creating both confusion and job opportunities: In response to an obvious and growing demand, a number of new professions will be created—among them, vitamin counselor.* ◀

In 1995, vitamins/supplements already constituted a $5 billion market, which was growing an estimated 7 percent a year. Well over half the country was taking some type of vitamin supplement. Everyone had the general sense that vitamins and supplements were beneficial, even crucial, but there was little or no specific knowledge.

The picture was further clouded by lack of education, special-interest groups, a drug-dependent medical establishment, marketers, and federal agencies, all of which offered confusing and often conflicting information. According to Trend Research Institute findings, fully 90 percent of consumers in the United States had little or no idea about what proper vitamin usage meant to them. Indeed, their knowledge of vitamins was even scantier than their knowledge of nutrition in general—and Americans were "nutrition-ignorant," according to Dr. David Kessler, commissioner of the Food and Drug Administration.

Vitamins were universally available in supermarkets, drugstore chains, mall-based nutrition centers, and specialized health-food stores. Even the Avon lady came calling with a full line of antioxidant products. Nevertheless, with a wealth of information readily available in books and magazines, consumers had little choice but to cherry-pick advice they felt they could live with and ignore the rest.

The doctors in your HMO plan were for the most part untrained in and unresponsive to this area of health. You couldn't expect knowledgeable advice from the minimum-wage checkout clerks at the supermarket, drug chain, or nutrition centers. Apart from occasional informed and interested personnel at your neighborhood health-food store, there was effectively nowhere to turn for specific personal advice.

Based on the understanding that no two people are alike, effective vitamin counseling must be individualized, just like effective medical advice. Your age, sex, lifestyle, profession, and eating, working, and sleeping habits must all be taken into consideration.

Anyone finding a professional vitamin counselor in the nineties was lucky. There was as yet no formal training. For the most part, the need was recognized by holistic M.D.'s, naturopaths, chiropractors, and other alternative practitioners who combed through the voluminous medical literature, both orthodox and alternative, creating a new discipline as they progressed.

The link between the earliest practitioners was a recognition of the importance of a holistic approach to health. Vitamin counselors were multidisciplinary practitioners. You needed a solid grounding of medical knowledge but not necessarily four years of medical school and a degree. For all its tremendous sophistication in so many areas, orthodox Western medicine was itself drug-dependent and vitamin-deficient; it had much to learn but little to teach.

Vitamin counseling was a wide-open and brand-new field—one of the disciplines within the quickly expanding Healthy U.

By January 1, 2000, vitamin counseling was on the way to becoming as professionalized and as respected as pharmacology.

Invariably, those who recognize a trend at the early stages of its life cycle are in the best position to profit from their foresight. Savvy retailers, professionals, and entrepreneurs were taking advantage of the myriad new businesses and professional openings.

CLEAN FOOD

Kicking the coffee habit was always tough. It wasn't so tough to give up Eggo waffles, Pop-Tarts, Kellogg's Frosted Flakes, or, indeed, any of the exotic-flavored "indulgence" cereals designed to lead you into temptation.

KELLOGG'S INTRODUCES NEW CEREAL, announced one headline. "Adults, like kids, look for products that taste great," said Kellogg's marketing spokeswoman, Karen MacLeod. "The baby-boomers want it to taste good first. They're not necessarily interested in eating it just because it's good for them."

But on January 1, 2000, you were looking for products that would improve your health. You *were* interested in eating what was good for you. You could not live on vitamins alone. What was good for you was "clean" food. This meant food free of artificial preservatives, coloring, irradiation, synthetic pesticides, drug residues, and genetic engineering. "Clean" food also retained its maximum nutritional value through processing, packaging, transportation, and storage. This meant food grown without chemical fertilizers. Where were you going to find that?

In 1995, 4 percent of the arable land in the United States was organically farmed; approximately 1.5 percent of the food grown was organic. But those marginal figures were deceptive in that organically grown food was less easily encountered than the figures indicated. Only rarely could you go into your local supermarket and find 1.5 percent of the space devoted to a little section of organic food or organic products.

Generally, if you insisted on clean food, you needed an enterprising local health-food shop or some private source, or you grew it yourself.

When shopping for food, most Americans shopped for price, not value. Between 1980 and 1992, the percentage of household income spent on food by Americans went *down* from 14.2 percent to 11.7 percent. By contrast, the average European household spent about 30 percent of income on food.

Food in the United States was cheap and plentiful. Agribusiness had standardized food production and brought everything from apples to yams into the supermarkets at bargain prices. Overall food costs actually declined relative to other consumer products. By 1995, with new trade agreements in place, the market was being flooded by cheap imports. Seventy percent of winter fruits and vegetables were being imported from developing countries.

HARVESTING PESTICIDES

Ninety-eight percent of produce imported into the U.S. is not tested for pesticide residues, and of the small amount that is tested, the pesticide contamination rate is approximately twice as high as that of domestically grown fruits and vegetables. (*Natural Health*, September–October 1992)

The downside of the situation was chemical-intensive agriculture: Everything was grown with chemical fertilizers, sprayed with chemical pesticides, and brought to market with the help of a variety of chemical preservatives. Increasingly, food was being irradiated not only as an alternative to chemical preservation but also to detoxify it. Many foods were being genetically engineered to produce higher yields and extended shelf lives.

Factory-farmed animals and poultry were fed massive doses of growth hormones to make them grow faster, then were treated with massive doses of antibiotics to keep them alive and disease-free in the crowded, unnatural, inhumane, cost-effective quarters they were confined to. More than twenty thousand chemicals were being used in the production of meats, and many hadn't been conclusively tested for harmful effects.

Throughout the nineties, there were numerous food scares, publicized in everything from TV's *60 Minutes* to *48 Hours*, from *USA Today* to the tabloids. Regardless of income, status, or education, it would have taken considerable effort *not* to know about rampant salmonella poisoning from chicken and eggs and *E. coli* poisoning from meat; the premature sexual development of children regularly fed on hormone-doctored foods; and scares about seafood and shellfish poisoned with mercury, PCBs, and lead or tainted with salmonella.

Some 6.5 million Americans become ill each year and 9,500 people die from acute food poisoning, according to the Centers for Disease Control and Prevention.

As the scares grew more widespread, warnings were posted not to undercook hamburgers or to soft-boil eggs as a matter of course. Eating had become so hazardous to health that the government sought legislation requiring "safe handling/cooking" warning labels on meat and poultry.

Over 2 billion pounds of pesticides were used each year in American agriculture. Forty-two different kinds of pesticides were used on tomatoes; thirty-eight on strawberries; and thirty-four on apples. Altogether, four hundred types of pesticides were being used on food crops. More than seventy, including most of the top-selling ones, caused cancer in laboratory animals. No one was sure what the long-term cumulative effects on the human organism would ultimately prove to be.

PESTICIDES FAR MORE HARMFUL WHEN COMBINED, STUDY FINDS

Pesticides that by themselves have been linked to breast cancer and male birth defects are up to one thousand times more potent when combined, according to a study.

"If you test them individually you could almost conclude that they were non-estrogenic, almost inconsequential," he [John A. McLachlan of Tulane University] said. "But when you put them in combination their potency jumped up five hundred- to one thousand-fold.

"Instead of one plus one equaling two, we found that in some cases one plus one equals a thousand." (AP, 6/7/96)

Over and above the repeated, predictable assurances of Professors Safe, Harmless, Risk-Free, Beneficial, and Unproven, a growing segment of the public was making up its own mind. It was concluding for itself that it did not want to spend in future health costs money saved on cheap but chemically dependent, mass-produced, irradiated, genetically engineered food.

Two billion dollars of the smarter money was being spent on certified organic tomatoes, strawberries, apples—produce that was pesticide-free.

► **TRENDPOST** *The trend for "clean" food is in the early stages of its life cycle. It will accelerate rapidly and will continue to grow beyond the foreseeable future.* ◄

While only 1.5 percent of the U.S. food supply was organic in 1995, this small fraction represented an annual growth rate of 25 percent over the preceding five years. And the rate was accelerating as the trend dynamics fused together a variety of reinforcing elements. By January 1, 2000, nearly 10 percent of the food supply was organic. Effectively, 10 percent of the food supply meant that enough organic food was being produced to feed 28 million people.

Those who saw the trend coming knew that health foods would become big business. Savvy mainstream food giants such as Smucker saw it, and they bought up the natural-beverage industry's top two brands, Knudsen & Son's and After the Fall. "They are one of the few big companies that's seen the health food industry for what it is instead of pooh-poohing it," said Kim Nilsen, marketing director at After the Fall. H. J. Heinz Co. also saw the trend and purchased Earth's Best organic baby foods.

▶ **TRENDPOST** *Huge demand for clean food will produce a pronounced ripple effect along the food chain that stretches from producer to consumer, farmers, chemical and fertilizer manufacturers, haulers, packagers, processors, and distributors. Individuals and corporations first to seize upon the foreseeable demand will capture the preemptive share of the growing market.* ◀

Despite stepped-up production, prices for organic foods were still high in comparison with those for products of chemically intensive agriculture. Increasingly, the aware and the unbuffaloed were realizing that cheap food meant cheap quality; it looked good, but it was nutritionally suspect. Organically grown fruits and vegetables have been found to have up to four times more nutritional trace elements and fewer toxic trace elements than foods grown using synthetic pesticides. Studies show that organic produce has 63 percent more calcium, 59 percent more iron, and 60 percent more zinc.

BUDDHA BURGERS AND KARMA-COLA

Just as the Health 'R' Us trend accelerated at the same time as the countertrend for alternative medicine, so the move toward clean food did not stop or reverse the growth of the junk-food/processed-food/artificial-food industry.

The food giants kept on growing—mainly through the expansion of overseas markets. At home, the trend was mature. Here, new markets were not being "grown" but new products were being launched (23,000 a year on average; fewer than 200 of these would be around five years later).

Consumers were telling pollsters they wanted wholesome meals, but more than ever before, they were choosing whatever was most convenient, especially when it was labeled "pure," "natural," or "healthy." While most sectors of the population were becoming more health-conscious, the time crunch forced most to compromise.

► **TRENDPOST** *For businesses looking to launch new products and services, the "fast and easy" trend will still be the main criterion for success.* ◄

Longer working hours, growing numbers of single-parent families, home-alone kids, widespread economic fallback— all of these were factors in keeping the industry profitable.

Most highly processed food products and junk foods were aimed at the impressionable young and people who couldn't afford to pay premium prices. The average American child saw ten thousand food commercials a year. For the 1.6 million children between the ages of five and fourteen left alone at home at least part of the day, what they saw on TV was what they ate.

Overworked Americans more than ever were eating on the run, devoting less and less time not only to preparing food but to sitting down at leisure to enjoy it. Nearly 15 percent of the meals bought outside the home were being consumed in the car. In offices, people got used to eating with one hand on the keyboard and the other gripping a sandwich.

The fast-food market would continue to expand, slowly topping $115 billion in the year 2000—though fierce competition would leave many casualties along the highways.

The junk-food/fast-food/processed-food industry stayed healthy; its customers didn't. For those determined to go on breaking down their immune systems, supply was always ahead of demand.

SOLD OUT

The rapid growth of the organic countertrend produced widespread clean food shortages. On January 1, 2000, and for much of decade beyond, clean food was very much a seller's market.

You knew it all too well: Like the Europeans, you were spending closer to 30 percent of your income on food. In the circles you traveled in, conspicuous-consumption status symbols had lost much of their status. The Mercedes in the garage, the wall-to-wall entertainment center or DKNY did nothing to counter the onslaught on your immune system. You put your money where your mouth was.

With only 10 percent of the arable land being farmed organically by January 1, 2000, demand for clean food was far outstripping supply.

The nature of the nascent industry made it difficult for opportunists to jump in for the quick buck. The art and science of producing clean food had been largely lost— future farmers did not learn it in agricultural science courses at universities, any more than future doctors learned about nutrition or homeopathy at medical schools. It had to be relearned and redeveloped.

Agribusiness had long since gobbled up the largest tracts of prime farmland—which was rapidly being depleted through overuse and misuse of chemical pesticides, herbicides, and fertilizers. Two million acres per year of former farmland was being converted to sites for condos, industrial parks, and shopping malls. Contrary to popular belief, most domestically grown fruits and vegetables do not come from isolated rural areas, but from farm regions near cities. Urban sprawl was seriously cutting into the local supply of fresh produce—which was increasingly coming in from abroad.

In 1994, the U.S. Census Bureau stopped counting the percentage of the population living on farms. At less than 2 percent, the number was no longer considered statistically significant. (The figure was 44 percent in 1880, 20 percent in 1945.) In the 1950s, an agribusiness-oriented Department of Agriculture told farmers, "Get big or get out." A few got big; most, forcibly, got out.

But now, quite suddenly, small became not only beautiful but also viable and profitable—at least for those willing to put in the time and effort to overcome the many difficulties presented.

► **TRENDPOST** *Under widespread, rapidly changing socioeconomic conditions, trend opportunities will arise all along the supply chain: teaching about, growing, raising, distributing, preserving, and marketing "clean" food.* ◄

MICROFARMS

In the late eighties and nineties, the return of the independent brewery (now known as microbrewery) made locally produced beer available after an absence of decades. Consumers willingly paid more for the local brew than for the priciest of the German and Austrian imports. Now a parallel demand for clean food inspired the development of the microfarm. But this food trend had infinitely greater growth potential as an industry.

There was much more at stake. You drank very expensive microbrewed beer because it tasted better, not because it was better for you. But you went out of your way to buy expensive clean food as much for health reasons as for taste reasons—this was a matter of survival.

By the year 2000, microfarms were beginning to challenge the food giants just as, earlier, microbreweries had confronted the beer mammoths. In the nineties, the independent breweries grabbed a small but noticeable market share in an otherwise-flat industry, prompting a flurry of copycat, pseudomicrobrews from Anheuser-Busch, Stroh's, Miller, and Coors. But unlike the big brewers, agribusiness farmers with millions of acres of chemically contaminated soil could not jump in at a moment's notice to get their share of the market.

By 2000, the specialty market for wholesome and natural food products penetrated some 45 percent of the population in varying degrees. (*Organic* meant both grown without chemicals and preserved without chemicals. *Natural* only meant no additives, preservatives, artificial flavors or colors.)

The new family microfarm had limited production and distributed most of its product locally. For people living in cities and suburbs, the clean food shortages were most severe. But if you lived in the newly developing exurban areas, now dotted with microfarms, you could get just about anything organic you wanted: chickens that did not need warning labels, eggs that could be eaten soft-boiled, hormone-free dairy products and meats, milk minus antibiotic residues.

Boutique producers within the microfarm segment found high-end niches for specialty foods, herbs, and organically farmed fish. Others cultivated heirloom vegetables, grown from seeds passed down through generations.

At the same time, technological breakthroughs in food preservation were making it possible to ship and store food without chemical preservatives. Over time, it became possible and economically feasible for the boutique farmers with their exotic specialty products to expand their range beyond local distribution.

▶ **TRENDPOST** *With demand so high and supply so short, clean land to grow clean food will be at a premium. Microfarm real estate will be among the coveted commercial properties of the twenty-first century—especially if it has an ample, dependable source of clean water on it.* ◀

WEIRD SCIENCE

If you didn't buy your food at the local health-food store, where did you buy it? The term *health food* was a telling choice of words in its own right. Chemical-free, organically grown food was health food. Then what was the other stuff everyone ate? Sick food?

During the nineties, you found that you were buying supermarket food less and less; mainly, you went there for staples—toilet paper, food wrap, garbage bags, detergent, paper towels—and for certain irreplaceable old favorites—ketchup, mustard, hamburger relish, Tabasco sauce, and the like—to gratify those occasional bouts of recidivism. You are, after all, only human. Nobody has ever figured out a way to produce an acceptable organic substitute for Heinz ketchup.

By 2000, much of your food came from the health-food store—especially if you had young children.

MONITOR PESTICIDES BETTER

A 1993 study by the National Academy of Sciences reported that data regarding the health effects of pesticide residues on children are almost completely non-existent. Particularly there is no understanding of how a variety of trace pesticides consumed together, as in a single pear, may affect a growing baby. (*USA Today*, 5/2/94)

Children have a higher metabolic rate and eat proportionately more fruit and juice than adults do—precisely those foods containing pesticide residues. Is it possible that trace amounts of poisons lethal to every kind of bug in the world would have no effect whatever over time on humans, especially small humans?

If you read the papers, you were well aware of the running battle between the $400 billion food industry (fighting to preserve the status quo, or roll back existing regulations) and the environmentalists (seeking to enforce existing regulations, impose more stringent controls, and ban many chemicals altogether). And since he who pays the piper calls the tune, the government put its mouth where the money was and gave into industry.

Many of the chemicals used caused cancer in laboratory animals. Less than 1 percent of all produce was tested by government inspectors. Residue levels of pesticides were routinely found in test samples. *The EPA had no standards for cumulative residue levels.*

A story headlined THE FOOD FIGHT OVER PESTICIDES represented the viewpoints of those on both sides of this controversy. "The EPA already requires an awful lot of scrutiny on these products" says Du Pont Company's Susan Shaw. "Used correctly there should be negligible risk to human beings . . . chemicals that fight weeds, fungus and pests provide a major benefit in producing abundant, affordable food supply." But since there was very little scrutiny and no standards had been set, there was no measure for "negligible risk." No one knew the risks—not Du Pont, not the EPA.

"More testing, more data," counseled Jeffrey Nedelman, of the Grocery Manufacturers Association, in the same article. But until the tests were run and the data collated, children of all ages kept on eating.

"Most people don't have time to wait for science," said Wendy Gordon, founder of Mothers and Others for a Livable Planet. "The question comes up at every meal."

The industry bottom line was an "abundant, affordable food supply." But "abundant" and "affordable" suddenly took a backseat. It was boom time for health-food stores.

HEALTHMART 2000

In the nineties, health-food stores were mostly small enterprises: mom-and-pop, his-and-hers, his-and-his, hers-and-hers, or any combination thereof. Except for a few small regional chains, shopping was mostly potluck. You never knew what you'd find. Choice was limited; space was limited; prices and quality were inconsistent shop to shop.

The health-food stores themselves were few and far between, and all too often, despite the merchandise, the people working there didn't *look* very healthy. Often you sensed a strange vibe in those places; you felt unwelcome.

By 2000, that intimidating more-wholesome-than-thou attitude has been replaced; health-food stores have turned pro. Inventories have become more extensive and dependable, and such stores are everywhere—moving into large prime locations vacated by unsuccessful twentieth-century supermarkets. The leaders in the field aren't just merchandisers looking for ever-new strategies to entice. In order to succeed in the field, they have to be fired by a vision that is as much mission as money. They are health impresarios. You no longer go to a health-food store just to shop for food; you go to shop for health.

► **TRENDPOST** *The American megamarketing mentality will be applied to the booming health trend. Entrepreneurs will take the best of the nineteenth-century general store, the best of the twentieth-century supermarket, and put them together to produce something entirely new: the Healthmart.* ◄

Along with full selections of the best clean food, the Healthmart provides you with informed advice. In the old days, if you were lucky, somebody at a mom-and-pop or his-and-hers health-food store might have had some knowledge. But it was hit-or-miss. By 2000, a knowledgeable staff is the rule. Customers expect service, and service means more than just pointing you to the aisle with aromatherapy oils or the bulk millet or the portable phototherapy units. Managers have to know their stuff, or have trained professionals on hand who do—someone who knows how to use the oils and cook the millet and discuss the merits and operation procedures of the phototherapy units.

Polls in the 1990s revealed that pharmacists were America's most trusted profession.

Just as you expect a certain level of medical advice from your pharmacist, so now you have come to expect reliable advice at Healthmart. You gave up over-the-counter symptom-relief drug remedies long ago. But now what do you do for your cold if you don't use Dristan and Contac? What was the natural replacement for Maalox and Mylanta? What herbs worked on PMS? Was it true that your hyperactive child could be treated by nutrition and homeopathy without recourse to Ritalin?

Healthmart functions as an information clearing house. Like a Home Depot of health, it provides a high level of do-it-yourself advice and information, and it steers you to professionals if the job needs more expertise. The ongoing exchange of information develops old-fashioned personal relationships that are, in turn, part of the larger social/community role Healthmart has come to play. Taking a page from Barnes & Noble, Healthmart is a place to go to browse through books and magazines, schmooze, and nibble in their Clean Food Café.

Taking the kids shopping is no longer the ordeal it once was. The point-of-purchase displays that attract childrens' attention aren't filled with overpriced junk: no Reese's Peanut Butter Puffs, no Lucky Charms, no Hidden Treasures (corn cereal blasted with artificially flavored fruit centers—the "hidden treasures"). You don't have to worry about your kids nagging you for a TV-hyped cereal laced with three teaspoons of sugar in each three-quarter-cup serving. New, interactive POP displays now entertain and inform. For the kids, just as for you, shopping has become an educational experience.

The massive Healthmart often played a central role in the rapidly changing fabric of society at the beginning of the new millennium, at once social and commercial.

Despite Healthmart's competitive advantage, there was still plenty of room for the little guy. Just as the gourmet deli and your local convenience store coexisted and thrived in the supermarket era, so the mighty health trend provided plenty of room for individual enterprise and specialized expertise.

TOFU HUT

You're doing your food shopping primarily at Healthmart or a specialty shop, but, like so many other Americans, you spend time on the road. Demand has made it possible to apply fast-food marketing skills to clean food.

In the eighties and nineties, a number of the major franchise chains had tried to cater to a perceived health trend. Salad bars were installed; baked potatoes were offered; leaner, diet, and fat-free versions of the standard franchise fare were appended to the menu. It was a mixed marriage that didn't work. Junkaholics stuck to what they were used to; the healthniks distrusted both the motives and the meals and went sprout hunting elsewhere. Like so many others, the franchise marketers had been taken in by all the media health hype and the sales figures for running shoes. The trend was not yet mature enough to support a mass-market approach.

It soon would be, however. Large segments of the population were becoming seriously health-conscious. There had been too many well-publicized incidents of mass poisoning and fast-food fatalities at too many places. When you had to stop to eat on the road, you avoided Salmonella Sal's. You wanted to eat food you knew you could trust.

TAINTED SOIL OK FOR CHICKENS

Raising chickens on land contaminated by radiation would be cheaper than cleaning up the sites and could provide a source of safe, inexpensive food, a study suggests.

A team of researchers at Savannah River Ecology Laboratory has been studying chickens foraging at the Savannah River site nuclear weapons plant near Aiken.

Chickens foraging in contaminated areas could be taken to a processing plant off the site and fed uncontaminated food. . . .

The radioactive material would pass from their systems and in about ten days, the meat and eggs would be fit for human consumption.

"If the meat is cheaper and you call it 'radioactively cleaned meat,' and you put it on the shelf for half price, I bet people in this country would eat it," he [I. Lehr Brisbin, one of the researchers on the project] said. (AP, 5/6/95)

But *would* people eat it? That was the question. Fried chicken was already suspect. Chicken that fried you back had even the unsuspecting suspicious.

By 2000, all over the country, on the roads, along the interstates, highways, and byways, wherever you would normally find only McDonald's and its standard bevy of burger clones, taco hybrids, and pizza kissing cousins, clean-food alternatives were sprouting up.

▶ **TRENDPOST** *Fast-food health-food restaurants, virtually nonexistent in the nineties, will be the hottest segment of an otherwise-saturated fast-food industry.* ◀

The continued success of the fast-food industry—on both its junk-food and health-food flanks—reflected its convenience. The big overriding trend, however, was toward the home. People were working at home, cooking at home, schooling at home; in the new millennium the home reestablished itself as home, not just home base.

12

TECHNOTRIBALISM

PIONEERING

With the pace of change accelerating, early-new-millennium USA looks as different from 1990 USA as 1990 did from 1890. On the positive side, a confluence of powerful trends created the widespread technotribal society flourishing in what had been rural areas.

These were the new pioneers, people escaping the congestion, noise, pollution, disease, crime, and violence of the cities and suburbs and taking their jobs with them to what had been the boondocks. You couldn't escape worldwide increased radiation levels; fallout fell everywhere. But outside the cities, a purifying atmosphere prevailed. You could lead a healthier life and take stronger measures to bolster your immune system.

Many in the vanguard were disenchanted achievers, seeing the American dream not as fame and fortune but as being their own boss. Others, downsized out of jobs, found new ways to use their skills, vowing to live new lives unbeholden to the corporation. Young retirees looking to stretch devalued pension money and angry citizens determined to avoid escalating big-city and suburban taxes swelled the wave. New communities took root, or took over and transformed traditional small towns and villages.

Technotribalism was a proactive, rational, and constructive survival strategy. There was no resemblance between it and the reactionary, head-for-the-hills, bunkered-down and fully armed Armageddonite response to the same set of conditions.

It was made viable by the digital decade of the 1990s and the energy revolution of the first decade of the new millennium. It was made necessary by the rapidly crumbling infrastructure and disintegrating institutions of a dying age.

Technotribalism was also a foretaste of the grander, global Renaissance that would rise from the shambles of the industrial past. For those who saw what was coming, and who had the skills and foresight to implement and live out their vision practically, technotribalism was the way to go.

▶**TRENDPOST** *Exurban commercial and residential real estate will be on an uptrend for at least twenty-five years. Buying into selected depressed small-town, exurban, and country markets in the nineties will prove a sound investment strategy in the technotribal society of the coming decades.* ◀

Between 1991 and 1994, more than 2 million urbanites moved to the countryside. More than four hundred rural counties whose populations shrank during the 1980s were growing in the 1990s. Hundreds of others stabilized or slowed their population declines.

Some were never spoiled by industrial development; others peaked early and subsequently declined into backwater drowsiness. All had workable infrastructures; they were ripe for resuscitation. (By contrast, the classic suburban community had been so overdeveloped and overpopulated that restructuring posed monumental, although not insurmountable, problems.)

Technotribes blossomed as prototypes, model communities for the twenty-first century. They balanced country life with high technology, functioning as service areas along the information superhighway. Depending on the natural environment, they interspersed residential and commercial/industrial districts with farms, forests, wetlands, deserts, rivers, and lakes.

HIPPIE ROOTS

Technotribalism had its psychological/physical roots in the hippie communes and in the self-sufficiency/ecological experiments of the sixties and seventies. It had its philosophical/metaphysical seeds in the typically American utopian schemes of the nineteenth century.

There is scarcely a boomer alive who does not remember the hippie/self-sufficiency movement of the 1960s and 1970s. Disgusted by rampant materialism, opposed to the Vietnam War, turned on by psychedelic rabble-rousers and a grab bag of drugs, raucously breaking free of the chains of Ozzie and Harriet's ersatz morality, a colorful coed bunch of beaded, bearded, braless young adventurers tried going back to the land—more often than not well supplied with dad's materialistically generated dollars.

They homesteaded tracts in rural or wilderness areas and tried to live out their respective visions. Some followed the guru of the month and tried to create the great American ashram; others were focused on the environment and sought ways to free themselves from the energy grid and live in an ecologically happy ever-after; still others experimented with new value systems or intellectually based sociological theories. Many just did drugs until the money ran out and the love-ins turned sour.

Highly visible but numerically insignificant, they generated a disproportionate amount of media attention. Americans thought they were seeing something brand-new and dangerous.

It wasn't dangerous, and it wasn't new. The beards weren't new, bralessness wasn't new (the bra wasn't invented until the early twentieth century; before that, it was bodices or nature), and even the drugs weren't new. Marijuana and opium were legal, readily available, and extensively used throughout the United States, often by otherwise staid, respectable, law-abiding, solid citizens throughout the nineteenth century and earlier.

UTOPIAN SEEDS

Utopianism was an integral element in America's eccentric and checkered history. Not everyone in the nineteenth century was taken in by the infinite promise of rational science or bedazzled by the prospect of a mechanized "progressive" world. Others thought the institutionalized church had lost sight of its spiritual origins. Still others revolted against Victorian sexual hypocrisy and experimented with "free love." Some of these precursor hippies were no less bizarre, irreverent, or free-swinging than their descendants.

The various utopias failed, or transmuted into some less radical, more viable form—forgotten, or reduced to footnote size in the pages of history books. The hippie communes of the sixties and seventies also failed, but for different reasons.

While the social structure of the nineteenth century was as constricted as the corsets its suffering presuffrage women were laced into, the United States was geographically open. There was plenty of physical room to be different, and it was not so very difficult to be economically self-sustaining.

The problem with the utopias was that they were . . . well, utopian. Flawed human beings could never put flawless ideals into practice. The free lovers couldn't detach the strings attached by a few million years of evolution and tens of thousands of years of conditioning. The brotherly lovers found it as difficult as ever to love their brothers, to say nothing of their enemies, and so on. Many of the utopias had a messianic intent. The idea was to set the shining example, and the rest of the world would follow suit. When the example could not be burnished to the requisite sheen, the world went its own way, and the brave experiments foundered.

By the time of the hippies, conditions were very different. Most of the communes were unconcerned with changing the world. They had their individual agendas—intellectual, moral, philosophical, political, ecological—and might have liked to initiate widespread change. But they were more in revolt than revolutionary. They were looking for viable ways to survive and live satisfying lives while dropping out of a society they perceived as hostile, increasingly frantic, and stultifying. The motto was Turn on, tune in, drop out.

The communes were vulnerable to the same disparities between vision and performance that scuttled the utopias, but economic factors were still more telling. Financial and agricultural self-sufficiency were realizable goals in 1870, but not in 1970. However much food was grown, it was next to impossible to get off the energy grid or to become tax-independent, especially if you were stoned most of the time. When dad's money supply dried up, the only way to keep the communes going was to earn the money, which could only be done in places far from the commune— usually just those cities that everyone had fled from in the first place in order to start the communes. By the 1980s, most had gone.

FREE RADICALS

The technotribe of the new millennium is not a commune, but it is community-spirited: The Me Generation turned into the We Generation. It is not utopia, but it is visionary—an ongoing practical exercise in the realization of shared social, political, economic, and spiritual ideals and values. There is no single cut-and-dried dogma, agenda, or manifesto, but wherever it has taken root, it has flourished.

The technotribe brought something precious to America, something it never had before: democracy.

From the very beginning, the American government had taken matters into its own high hands, maneuvering around the original "Contract with America"—the Constitution—to suit itself. It made and broke treaties on its own, declared wars, conned and deceived the public, and enacted legislation that had little or no public support. As the good Quaker William Penn said, long before the Constitution was dreamed of, "Let the people think they govern and they will be governed."

The government carried out the genocide and humiliation of Native Americans and then willfully broke every signed treaty with the few who survived. For centuries, the well-known big stick was employed in the service of big business.

In his 1995 book, *In Retrospect: The Tragedy and Lessons of Vietnam,* former Secretary of Defense Robert McNamara finally revealed what an entire generation had known for thirty years: that our "democratic" government foisted the Vietnam War upon the public, knowing full well that Vietnam posed no threat to our national security, that "the war was wrong, terribly wrong," and could not be won anyhow.

Robert McNamara now states that "we were terribly wrong." He should be tried as a war criminal.

His dogmatic policies resulted in the most terrible tragedy this country has suffered since the Civil War. . . . We call for a tribunal for Bosnia. Why not for McNamara? Do the Israelis forgive the Holocaust because the perpetrators have aged? Neither should we! . . . McNamara ranks with Hitler and Stalin as a perpetrator of crimes against humanity. (Curtis D. Westphal, retired air force colonel, Austin, Texas, letter to the editor, *USA Today*, 4/11/95)

Washington deliberately sacrificed the lives of 58,000 American soldiers, ruined the lives of millions more, killed 3.3 million Vietnamese, and ravaged a foreign country whose destiny, for better or for worse, was none of our business. In the process, it exalted the CIA and FBI to inviolable KGB status, producing a situation in which dissent by private citizens meant ruin or jail.

Despite the endless list of proven enormities, pronouncements from the lunatic middle continued to disseminate the fiction that America was a democracy dedicated to peace.

In April 1995, President Clinton stated, "There is no right to resort to violence when you don't get your way. There is no right to kill people. . . . Those who claim such rights are wrong and un-American."

President Clinton had evidently forgotten the massacre at Waco, Texas, or his own 1993 bombing of Iraq. (This was in retaliation for a discovered Iraqi plot to assassinate former President George Bush on his visit to Kuwait. But since a CIA pamphlet teaching operators how to assassinate unacceptable foreign leaders had been made public not long before, a moral stance on the issue was hardly justified.)

On pretexts of manifest destiny, national security, falling dominoes, and American interests, Washington had been "resorting to violence when you don't get your own way" every time it didn't get its own way. If a willingness to resort to preemptive violence is un-American, America had been un-American since the Battle of Bunker Hill.

What can be said in defense of American democracy is that the governments of other countries are worse, usually much worse. It's no accident that millions of people have immigrated here and that very few have left.

As usual, government in the nineties was not a democracy—it was not a government "of the people, by the people, for the people"; it was a government of the people, by the politicians, and for the special interests. The difference was that now everyone was beginning to see it.

People were angry but confused. They were expecting democracy and politicians were talking democracy. The public did not see that the traditional words had lost their intended meanings and had been Middle-Muddled into their opposites.

So-called conservatives no longer conserved. They no longer showed "a disposition to preserve what is established." The environment had been established for millions of years. Conservatives clear-cut the environment whenever the environment stood in the way of a cost-benefit analysis. *Conservative* no longer referred to people "preferring gradual development to abrupt change." Conservatives were those who felt morally justified in casting the first bomb at any other nation or institution with a different value system.

Liberal no longer meant "broad-minded, tolerant, and not bound by authoritarianism." Liberals enacted legislation to suspend civil liberties, cancel constitutional rights, and initiate broad police-state powers. *Liberal* no longer meant "a belief in economic freedom and the greater individual participation in government." Liberals legislated policies that resulted in more government intrusion rather than less, more control, more centralization, more foreign entanglements, and more secrecy.

As for *democracy:* Abroad, this word was now applied to any country doing business with us. At home, this meant overriding dissenting 70 percent and 80 percent popular majorities on one issue after another. The government systematically implemented policies dictated to it not by the people but by the people who paid for political campaigns.

On the state, county, and local level, things were no different. Hometown USA was a mini Washington, just that the big stick was smaller and contracts given out to cronies had fewer zeros attached to them. Abuse was inevitable; it could not be otherwise. Our vaunted two-party system was, in practice, an illusion.

BEDTIME FOR BONZO

At school, we had it drummed into our heads that the American two-party system was central to our brand of democracy. Though the two-party system was not perfect, it gave working expression to two fundamentally opposed socio/political agendas. It was understood from the very beginning that conflicts and differences of interest and opinion were inevitable in a democracy. The two-party system—we learned—had evolved over time to deal with this inherent polarization: Right versus Left, conservative versus liberal, Republican versus Democrat. Through the two-party system, the will of the majority could be both expressed and implemented in the most efficient manner known to history.

Belief in both the superiority and necessity of a two-party system is an article of faith in political science circles.

"The American political system is susceptible to occasional third-party candidacies," said Ken Janda, a professor of political science at Northwestern University. "But I don't think it's a long staying virus."

However, by the latter half of the twentieth century, the

parties had lost their identities. There was no two-party system. Washington provided unilateral support for issues that had the voting public strongly polarized: high levels of defense spending, the War on the Environment, the Mexican and S&L bailouts, GATT, NAFTA, foreign aid, corporate welfare.

"The Cato Institute calculates that Congress finances more than 125 programs that subsidize private businesses at a net cost of about $85 billion per year. Add tax breaks, and the price tag exceeds $100 billion a year—or half the annual Federal deficit," said Stephen Moore, director of fiscal policy studies at the Cato Institute.

Every major cabinet department was funneling the public's money into corporate treasuries. McDonald's, Campbell Soup, Mars, Inc., Gallo, Cargill, Pillsbury—all received millions of taxpayer dollars to help them to market their products. Asked if these programs were "corporate welfare" as critics charged, Senator Nancy Kassebaum, R-Kans., replied, "To a certain extent, if you're completely honest, I suppose you could look at it that way." Unconcerned with honesty, complete or otherwise, the Senate voted to retain subsidies that enriched huge corporations then voted to cut billions from welfare programs for the poor.

There were no real Democrats opposing real Republicans; no two distinct parties. There were just two wings of a single party: the Wall Street party, with branch offices in every village, town, and city hall. The apparent differences were in character traits rather than in doctrine: insensitivity and greed on one side, hypocrisy and greed on the other.

But the days of the two-party system were numbered. This time, the multi- or antiparty "virus" did not respond to political penicillin—just like those wonder bugs currently outfoxing the wonder drugs and the microbiologists.

Fifteen years of trends research told us at the Trends Research Institute the "virus" would reach epidemic proportions, and was here to stay. In 1988, we forecast the formation of a third party in the 1990s. As politicians progressively alienated themselves from the people, this trend toward a third (fourth, fifth, and beyond) party would gather steam.

Within decades, the technotribal town hall will be doing away with parties—in their present form. We will be voting for people, not parties. It will be bedtime for Bonzo.

Just as the technotribalists reclaimed and exalted the land, so now, in the new millennium, they have reclaimed and reconstituted democracy. People were now putting into practice what had been promised in principle for over two hundred years. As Thomas Jefferson noted, "Democracy is cumbersome, slow and inefficient, but in due time the voice of the people will be heard and their latent wisdom will prevail." Democracy at last.

TECHNOTRIBE TOWN HALL

It began in isolated little communities where—for better or for worse—the voice of the people can override the voice of the power brokers, money brokers, and stockbrokers. Out in the boondocks, when conditions were right, a new value system supplanted the old one.

Voting had never been fair or easy. From the beginning, it was hedged about with restrictions: Poll taxes excluded the poor and minorities; gender, race, property ownership, and registration requirements all impeded the process. It was further complicated by the sheer physical distances required to cast a vote. Even in the digitalized nineties, a push-pull Model T technology prevailed in the polling booth, often in an intimidating atmosphere, as scowling local ward-heelers, party hacks, and precinct captains monitored the proceedings.

Over the years, the manifestly undemocratic restrictions

were lifted. The right to vote became universally available. Everyone over eighteen could vote, but elected representatives did what they pleased—particularly on state and federal levels. Deals were cut, and decisions were made in trendily smokeless, locked back rooms. Having the vote wasn't much better than having no vote at all, and voters responded by not responding. Typically, presidential elections drew around 50 percent of eligible voters to the polls.

The information superhighway would change the entire process. During the 1992 presidential campaign, the feasibility of an "electronic town hall" was raised—a multimedia hookup that would bring televised government debates—at all levels—into everyone's living room—with a built-in capacity for voting individually, issue by issue, at the press of a button.

The first, easy half of this two-step revolution began in the eighties when C-Span and local cable both started televising government meetings and debates. Everyone could now tune in on what was being said—on certain carefully selected issues. On the others, the customary cloak of secrecy prevailed. But there was no easy and immediate way to influence the outcome of the debate. You could call or write your representative with your opinion; you had no vote on any one issue. Your only recourse was to vote him out of office—by voting for his twin brother in the next election.

The second, more difficult half was legislating the hookup and making it happen. By the mid-1990s, the technology was in place, available, and cheap. But since both the judges and the legislators were members of the Wall Street party, any action that threatened the life of the party was stonewalled.

Instant on-line voting would make everyone his/her own representative. But since both wings of the one party were acting in opposition to the will of people, politicians were opposed to democratizing democracy. The difficulty lay in passing the electronic town hall legislation, not in the technology.

ACT LOCAL

By January 1, 2000, only a handful of the most advanced technotribes were voting on-line. They were using their votes to act and proact at the local level.

Technotribalism made real a principle that had been carefully written into the American Constitution by our Founding Fathers but which had been less successful as a practice: the principle of mutual respect.

People's religious beliefs, philosophical and artistic interests, sexual preferences, and what they chose to do or not to do to their bodies was their own business, and not the business of busybodies—period. Individuals bore the consequences of their own actions. For those who chose to drug or drink themselves to death, there were no bailouts or handouts.

A polygamist might coexist alongside a monogamist; an atheist alongside a staunch Catholic. The technotribe was not fertile ground for meddlers; they went elsewhere.

Technotribes preserved privacy in lives, fostered communal action in services, and retained hippie tolerance and utopian zeal and gumption—along with a bit of the medieval village in the mix. There was a sense of self-containment; each tribe was its own little island continent.

Members of the technotribe lived as individuals but subscribed to a set of broad-based environmental values shared by all. Stewardship of the planet called for careful communal action; individual action was not enough.

In the pre-technotribe age, people were often out of the house at 7:00 A.M. and not back until 8:00 P.M., often commuting long distances just to get to work. There wasn't much time or energy for community consciousness. But now, living at home and working at or near it, the community became the new priority. A growing sense of tribal consciousness, loyalty, and organization extended beyond a local town's borders.

To the technotribal We Generation, community interests took precedence over selfish interests; harmonious habitat took precedence over economic development. Cooperative confederations of neighboring cities, towns, and hamlets were finding ways to pool and share resources.

Within the technotribe, goods and services that might otherwise have been prohibitively expensive were often bartered—dental fillings exchanged for organic food, arts and crafts for martial-arts instruction, auto repairs for roof repairs. People created new internal systems for education, health care, and adult and child care, putting into practice the old adage, It takes an entire village to raise a child. Or to care for a grandparent.

The technotribe, with the aid of the information superhighway, created a loosely knit autonomous entity able to immunize itself against the Millennium Fever raging outside. It could act locally.

But on January 1, 2000, it was not yet sufficiently connected to implement the principle of thinking globally. The technotribes could not prevent the Wall Street party from embroiling the country in further unpopular schemes: expensive bailouts, hidden corporate welfare (tax breaks, subsidies, grants, and loans), costly, useless military interventions, and Social Security and health-care sabotage.

HOME SWEET HOME

In 1988, according to the Bureau of Labor Statistics, 18 million people worked full- or part-time out of their homes, an increase of 40 percent since 1985. By 1995, this figure had swelled to 48 million, roughly 40 percent of the 120 million in the domestic workforce. A mighty $25 billion home-office industry for goods and services (excluding furniture and supplies) sprouted to cater to this huge new sector.

Major advances across the technological/electronic/computerized/digital board were enabling people to do at home—often more efficiently and economically—everything they used to have to travel to the office to do. By 1995, 10 million employees were "telecommuting," up from 3 million in 1990. The figure was estimated to rise to 25 million by the decade's end, according to JALA International, Inc. Most businesses hailed the trend.

WORKING AT HOME

Nearly one-third of U.S. companies are encouraging their workers to telecommute, according to a survey by Olsten Corp. Companies reported that about 9% of their employees work at home using a computer and modem. Among companies with telecommuting programs, 86% experienced increased productivity. (*Staffing Industry Report,* first and second quarter 1995)

Further advances over the last few years of the decade removed many of the remaining home-office rough spots and glitches. By January 1, 2005, tele-videophony had become foolproof and cheap. It swiftly swept the nation, vastly reducing the need for personal meetings—a development that had its pluses and minuses.

No machine can ever wholly replace personal, physical one-on-one contact, and you couldn't go out for a chat, a meal, or a shared cup of coffee. On the other hand, even as technotribalism depersonalized, so it depoliticized the office—just as it depoliticized town hall. It shattered glass ceilings and implemented affirmative action. It was very difficult to play all those hateful yet familiar office power games over the videophone.

Being on-line instead of on-site put brownnosers and elbow-rubbers at a disadvantage, making it physically difficult to schmooze their way up the corporate ladder. And with reengineered companies outsourcing more and more work to self-employed professionals who stayed in touch from afar, work tended to be judged strictly on its merits.

The nation's productivity and creativity would increase as people both within and without the corporation put their energies into constructive applications rather than office politics.

HEIGH-HO, HEIGH-HO . . .

Nevertheless, most corporations still needed corporate headquarters. Throughout the seventies, eighties, and nineties, many of the largest corporations had moved out of the cities into the suburbs, where their huge staffs could be more easily accommodated and/or recruited. But by the new millennium, between brutal downsizing and intelligent digitalization, the physical size of most corporate headquarters had miniaturized into a fraction of what it had been. Corporations were no longer tied to massive personnel pools. Many were finding ways to move still farther into the sticks, to take advantage of the innumerable benefits, corporate as well as personal, of technotribal society.

In 1995, Link Resources Corp., a marketing data organization, had forecast an annual growth rate for the home-office trend at from 7 to 8 percent. Figures like these had card-carrying digital revolutionaries predicting an entire society working at home on their PCs.

Followed to its logical conclusion, an 8 percent annual growth rate meant that by the year 2005 or so, everybody would be working at home full- or part-time. But society follows a different logic. The trend could go only so far. Not everybody could work at home. Not everybody was a computer jockey galloping along the information superhighway.

There were also the technotribal butcher and baker, and the silicon-chip maker. They all had to travel to work. But if they couldn't work at home, at least they didn't have to commute; facilities were located nearby.

Despite the downsizing, and the mass exodus overseas, the United States had never stopped producing. There were still plenty of factories based in this country, and they were humming. American know-how knew how to get back on-trend. High-skill specialty manufacturing thrived within our borders, compensating to some extent for the decline of heavy and labor-intensive industry.

Yankee ingenuity isn't an invention of Madison Avenue. It's a bona fide American quality. From hardware to software, many of the products that fueled the emergent economies of the post–World War II era were invented, patented, and developed in the USA. But they carried "Made Elsewhere" labels by the time they were sold. More than 3 million high-paying U.S. manufacturing jobs were shipped abroad between 1979 and 1994. (A small but positive countertrend produced 483,000 new manufacturing jobs between 1988 and 1992, at firms with fewer than one hundred employees.)

Wall Street built portfolios, not economies. And relentless pressure on American business by Wall Street to produce short-term profits prevented many farsighted corporations from implementing sound long-term strategies. Other massive corporations, grown sedentary and obese, sat back and took few chances. We watched as Japan's nimble, economical cars supplanted our rolling, voracious dinosaurs; we waved farewell as the vast electronics industry took root abroad.

We did the research; they did the development. Huge one-time-only business opportunities emigrated abroad. America's reward was a giant trade deficit and the glory of original invention.

Still, all was not lost.

Genius, though rare, is a renewable resource. American genius had not emigrated with the factories. It was still here; it just had to be implemented. The cultural diversity and freedom that fostered American genius and Yankee ingenuity reasserted themselves in the technotribe.

Freed from the assembly-line assault upon individual creativity, and from the imposed conformity of an Industrial Age corporate caste system, people at every level of training were finding ways to express their individual creativity.

▶ **TRENDPOST** *By January 1, 2000, a resurgence of environmentally clean industries based in the United States will be providing high-end wages for high-skill workers. New products will be produced and new services developed to meet growing demand in on-trend fields: health, technology, communications, the environment, transportation, energy, housing, agriculture—and the booming home-business business.* ◀

13

INVOLUNTARY
VOLUNTARY SIMPLICITY

DUMBSIZING

Throughout the nineties, there were millions of variations on a single theme. It was happening everywhere and at every level. You heard the same story over and over and over again.

When you signed on, they said the only way you would get fired was for cause. You really had to screw up. But if you did your job, were loyal, and met the company's goals, you had your job for life.

You gave them your best years. All those weekends you went to the office and all those weekends you were on the road; all the office work you took home at night, and all those nights you stayed late . . . and those fights when you finally got home. The vacations cut short, the kids' long faces when you had to cancel long-planned trips. You were a team player and they needed you back at the company to help finish the "important" projects. But most of them were never implemented, or they did them wrong. And then all those days you went to work sick, and the kids' birthdays missed, and the . . . "Like one big family," they told you way back when—you remember the hearty handshake. You made the sacrifices—willingly; sacrifices have to be made to keep a "family" together.

When they called you into the office that day, it wasn't a total surprise. It had been going on all over the country for at least a couple of years. With foreign competition cutting into profits and with the company moving some of its operations abroad, they were saying the nation's workforce had to get "lean and mean."

Only you did not think you would be one of the victims—not with the seniority, and all the extra work taken on as others were let go.

Your boss told you she was sorry; the decision wasn't hers. But you know company politics. She was told she had to cut five jobs out of twenty. Five heads had to roll. Yours was one of them.

At first, the only emotion you felt was anger. You wore the temporary pass they gave you to clean out your office like a scarlet letter. The security guard watched you like a criminal as you emptied your desk.

In the language of Middle Muddle, firing thousands of loyal employees was called "downsizing." The Trends Research Institute called it "dumbsizing." Morale was shattered. Nobody felt safe.

"Everyone has a sense of insecurity sitting in the back of their minds," said Lawrence Katz, the Labor Department chief economist, referring to the layoffs and cutbacks that have characterized the 1990s and have touched millions of Americans.

The jobs downsized out were supposed to save the company millions; it no longer had to pay all those salaries. But it wasn't as though the people who were let go had been sitting around doing nothing all day long. Those who were left shouldered the extra work. The money saved from downsizing was supposed to "rightsize" the company, bring it back to efficiency, and boost the bottom line.

Boosting the bottom line came to mean buttressing the top. The CEO took a huge raise; another couple of mil went to a handful of top honchos, and the rest to the stockholders. "Lean and mean" indeed! The people who were cutting out the pork were riding high on the hog.

LAYOFF PAYOFF

The Clinton administration has agreed to use $31 million in taxpayer money to pay a third of the $92 million in bonuses that top officials of Martin Marietta Corp and Lockheed Corp granted themselves for staging the largest merger in Pentagon history. . . .

The government-subsidized merger of Lockheed and Martin Marietta which will eliminate 30,000 jobs . . . Stockholders argued that bonuses including $8.2 million for Martin Marietta chairman Norman Augustine were excessive and unwarranted. (*New York Newsday,* 3/17/95)

Defense Secretary William Perry and CIA Director John Deutch had been consultants to Martin Marietta and were said to maintain close personal relationships with Augustine, according to *Newsday.*

RAKING IT IN

CEO pay is soaring again thanks to rising profits, directors' pursuits of outside talent and reduced public criticism.

"Greed clearly is back in style," says Robert Monks, a principal of Lens Inc, an activist investment fund in Washington. "There is almost a feeling (among CEO's) that the money is there to be taken." (*WSJ,* 4/12/95)

CEOS BENEFIT FROM LAYOFFS

A study released Friday says pay for chief executives at 23 major corporations rose 30% last year even though the firms laid off hundreds of thousands of workers since 1991. (AP, 4/30/94)

As CEO paychecks went up, worker paychecks went down. The Labor Department reported that between 1994 and 1995 wages for American workers had fallen 2.3 percent, possibly the biggest drop in American history, according to economic historian Bradford DeLong. To put the matter into perspective: In the mid-1970s the average CEO of a large company made forty-one times the salary of the average worker ($326,000 to $8,000). By 1995 the ratio had tripled to 187 to 1 ($3.7 million to $20,000).

Even through the anger, you could put your own position into perspective. If misery loves company, there was plenty of company.

In 1993, IBM laid off 105,000 workers, one-third of its workforce. Not long after, the company announced it was slashing secretaries' salaries by as much as 36 percent as part of its cost-cutting strategy.

Despite the most extensive downsizing program in American corporate history, Louis V. Gerstner, Jr., IBM's chairman and chief executive, hired an executive chef in 1995 for almost $120,000 a year. Gerstner himself was earning $12.4 million a year.

For decades, IBM had been the role model, the bellwether, the American corporate Big Brother. IBM led; the rest followed.

It was happening everywhere. Wherever there was injury, there was insult. The anger gave way to deep resentment, panicky confusion, and finally depression and despair. But you couldn't afford the luxury of despair. There was the mortgage, the car payments, the kids' school tuition, taxes . . . life. Whatever problems your job may have presented—the long hours, the hassle, the stress, the office politics—one sound you'd never heard was the wolf baying at the front door. Paying bills had always been a problem. You were often at your credit limit, sometimes borrowing or refinancing. But you knew where the next dollar was coming from.

Now you didn't. You went looking for work that would keep the wolf at bay. After the initial shock wore off, subliminal relief set in. It wasn't as though you'd gotten kicked out and were left helpless. You took your skills with you, even as you left your pride, your loyalty, and your esprit de corporation behind.

NICE WORK IF YOU CAN GET IT

The problem was that most of the jobs out there paid less than people were used to getting. Those who lost jobs and found new work between 1991 and 1993 took an average 47 percent cut in pay.

Federal and state funds were used to finance widespread retraining programs, but who was being retrained to do what? Operations managers retrained as home health aides? Marketing managers retrained as human service workers? Secretaries retrained as retail clerks?

The jobs of the future as projected by the Bureau of Labor Statistics told a poignant story.

The highest percentage growth in jobs will take place in the categories of home health aide, human service workers, and personal home care aide. In other words, by 2005 there will be 138 percent more home health aides and 136 percent more human service workers than there were in 1992.

There will be 110 percent more systems analysts. The Labor Department estimates 26 million jobs will be created over the next thirteen years. Of these, 25 million will be in the service sector.

In terms of sheer numbers, the most job increases will be in the categories of retail salesperson, registered nurse, and cashier. In 2005, there will be 780,000 more retail salespersons, 765,000 more registered nurses, 501,000 more systems analysts, and so on.

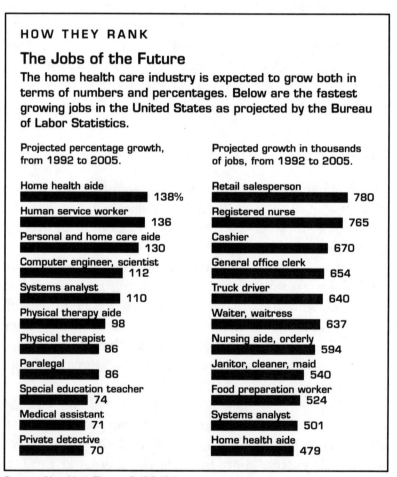

HOW THEY RANK

The Jobs of the Future

The home health care industry is expected to grow both in terms of numbers and percentages. Below are the fastest growing jobs in the United States as projected by the Bureau of Labor Statistics.

Projected percentage growth, from 1992 to 2005.

Job	Percent
Home health aide	138%
Human service worker	136
Personal and home care aide	130
Computer engineer, scientist	112
Systems analyst	110
Physical therapy aide	98
Physical therapist	86
Paralegal	86
Special education teacher	74
Medical assistant	71
Private detective	70

Projected growth in thousands of jobs, from 1992 to 2005.

Retail salesperson	780
Registered nurse	765
Cashier	670
General office clerk	654
Truck driver	640
Waiter, waitress	637
Nursing aide, orderly	594
Janitor, cleaner, maid	540
Food preparation worker	524
Systems analyst	501
Home health aide	479

Source: New York Times, 8/30/94.

Both numerically and in terms of percentages, the jobs of the future are not what people spending $100,000 on a college education would consider a satisfactory return on investment. Out of the list, only four high-skill, middle-income jobs figure in the percentage chart (computer engineer/scientist, systems analyst, special education teacher, and registered nurse). Only two of these (systems analyst and registered nurse) cross over into the top eleven in growth in numbers.

These jobs of the future represent an extension of the job trend prevailing in the early nineties. According to the Labor Department, most of the 4 million jobs added from 1988 to 1993 were in low-paying industries such as services and retailing. Washington and the financial papers pointed to decreasing unemployment statistics as proof the fiscal policy was working. Jobs! More jobs! exulted the politicians.

Sure, there were more jobs than ever at the Quackenomic Country Club: Waiters, groundskeepers, locker room attendants, valets, lifeguards, bartenders, busboys, janitors, and dishwashers all found work.

Going out job hunting wasn't what it used to be. Armed with skill and experience, millions of out-of-work workers looked elsewhere: toward home.

One business that was booming was the home business business—spurred on by massive downsizing and made feasible by the information superhighway.

The powerful and pervasive work-at-home trend, (re)-born in the eighties and growing through the nineties, preceded the technotribe and was more broad-based, affecting almost every level of American society.

By 1995, 25 million full-time home-based businesses were generating nearly $600 billion. This unexpected but huge development provoked universal expressions of surprise and astonishment. Newsletters proliferated, home business trade associations were formed, and how-to books were hot sellers. Working at home was treated as though it were something new. Actually, it was older than the pyramids.

THE PRICE OF PROGRESS

Before the nineteenth century, nobody traveled far to get to work. Everyone worked at or near home. It was the Industrial Age that forced workers to leave their homes to get to vast factories and centralized offices. Early Industrial Agers lived nearby in grimy towns sprung up around the factory or mill. But with railroads, trams, and then the automobile, the workforce was no longer obliged to live in the immediate vicinity. The miracle of modern transportation freed modern workers to live where they pleased.

The downside of freedom was that many blue-collar workers moved far away, where housing was cheap. White-collar workers also moved far away, usually in a different direction, to where peace and quiet could be purchased—at a price. Going to work suddenly became work, a second job that didn't pay you; you paid for it—not just financially but also emotionally: the rush-hour subway or bus, the long, crowded commute from the suburbs, the traffic jam.

It was understood that all of this was a price that had to be paid for "progress." But that understanding was never universal. In the earliest days of the Industrial Revolution, social critics argued that taking people from their homes to work in centralized locations was unnatural and inhumane.

That argument was generally dismissed or ignored throughout the Industrial Age. In school, we were taught that progress freed workers from the farms for more "productive" work in the factory or office. But to the millions regularly subjected to the rush-hour subway, the rush-hour freeway, and the long commute, leaving home to go to work seemed just that: unnatural, inhumane . . . and sometimes deadly. According to the Bureau of Labor Statistics, there were a record high 160,000 physical assaults and 1,070 murders in the workplace in 1994.

WORK WEEK

WORKING ON MONDAYS may be hazardous to your health. Workers suffers more back injuries and heart attacks on the first day of the work week, new evidence shows.

Blue collar workers have a 41% increased rate of a heart attack on Mondays while white collar workers have an 18% increase. (WSJ, 5/9/95)

The statistics were significant. People were getting killed in the workplace and a lot of others were deciding they would rather die than go to work. It had not always been like this.

Without for a moment minimizing the iniquitous sociopolitical structure of preindustrial society—its lack of individual freedom, the squalor of its poverty, and an oppressive religious structure—most preindustrial people had something very few had in the Industrial Age: a sense of accomplishment in whatever they did.

There were no jobs back then. There were arts, skills, crafts, trades, professions, but no jobs in the modern sense.

To be a good cobbler, cooper, or candlestick maker calls for expertise and creativity. Even the good peasant is thinking and making decisions all day long: how to plant, when to plant, where to plant, when to reap. Building a stone wall, laying a hedge, caring for livestock, fixing the barn—every task takes skill. Every task done well provides its own sense of satisfaction.

There's not much room for creativity and satisfaction on the assembly line, at the checkout counter, in data entry at the office, in flipping hamburgers, or in stocking shelves.

The Industrial Age brought boredom to the workplace, and took most artistry out of it.

On higher coveted executive levels, work was more war than art—defeating the competition, planning strategies, problem solving—more putting out fires than stoking up the creative fire within.

With the Industrial Age dying, and the Global Age before us, a return to the pre–Industrial Age was neither a choice nor a desire. However, like it or not, millions were abruptly obliged to stop paying their customary price for progress. They were on their own.

THE UPSIDE OF DOWNSIZING

Starting in the eighties and continuing throughout the nineties, the reborn work-at-home trend gathered momentum. The multitudes of downsized were forced into it; they cold turkeyed out of the corporate/industrial world—experiencing all the inevitable trauma of that brutal therapy.

Many went down, but not many went under. The adaptable, the versatile, and the skilled did not end up on the streets or the welfare rolls. Confronted by necessity, millions of people suddenly had to do something they had been discouraged from doing before: act for themselves, think for themselves, implement their innate creativity.

In school, from day one to graduation day, you conformed to a regime. The bell rang; you sat where you were told and learned what they told you to learn when they told you to learn it. Emotional scars remind you of the consequences of trying to assert your individuality.

In many ways, the job world was no different. The sign on the door said: Welcome aboard. Don't rock the boat.

Kicked off the ship and on their own, millions of the downsized were charting strange new waters: themselves.

The repressed creativity and individuality of two generations were unleashed.

Within the corporate structure, downsizing combined with two decades of mergers and acquisitions provided a niche-rich climate for the enterprising. Fill a hole with sand and there's no room between the grains for anything else, but fill it with boulders and there are all kinds of spaces and gaps. This is what happens when large corporations merge or acquire one another to fill a market: They leave spaces in between, especially when they abandon segments of that market and concentrate on what they then define as their "core business." Downsizing created still further niches. Because of the brain drain, and the focus on short-term profits instead of long-term growth, companies lost their proactive capacity to develop future markets.

Cut free from the corporate net, stifled creative talents now had the chance to make good on all those scuttled or bungled bright ideas: inventions, bold new marketing programs and distribution systems, ingenious recycling/reuse money-saving and moneymaking projects—all the new products and services designed to meet the needs of changing times.

Downsizing also inspired a new corps of freelance consultants. Cost-cutting mania often left corporations without the basic human resources they needed to function. Now they found they had to go back to their axed employees for the skills and expertise they had taken away with them. The first wave of work-at-homers included many former specialists turned consultants.

Downsizing, perceived by the government and the media as a grave concern, and by the downsized as a catastrophe, proved to be a blessing in thin disguise. Forced into freedom, millions of people on every level started finding ways to take control of their lives and do what they had always wanted to do. In 1996, 12 percent of downsized workers were starting their own businesses, double the rate of 1993.

If the Trends Research Institute were asked to define the most important trend of the new millennium, it was this focus on freedom. Freedom is big time; it is what everyone wants and has always wanted but rarely has had. The simultaneous combination of factors responsible for bringing about the demise of the Industrial Age and the beginning of the Global Age all enhanced the emphasis on freedom: the external freedom made possible through technology and social action, the inner freedom made possible only through individual directed will and effort. Freedom, and the newly acquired widespread capacity for the exercise of individual creativity, would be the single most important driving force behind the global Renaissance.

INVOLUNTARY VOLUNTARY SIMPLICITY

By January 1, 2000, the anger, resentment, panic, confusion, depression, and despair have become memories. Sure, the new life was not all peaches and cream. Family problems were still family problems. The bills still piled up. For the downsized and out, there was no guaranteed paycheck, and less income, a lot less. And nothing went down after the downsizing: the mortgage payments, the car payments, the taxes, the heating bills—no breaks there.

Most Americans were earning less and buying less, but those on-trend were living more fully. They were learning to distinguish between the quantity of life and the quality of life.

▶ **TRENDPOST** *Voluntary simplicity, an unrealizable counterculture ideal in the seventies, will become a reality and a significant trend in the new millennium. Entrepreneurs able to provide goods or services that enhance the quality of life while at the same time saving money will make money.* ◀

Cutting-edge baby boomers led the charge. Growing numbers were willingly trading down high-paying, high-stress, high-power jobs and professions for lives that gave them more free time, more time with their families, more satisfaction—more control. Larger numbers of the out-of-work workforce unwillingly did the same, but eventually they came to the same conclusion. They had been forced to give up the trappings of success and now would not trade their new lives for their old ones.

Voluntary simplicity did not mean wearing a loincloth and eating locusts and wild honey in the desert; it was not deprivation. Voluntary simplicity called for moderation, self-discipline and training of the mind and body, and spiritual growth over material accumulation. It didn't mean doing one big thing differently; it was doing many little things, all in answer to three main questions: How much do I really need? How much do I really want? How much am I willing to do to get it? Like working at home, voluntary simplicity was nothing new; it was rampant consumerism that was new. This was old-fashioned, forgotten Yankee frugality, rediscovered and redesigned from the chassis up for the Global Age.

It was a lifestyle lost for so long, almost no one knew how to do it anymore; those who did, or who learned it from scratch the hard way, wrote books and newsletters about it. (*The Bankers Secret* by Marc Eisenson and *Your Money or Your Life* by Joe Dominguez and Vicki Robin are among the best. The New Road Map Foundation, P.O. Box 15981, Seattle, WA 98115, and *Pocket Change Investor*, Box 78, Elizaville, NY 12523, provide information on voluntary simplicity.

An old saying goes, Use it up; wear it out; make it do; do without. Everyone did it differently; there were no rules or general guidelines. Grow it yourself; fix it yourself; make it yourself; cook it yourself; buy it used (or get it free). If you don't really need it, it's a luxury (nothing wrong with luxuries, just don't confuse them with necessities). Pay a few dollars additional on your mortgage each month; save tens of thousands over its span. Pay off your credit cards, and then buy nothing with them that you can't pay when the bill comes in. Swap services; barter goods. In the hippie days, these ideas and ideals seemed quaint and cute, but in the do-or-die nineties, that was what many had to do to survive.

The Involuntary Voluntary Simplicity Corps took on millions of new draftees when the baby boomers came of age.

Surveys conducted in the nineties revealed that the vast majority of boomers had not taken steps to ensure retirement for themselves at the level of their customary lifestyle. To maintain a fifty-thousand-dollar-a-year lifestyle in retirement, boomers had to have close to a million socked away. Few did. On average, boomers were saving only 38 percent of what they needed to retire at age sixty-five.

Among the lower-middle and working classes, the situation was much worse. According to a 1993 Merrill Lynch survey, half of all American families had less than a thousand dollars in net financial assets. In the nineties, the savings rate among Americans hovered around 4 percent, compared with 9 percent in 1974. Two-thirds of the nearly 90 million Americans in the private sector had no pension plans. Half of all Americans had no retirement plans.

▶ **TRENDPOST** *Financial planning experts will find a booming business helping boomers prepare for the future. Up-and-coming generations will learn to make use of financial planning services earlier rather than later in life.* ◀

Huge numbers would have to survive on Social Security alone—difficult in the best of times. Now, the entire Social Security program was groaning under the weight of demographic overload. With benefits shrinking, boomers would find survival harder than ever. Increasing numbers of people were fighting for a decreasing slice of the pie.

GAP IN WEALTH IN U.S. CALLED WIDEST IN WEST

New studies on the growing concentration of American wealth and income challenge a cherished part of the country's self-image: They show that rather than being an egalitarian society the United States has become the most economically stratified of industrial nations.

Even class societies like Britain which inherited large differences in income and wealth over centuries going back to their feudal pasts, now have greater economic equality than the United States. . . .

Economic inequality has been on the rise since the 1970's. . . .

Federal Reserve figures from 1989, the most recent available, show that the wealthiest 1% of American households . . . own nearly 40% of the nation's wealth. By contrast the wealthiest 1 percent of the British population owns about 18% of the wealth there. (*NYT*, 4/17/95)

America was the place where "all men are created equal." But throughout the eighties and nineties, America was becoming more and more unequal—even as the Global Age took root.

Apart from the tiny percentage of the very rich, the vast majority, on every income level, from upscale to subsistence, was going to have to make do with much less when retirement hit (between the years 2010 and 2030).

► **TRENDPOST** *Retiring boomers will generate a real estate and building boom south of the border, seeking locales where a high quality of life can be lived on diminished means. Favored sites will be Cuba, shortly to become accessible, the Dominican Republic, Costa Rica, and other politically stable Caribbean* *and Central American countries. Low-end boomers will also be moving south for the very same reasons, but financial constraints will direct them to the poorer southern states within the U.S. (West Virginia, Mississippi, Arkansas, etc.). Boomers looking toward retirement will do well to stake out claims in desirable areas before the landrush hits. Architects and builders servicing the trend will prosper.* ◀

14

REENGINEERING
THE HOME

EDIBLE ASSETS

Although hard times were finally in the numbers as well as in the air, the quackenomic rhetoric did not change. But the public perception did. By January 1, 2000, repeated assurances of economic recovery, soft landings, and a Goldilocks economy (not too hot, not too cold, but j-u-u-u-st right!) were recognized as fairy tales. For a growing majority—young and old, seniors, boomers, Xers—times were not getting better, and they were not going to get better.

Practical measures had to be taken to ensure a satisfactory lifestyle on less—and a way to enjoy it more.

One major plank within the technotribal, involuntary/voluntary simplicity trend was: Do yourself, your health, and your pocketbook a favor by growing as much of your own food as you can.

But how many people could do this? A relatively small percentage of Americans lived in wilderness, rural, or exurban areas and had—or had room for—the kind of extensive garden needed to produce a substantial portion of the year's food. City dwellers were out of luck. A couple of pots with tomato plants in them on the fire escape weren't going to make much difference. And the suburbs? Who had room in the suburbs? With the lawn in front and a little patch of backyard, there was no room for a garden there.

Somewhere around the year 2000, it came as a simultaneous revelation and revolution. The lawn! Lawns were everywhere—millions upon millions of costly, intensively cared for, carefully manicured suburban lawns . . . doing nothing but growing grass (the kind that Bill Clinton could inhale and sheep could eat). A lawn turned into a vegetable garden would produce fresh food!

Just as there was nothing new about the work-at-home trend or the voluntary simplicity trend, there was nothing new about using a portion of the land around the house to grow food. It just felt new because, relatively, so few people had been doing it. The art had to be relearned, and as with work at home, alternative healing, and voluntary simplicity, it combined the best of the old and the new.

People planted and grew organically, the way their great-grandfathers had, but made use of leading-edge technologies in equipment, advanced growing and harvesting procedures, and cultivation and irrigation techniques.

▶ **TRENDPOST** *Home garden–oriented businesses will experience tremendous growth in every sector—vegetable, ornamental, aquatic ($26 billion in 1994, up 59 percent since 1989). This trend will be a bountiful producer of jobs, products, and services. The trend is in the adolescent stage of its life cycle.* ◀

In 1994, home vegetable gardening was a $1.2 billion business and increasing. Growing consumer demand was already enticing on-trend retailers. Central Tractor Farm & Country was on a forty-six-store building spree and Home Depot was testing stores with a farm motif.

As the trend reached maturity in the new millennium, it had a significant impact—in the way people lived, in the way they felt, and in the way they ate. It was part of the art of living better for less. America was going back to the land and back to basics—the sixties pipe dream became reality. Billions formerly spent on lawn care were now either saved or redeployed in producing fresh food.

The conversion of millions of lawns into gardens also cut a substantial chunk out of the 90 million buzzing, roaring, whirring, fume-spewing mowers, leaf blowers, and weed trimmers in the process. Studies reveal that these are responsible for some 15 percent of total summer air pollution. An inefficient 3.5-hp gas mower emits the same amount of hydrocarbons in one hour as a new car driven 340 miles. The 70 million pounds of pesticides and the millions of pounds of chemical fertilizers needed annually to keep all those lawns in golf-green condition would no longer poison the land, the streams, the aquifers, and the people. Huge quantities of what had been thrown out as garbage was now recognized for what it was, valuable organic matter. Instead of filling up the landfills, it was composted and returned to replenish the land, where it belonged.

The American lawn did not disappear. Kids still romped on them; barbecues were cooked on them; badminton was played on them. But a significant percentage of the nation's arable lawn area was steadily converted to food production.

A modest twenty-by-thirty-foot plot of garden can produce up to one thousand dollars' worth of organic food in a year. Just two mature standard fruit trees will produce 250 pounds of fruit a year. With millions struggling to make ends meet, a thousand saved here and a thousand saved there made a real difference.

By 2000, the familiar Norman Rockwell American lawn, symbol of stability, security, and conformity, was newly perceived as an unaffordable luxury, a fashion that had outlived its day.

Once the great lawn-into-garden trend hit, it hit everyone. Even the well-to-do saw that money formerly spent on professional lawn care could now be more productively spent on professional gardening. It made sense. You could eat the result.

EDIBLE LANDSCAPING

The traditional American lawn was a miniaturized Everyman's version of the great English and European estates of the seventeenth and eighteenth centuries. But it did not have the same artistic effect. Developers, especially in the post–World War II period, went at landscaping with an assembly-line mentality. These "Bronx builders" began by clear-cutting every tree, a "money saver" that made it easier to move machines and material around the site.

Cookie-cutter houses and cookie-cutter plots may have maximized short-term profits for the developer, but in the long term, it was economically, ecologically, and aesthetically costly. Home owners started off life with a clean slate: a bleak expanse of newly planted lawn ready for a few azaleas, a flower bed, a bit of hedge, and a couple of flowering saplings. The grounds had only a recreational and cosmetic function. Food was grown, if it was grown at all, in the occasional hobby garden.

But now, the purely pragmatic decision to grow food spun off into a creative and aesthetic trend. Suddenly, with lawns—especially front lawns—being converted into gardens, there was room for individual creative expression. Nobody wanted a front lawn that looked like a victory garden, with its neat, uniform rows of a dozen different vegetables.

The concept of edible landscaping took hold; interspersing edibles with ornamentals, berry bushes, arbors, fruit trees patched together with mosaics of culinary and medicinal herbs. The average American home became the scene of a landscaping renaissance.

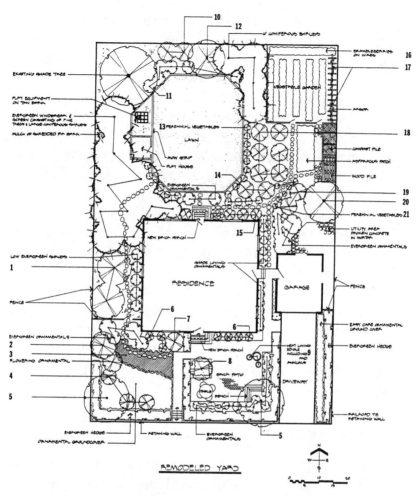

REMODELED YARD

5.5. A completed architectural plan of the design chosen for the sample yard ("bubble drawing" 5.4). It includes the following edibles, keyed by number:
1. Filbert 2. European semidwarf plum 3. Strawberries
4. Gooseberries 5. Apples
6. Blueberries 7. Genetic dwarf apricot 8. Genetic dwarf almond
9. Kumquat 10. Elderberries
11. Salal 12. Sour cherry
13. Artichokes 14. Genetic dwarf nectarines 15. Currants
16. Raspberries 17. Grapevines
18. Genetic dwarf peaches
19. Genetic dwarf pears 20. Japanese plum 21. Rhubarb

A new breed of gardener/artist found ways to lavish creative energy on the land. The models were being created first on the grand scale at the longevity centers, at Healthmart locations, and in communal technotribe gardens.

As the trend took hold, acres of university and corporate campus lawn were transformed into edible landscape, providing students and employees with practical, enjoyable therapeutic respite from study or work. Sprawling, barren, glum, grimly misnamed industrial parks eventually acquired a right to be called that, sprouting character along with carrots. Building upon a handful of nineties token experiments, larger and larger tracts of inner-city wasteland were reclaimed, planted, and flourishing—when the spirit and energy were there.

For the land-challenged, a new science of miniaturization developed to capitalize on the demand, combining Zen artistry with high-tech innovation and producing unheard-of yields in beautifully orchestrated tiny spaces. No plot of land was too small to become its own little piece of paradise.

HOME HEALTH

The stay-at-home/work-at-home trend was like a mighty river, swelled by strong trend tributaries: technotribalism, the information superhighway, involuntary voluntary simplicity, economic fallback, downsizing, and a generation of Depression baby retirees, soon to be followed by the baby boomers.

Whatever it was that compelled or induced people to return to their homes, one overriding concern at every income level was health. Millions of people living and working at home coincided with sharply escalating health-care costs and declining services. The result was a boom in home health care.

▶ **TRENDPOST** *Bringing health to the home will provoke new businesses, big and small, and a spectrum of new jobs for enterprising and inventive individuals. The trend is in the early stages of growth in its life cycle.* ◀

With America's middle class suffering from economic fallback and unable to afford traditional health care, less costly options became a necessity.

In 1991, home health services were already grossing $15 billion a year. Having produced trend studies for the home health-care industry, the Trends Research Institute was quoted in the *New York Times* as forecasting that this would be the quickest-growing segment of the health industry. "Most products and services for the home-health-care market haven't been invented yet," we said.

By 1995, the gross had topped $30 billion. By 2000, 60 million Americans were fifty-five or older, and the industry's growth rate was accelerating. The advantages of home health care were becoming known to the population at large, not confined to the aged and aging. Beginning as a way to keep the aged and chronically but not dangerously ill from filling up the hospitals, home health care swiftly grew in sophistication and in the range of its services.

Many high-tech procedures and treatments that had formerly been hospital-based were routinely performed at home. "There is practically nothing that cannot be treated in the home," said Allen I. Goldberg, head of pediatric home health at Loyola University Medical Center in Chicago and president of the American Academy of Home Care Physicians.

In general, patients preferred to be treated at home, for a number of reasons. It was cheaper. On average, twelve to fourteen visits at home cost two thousand dollars, which couldn't buy a day and a half in a hospital. Apart from lower costs, patients liked being treated in the comfort of their own homes. The attention they got was more personal. By not checking into the hospital, there was no risk of checking out with something they hadn't checked in with.

HOSPITAL INFECTIONS ON THE RISE

In 1992 the Centers for Disease Control and Prevention reported that two million patients annually suffer from infections while in the hospital, requiring an estimated $4.5 billion to treat. That year, 19,027 people died from infections contracted while in the hospital, and another 58,092 died from causes to which such infections had contributed. (*Natural Health*, January 1994)

Like going to work, going into a hospital could be deadly.

Home health care reprieved patients from the horrors of hospital food and the myriad indignities of hospital treatment (middle-of-the-night wake-up calls, uncaring care, unannounced visits from unknown doctors, unasked-for conversations with unchosen wardmates).

The home health-care trend inspired a number of new ancillary businesses: from high-tech to home-delivery, from basic needs administered to by freelance paramedics to mobile pampering provided by wandering massage therapists. The old-fashioned house call staged a revival, but instead of arriving with a black bag, the doctor carried compact high-tech equipment networked to client-server diagnostic centers and hospitals.

New millennium home health care extended to the whole range of new medical services: The friendly neighborhood acupuncturist, homeopath, naturopath, herbalist, vitamin counselor, chiropractor, and dentist also paid house calls. Small new businesses delivered safe, healing, high-nutrition meals specifically designed to satisfy the patient's individual dietary needs.

By 2000, the home health-care industry expanded to meet growing needs. Innumerable work opportunities were created on every level. While many such jobs were strictly work-a-day they provided millions with a day's work they might not otherwise have been able to find.

In 1994, home health aides, the most common and the poorest-paid home-care service providers (1994 average: $281 per week) accounted for 31 percent of home health employees. This was a harbinger of the best that a huge and growing sector of uneducated, underskilled Americans could hope to find. Home health care was the quickest-growing segment within the trillion-dollar health-care industry, itself the fastest-growing industry overall in the United States. Between 1988 and 1995, one in five new nonfarm jobs was in health care. And the industry could only grow, servicing both proactive and reactive streams of society.

No one was immune to environmental poisoning, increased radiation levels, and newly mutated wonder bugs. No one was immune to aging. But the proactive were taking preventative steps to get healthy and stay healthy. The reactive majority—sedentary, "virtually relaxed," and on-line—moved toward the millennium immobile in their armchairs, hoping wistfully to preserve an ailing status quo. Both proactive minority and reactive majority needed health care.

FROM CHIMNEY SWEEP TO ACUPUNCTURIST

Individuals looking for new ways to earn useful and honorable livings met the challenge with ingenuity. Some of the new health-related services provided upscale, creative, inventive, highly individualistic, and deeply satisfying livelihoods on a personal and community level. The personal success stories of such individuals stood as exemplars for the global Renaissance.

Clued-in people, dissatisfied with their lives and life-styles, or sometimes forced by circumstances to find new means of livelihood, turned to health care, in its broadest application.

The individual stories were legion: the chimney sweep who put himself through four years of training and became an acupuncturist; the advertising executive who opened a health-food store; the police officer who became a martial-arts master and instilled in people the kind of physical self-confidence that is essential to health; the many orthodox doctors practicing various forms of yoga and meditation and inspiring their patients to follow suit.

Anything having to do with health was good business—big and small.

HOMING IN

Anything having to do with the home was good business—big and small.

Returning home did not mean retreating into a cave. Rather, it meant turning the cave into a castle. By choice or by force, people were using home as more than a rest stop at the end of the workday, or as a weekend sanctuary.

▶ **TRENDPOST** *Home improvement and remodeling, from the architect/designer level to do-it-yourself, will be a strong growth sector.* ◀

The figure for home-remodeling sales for 1995 was $123 billion. By 2000, this had become a $200 billion industry. It was no longer just home improvement; it was life improvement.

With America spending much more time at home than

ever before, much more thought and effort went into every aspect of home. The most obvious beneficiary was the home office—which for most people had simply never existed before in any form. Usually, the home office had to be created from scratch. The kitchen and bathrooms were the traditional recipients of the lion's share of the attention, but now careful thought went into nontraditional areas— health/fitness rooms, meditation spaces. Pools, saunas, and steam rooms were becoming standard equipment.

In the fifties, the swimming pool was strictly a rich man's status symbol. If you had a pool, you were *rich,* and that was that. By the eighties, the pool had become commonplace, but it was still a recreational luxury. Did you put in a pool or buy a motorboat?

By 2000, the previewing segment of society, faced with the prospect of wheelchairs and walkers, was making the home pool a fixture, an integral part of its health-conscious, home-centered lifestyle. It was no longer just expensive cool water to party around and jump into on hot weekends.

"Whether you simply jog around in a pool, or engage in a more studied workout consisting of stretches and kicks . . . water workouts provide good cardiovascular returns without hurting bones, ligaments or joints. Not only is it excellent for lower back problems, it helps improve breathing. It's meditative and relaxing. In a stressed-out society, swimming is a perfect stress reducer," stated Dr. Mitchel Skolnik, chiropractor, holistic practitioner, and sports medicine expert.

Pools still weren't cheap, but to the many staying home much of the time, the pool became a cost-effective adjunct to life—almost a necessary expense. The private pool was a health and longevity investment, a price to pay for staying healthy, especially for an aging America. Only two in ten people living past sixty-five are fully functional in the last years of their lives. Swimming and pool exercises are tailor-made to maintain a self-sufficient lifestyle.

The private sauna or steam room played an analogous role to the pool. These high-tech versions of the Native American sweat lodge and its Nordic cousins could no longer be dismissed as Yuppie luxuries; the health benefits were proven.

Greenhouses were also becoming commonplace. They could be used to grow organic food, and, utilizing new heat-storage and transfer technologies, they cut down on fuel bills. When the free-energy revolution hit early in the twenty-first century, greenhouses became standard.

UNWELCOME GUESTS

Health maintenance also meant home maintenance—of a particular sort.

For several decades, the aware and the unbuffaloed had been acknowledging the stiff price paid by one and all for the "profit at any cost" philosophy of the Industrial Age. Most of the early attention was focused on nature: endangered species, polluted air and water, clear-cut forests, dwindling wetlands.

By the eighties, it was realized that the degradation of the great outdoors had moved indoors. Millions of office workers reported headaches, dizziness, nausea, exhaustion, and a variety of other symptoms suffered while at work. The term *sick building syndrome* was coined. An estimated 25 million people in an estimated 1.2 million U.S. commercial buildings were affected. Its reality was acknowledged.

But it was not until the nineties that the alarm sounded for the private home and the modern apartment. Materials developed to make building and maintenance cheaper and easier often proved to have a high price attached, as well. Increasingly sophisticated studies were showing that many of the materials commonly used in modern homes had long-term harmful effects.

HOUSEHOLD MATERIALS MAY BE TOXIC, A STUDY WARNS

Chemicals found in everyday products like carpeting and particle board may pose greater longterm environmental hazards than industrial chemical wastes, a study conducted for the influential environmental group Inform has concluded.

For example, formaldehyde which the Environmental Protection Agency classifies as a probable human carcinogen, is contained in carpeting and particle board, and is gradually released into the air over the long life of those products. Concentrations of 16 contaminants under study are greater indoors than outside, according to an E.P.A. study cited in the report.

Morton L. Mullins, vice-president for regulatory affairs for the Chemical Manufacturers Association, said he was "disturbed by the tone" of the group's announcement and feared that it was using "alarmist rhetoric to create a new set of concerns" for the public. (*NYT*, 3/15/95)

Standard operating procedure for industry spokesmen and lobbyists was immediately to label any identification of danger as "alarmist rhetoric," or an "unnecessary attempt to scare the public."

Not all of the newly discovered culprits were man-made. Naturally occurring radon gas, found in high concentrations in many homes, was being blamed for up to one-tenth of U.S. lung cancer deaths.

There was not much point in doing push-ups in a polluted home.

Even before 2000, some old houses were retrofited with state-of-the-art air-filtration and water-purification systems; by 2000, they were standard equipment in new ones.

Natural or proven neutral synthetics became the building materials of choice. The physical environment of the home had to undergo its own detox regime.

Numerous new products were designed to maintain or restore house health: nontoxic, nonpolluting cleaners and detergents that actually worked, high-filtration vacuums and dust filters, anti-allergy equipment, and so on. Devices and products once considered costly, experimental, or flaky gained increasing acceptance as global environmental conditions worsened and radiation levels increased. The home had to be made as immune system–friendly as possible.

▶ **TRENDPOST** *The need and desire for healthy homes and environmentally sound architecture will generate new products and new specialties within traditional construction industries, trades, and professions.* ◀

HOME DELIVERY

Meanwhile, an array of home-oriented services surfaced to cater to the homing trend. Highly publicized high-tech, state-of-the-art new businesses like electronic shopping and electronic banking blossomed. Some created major shifts in national shopping habits as the local supermarket and Healthmart went on-line and delivered the entire shopping cart full of goodies to the door.

By 2000, home delivery of full dinner menus had become the fastest-growing segment of the food industry. High-volume, low-overhead buffet-style home-delivered meals filled the big market niche between pizza or Chinese food and upscale fare.

Despite the reality of accelerating massive change, some things did not change. There were still twenty-four hours in the day, and many of the work-at-homers were working longer hours than ever.

Convenience remained a valued quality, and where the population density would support it, a new breed of traveling salesperson came knocking at the door, or responded to SOS's. The revival of door-to-door selling was yet another example of how much of what was new was old. But now they were selling organic produce, specialty foods, and prepared meals. Electronic tinkers and cobblers made rounds to repair all the new technology.

Old standbys that had survived the long eclipse were joined by newcomers: The Avon lady and the vacuum salesman rang doorbells with New Age purveyors of environmentally sound household basics, software, and high-end ergonomic furnishings. New on the route was the traveling high-tech nursery salesperson with an array of the latest products to help you grow your own year-round—specialty seeds and plants, equipment, and gardening paraphernalia.

The rag and bone man of old (minus his horse and cart) was reborn as the recycle man, traveling door-to-door to collect and pay for an increasing number of products that were being reused or recycled. Beginning in the eighties as a token noble gesture, recycling became economically feasible by the mid-1990s. Later, a combination of steadily rising costs for raw materials and waste disposal, along with improved recycling technology, made recycling profitable. In 1995, recyclers were paying $1.34 billion for aluminum cans, and old newspaper was selling for from $150 to $200 a ton, five times the rate of the previous year. A brisk stolen-newspaper industry was flourishing, netting an estimated $100 million a year, according to *Resource Recycling* magazine.

Nevertheless, like any other business, recycling had its risks. Prices were subject to market fluctuations—but for the foreseeable future, recycling would be on an uptrend.

▶ **TRENDPOST** *Enterprising businesses and individuals will find ways to make livings from the home delivery trend. Many of the foot soldiers in the door-to-door corps will be recruited from the ranks of middle managers and other downsizees unable to find work in their own fields or at their former income levels.* ◀

SACRED SPACE

For two centuries, the machine had been more important than man, and economic goals more important than human needs. By January 1, 2000, humanity was beginning to reassert its humanness. As the Industrial Age died, the philosophy that had brought it to life and sustained it died with it.

The Global Age that replaced the Industrial Age subscribed to a different set of values. The difference was easy to see but not easy to define. It was like the difference between the face of a dying octogenarian and the face of a newborn baby.

The past was etched unmistakably into the features of the old Industrial Age. The features of the future were written no less indelibly into the face of the coming new age, but they were as yet subtle and amorphous; only maturity would stamp them with their ultimate emotional, spiritual, and psychological character.

Over the first decades of the new millennium, a renewed sense of the sacred was taking root, not yet doctrinaire, formalized, and institutionalized.

The new role played by the home in the lives of so many was central to this emerging philosophy and the lifestyle that accompanied it. Home was more than a place to hang your hat; it became even more than the place that now actually produced the bacon. By the year 2000, the home was becoming a place where the spirit could reside.

15

COMMUNITY SPIRIT

THE WAL-MART WARS

The technotribe represented the vanguard of the Renaissance, the prototype of what would ultimately prevail. By January 1, 2000, it was still gestating; there were as yet no full-fledged technotribes that might serve others as a model.

But the spirit of community that would characterize this Renaissance and the technotribe was beginning to take root throughout the United States as a consequence of the enormous homing trend. The combination of economic need, the urge for creative expression, the dissolution of the rigid old social, political, and economic forms and institutions, and the huge, inescapable fact of tens of millions of people working at or near home threw local community life into a new and bright light.

The home went beyond the house, and health was a principle that had to be applied to the community as well as to the individual. Community health could not be determined with the standard Industrial Age thermometer that measured only dollars. The community itself had to be consciously fed, nurtured, cared for, and supported.

Wherever this understanding was implanted, a new sense of community grew. Neighborhoods within the larger city, as well as many small towns and villages, reacquired something of their vanished original personalities. Even the worst of the inner cities had the infrastructure, and therefore the potential, to "recommunitize."

The only major exceptions were post-1960s suburbs. Built without a core, dependent upon malls for their supplies and highways as their arteries, these monotonous developments had no heart—and no soul. And with very little potential for acquiring either, they would have to await the drastic suburban renewal of 2020 before fully participating in the Renaissance.

Revitalizing the community did not just mean bringing more business to it; it meant supporting the business *in* the community. Local retailers joined with environmentalists and preservationists to implore residents to repel the mass-discount invaders that were destroying their town commercial centers along with the individual character of their communities. The "buy local" trend was a way of saving local economies.

In times of economic downturn, giant retailers held out the carrot of cheaper prices for all and the creation of jobs in return for access to the local markets. If the pitch was successful, the result was indeed cheaper prices—everyone paid a few dollars less for their jeans and microwaves. But the profits were exported to swell distant corporate coffers, while the promised jobs created at home were at checkout counters and in stockrooms, and scaled to the minimum wage.

A few dollars saved on today's clothes and appliances carried a heavy burden in hidden long-term socioeconomic costs. Money spent in hometown businesses tended to stay in the community and get recycled, not only as more business but also into community services and activities. Money that was exported as corporate profits was gone for good.

By January 1, 2000, historic preservation movements were commonplace. Saving Main Street and preserving the hometown flavor and the hometown past became passionate campaign issues in local politics.

Just as the medieval village or the American small town once supported its local miller, brewer, butcher, baker, wheelwright, carpenter, cobbler, mason, and half a dozen other highly skilled tradesmen, so, now, with significant additions and deletions, craftsmen, tradesmen, technicians, and other professionals returned to enrich the life of the reborn communities of the new millennium.

The Industrial Age assembly line worked brilliantly for automobiles, computers, electronic equipment, plastics, and many other products. But when the same principle was applied to bread, beer, beef, and much that was inherently qualitative in human life, quality was destroyed.

The successful microbrewer of the eighties and nineties was joined by the microfarmer, the microbutcher, the microbaker, and even the micro–candlestick maker here and there. These were nothing more than boutique names applied to enterprising individuals doing exactly the same things individuals had always done—before their lives and livelihoods were preempted wholesale by big business and Big Brother, the ruling partnership over the two centuries of the Industrial Age.

▶ TRENDPOST *Microbusiness will amount to an entrepreneurial explosion over the next three decades. In the mid-nineties, the trend was only in its early growth stage, with successful microbusinesses taking on average 1 to 3 percent of total industry market share.* ◀

WONDER (IF IT'S) BREAD

In 1980, there were one hundred retail "bread boutiques" nationwide selling fresh home-baked bread. In 1995, there were one thousand, and the number was expected to rise to five thousand by the end of the decade. Microbakeries grinding their own flour accounted for about 1 percent of total bread sales in 1994, or $216 million. A white-bread America grew up without ever tasting real bread. Nevertheless, those who remembered missed the fresh, crusty, wholesome loaf that once had come from the local baker and was no longer available at all. Even people who'd never had the real bread experience felt a vicarious nostalgia.

Great Harvest, a franchise microbakery chain with eighty-eight bakeries in 1995, began back in 1978 in Great Falls, Montana. On the day it opened its doors, there was a line around the block. The bread sold out in an hour, and the company has gone on from there.

The micro principle found application in hundreds of different forms as the American community revitalized itself from within. The secret to success was seeing and filling a real niche or gap within the existing framework of society.

The post–World War II framework ushered in "the Reign of Quantity" (René Guenon), the application of assembly-line principles to Everyman's lifestyle. It was a Wonder bread world—homogenized, standardized, depersonalized, McDonaldized . . . and usually cheap.

Mom-and-pop stores couldn't compete. Most of the local men's stores, women's wear stores, groceries, bakeries, shoe stores, and appliance stores went under as Downtown USA disintegrated. The supermarket, the superstores, and the megastore put everything together into one vast building.

The small shop appeared to make a comeback in the great shopping mall trend of the sixties and seventies. But for the most part, these stores were links in huge retail chains.

There was not much room for individual enterprise or creativity on any level. Nevertheless, in an age dominated by brands, there were notable success stories—the few who started small with something new (the PC) or qualitatively superior (gourmet ice cream) and parleyed quality into quantity. These were exceptions, but they set the stage for a reappreciation of quality, and the return of the individual.

In 1990, the Trends Research Institute presented a report before the National Coffee Association that forecast a bright future for specialty coffees. Back then, a handful of major consumer-product companies dominated the market. If it wasn't put out by Procter & Gamble, Kraft, or Nestlé, it wouldn't be on the supermarket shelf. In the coffee world at that time, Dunkin' Donuts was regarded as the quality standard.

By the mid-1990s, specialty coffee sales were growing at a rate of 60 percent a year. Like the huge breweries with their mock microbeers, the huge processing giants soon had their own gourmet coffee labels. So great was the demand for quality that the trend swiftly proliferated into thousands of coffee bars (5,600 in 1996, only 200 in 1989) serving a brew that was actually good to the last drop. It had taken just four hundred years to arrive, but the Elizabethan coffee shop finally took root on American soil.

Quality coffee was just one small cog in the quality bandwagon rolling across America. From beer to bread, from soft drinks to snack foods—suddenly, if you could eat it or drink it, you could find a genuine quality version of it. Madison Avenue's marketing mavens did their best to reduce to a marketing strategy this awakened appreciation of what had been lost. Bread, the staff of life, baked with care from top-quality ingredients, was described as "indulgence food." It was no such thing. It was just good bread, the kind you used to be able to get anywhere. People knew the difference. It tasted good—and it was good for you.

Nor was the new Reign of Quality restricted to food and drink; it extended to every aspect of external life. Large numbers of on-trend consumers bought fewer but higher quality products. A parallel movement took place in products directed at the inner life. Large numbers of people came to understand that most pop culture is the artistic equivalent of junk food. Arrogant radio shock-jocks, sensation-based daytime TV talk shows, the tabloid press, most prime time TV, and violent Hollywood spectaculars represent literal psychic poison. Those who did not want their souls poisoned now filled their emotional and intellectual lives with quality art, philosophy and literature, and quality entertainment.

FILLING THE HOLE

While each contributor to the Return to Quality trend comprised just a few percentage points of its respective industry's gross, the growth rate was well into double digits. It was just gaining a foothold but would become a significant psychoeconomic element in the global Renaissance.

By filling the economic hole with bigger and bigger boulders, the handful of corporate giants left bigger and bigger spaces in between. By 2000, small enterprises were filling the gaps. Individual businesses and microchains were outmaneuvering the national giants.

Assembly-line thinking could not compete with individual creativity on the local level. Foxy Thelma's Chicken outfoxed the Colonel's. Barry's Backwater Burgers beat out Burger King. The micros used locally raised, free-range, organically fed animals. The chains used animals that had been factory-farmed, brutally caged, and chemically fed. The microchains flourished in the technotribes and the revitalized communities where word of mouth spoke louder than marketing clout.

The chains still did big business in inner cities, on the road, and in the malls, but the market had long since matured. New growth took place only in foreign countries, particularly Third World countries and former Soviet satellites. These so-called emerging markets would have to experience the same destruction of their own traditional ways before realizing the value of what they had lost and then initiating their own quality revolutions.

The United States, the first country to succumb to "the Reign of Quantity," was also the first to recover from it.

THE PALL OVER THE MALL

But recovery did not take place across the board. In the huge world of retail sales, the trend toward bigger and cheaper marched forward to its logical conclusion. The shopping malls that put mom-and-pop stores out of business in the sixties and seventies were themselves falling prey to the power centers and megastores of the nineties: the barracudas eaten by the killer whales. Between 1993 and 1995, regional mall net profits fell 6.4 percent, while power center profits rose 15 percent. In 1995, 14 percent of the nation's mall space was vacant, up from 7 percent in 1993.

Dealing entirely in standardized, mass-produced products, whoever could sell cheapest beat the competition. By locating in out-of-the-way, hence cheaper locations, by ruthlessly eliminating any hint of atmosphere or design, and by dealing in massive volume, the power centers prevailed. Around the country, the shopping mall—which in two short decades had come to feel almost like an American institution, a kind of architectural processed apple pie—had become an endangered commercial species.

With economic fallback increasingly severe, price-conscious shoppers bought their staples at bottom dollar. Since power centers were normally inconveniently sited, people planned shopping forays in advance and bought everything at once.

In areas where it usurped the former city, town, or village commercial center, the mall had served for a generation as an unsatisfactory surrogate social community. It became a sort of dysfunctional indoor Main Street—when Main Street turned into Mean Street.

In the start-from-scratch, faceless, soulless suburbs, the mall was an even more unsatisfactory quasi-community. Developers and economic-development agencies, motivated by bottom-line interests rather than human/social needs, had created a suburban wasteland. There, the mall was effectively the only game in town.

The mall was never a genuine substitute for the village green. But the mass warehouse steel and asphalt atmosphere of the power center provided no possible socializing context at all. Like the dying downtowns before them, the stricken malls would acquire a nostalgic glow of their own, and efforts were made to preserve these surrogate Main Streets. The malls looked for survival strategies as power centers pulled away a big chunk of the commercial action.

THE WRITING ON THE MALL WALL

The malls began developing a potential they had never been designed for. In a long-term recessionary economy, with scant funds to build, thousands of square feet of unused space could be turned to innumerable other uses. The typical mall had evolved over time into a virtual community. Now, new, actual community-oriented uses were found for commercially obsolete malls. Individual situations demanded individual solutions, and often these were found. There were relatively few ghost malls.

Higher-tier malls, well-positioned, strategically located, and solidly established, went through the hard times relatively unscathed. This pertained particularly to those in prosperous, high-density suburbs where real estate values, taxes, zoning laws, and community action combined to keep the power centers at a distance.

Upscale specialty shops still did good business. Middle-scale stores selling products you could get anywhere at a cheaper price were driven out and department stores again consolidated. Burgeoning high-tech entertainment emporiums filled some of the vacant spaces, along with craft and hobby centers.

▶ **TRENDPOST** *Prosperous malls will increasingly function as social venues. Evacuated department stores and national retail chains will be converted into multipurpose, multimedia entertainment/fitness/sports/recreation units, catering primarily to a market ranging from preteenagers to young adults.* ◀

Along with the middle class, middle-tier malls were taking an economic pummeling. Nevertheless, by 2000, many were able to recast their priorities and reengineer facilities and services. The phased-out former shoe stores, apparel shops, and houseware outlets were converted into inexpensive municipal and private office space and annex classrooms for overcrowded schools, existing together with a mix of surviving shops and entertainment facilities.

On the low end, malls that would have become derelict were transformed completely. The worst became shelters for the homeless and/or temporary subsistence housing, as well as emergency medical clinics. While hardly ideal, this was a way of grappling with costly, intractable social problems that otherwise could not be funded. One tier up found malls serving as training centers, storage areas, and elder- and day-care centers.

TECHNOSHOPPING

Just as the assault of the power centers in the nineties forced the malls into retreat and restructuring, so, by 2010, the power centers were under attack from technoshopping revolutionaries.

As the homing trend took hold and travel increased along the information superhighway, consumers changed their shopping habits.

► **TRENDPOST** *Factory-direct or distributor-direct shopping will revolutionize American buying habits. Easy-to-access, easy-to-use computer services, available to every American home, will make it possible to buy a wide array of mass-produced consumer products more cheaply and easily.* ◄

The catchword was *interactivity*. Once you could discuss a potential purchase with someone knowledgeable or pull up specifications, consumer reports, expert opinions, and just about any other information you might need on any given product at the touch of a button, there was no need to shop around for it.

People will still want to test-drive a new car, but no one test-washes a washing machine prior to purchase or test-freezes a fridge. However, sophisticated hardware and software technology will make it possible to test-load a virtual washing machine and test-stock a virtual refrigerator.

While it is impossible to experience the actual sensation of the real article by trying on a virtual shirt or sitting in a virtual sofa, it is an experiential quantum leap up from catalog shopping. Most consumer durables—appliances, electronics, home-office equipment, furnishings—lend themselves to technoshopping, the virtual mall of the millennium.

The hegemony of the power centers was shorter lived than the twenty-year-plus reign of the malls. But there was no nostalgia as, one by one, they failed. Few attempts were made to reengineer them. It was difficult to find new uses for the huge, cavernous, empty shells. They were torn down and recycled, or abandoned by bankrupt retailers and developers and left to rot away.

People shopped on-line from their homes. Purchases were delivered to the door. Buying habits changed. Computer shopping cut down drastically on time spent shopping and also on money spent on impulse items.

A new breed of stay-at-home consumer was evolving, and with it, a new set of priorities for how the day was spent.

16

FAMILY VALUES

QUALITY TIME

The time it takes to take care of yourself takes a lot of time.
You wonder how you did it before. Only now do you realize
that you weren't really doing it. Nothing was given the attention it needed—kids, family, home, your health . . . life.
Everything suffered. Yet, it's a curious thing. Looking back,
you can see that it's only when things got worse that things
got better.

Compelled by circumstances into making do with less
money but with more time on your hands, your life in 2000
(and the life of millions like you) looks very different from
the life you lived just ten years earlier. Aware of the need to
survive and stay healthy in the midst of a worldwide health
crisis, forced into expanded personal freedom, driven to exercise greater creativity and to practice voluntary simplicity
within an atmosphere of heightened community spirit,
you've had to rethink your life, even as you live it day to
day.

You no longer make a false distinction between "quality"

time and the rest of the day. All time is quality time (except for filling out tax forms and that sort of thing). You've learned to manage your time differently.

It takes time to meditate. It takes time to cook a good meal. It takes time to play with the kids. It takes time to nurture relationships. Once you learned that the quick fix fixed nothing, and you stopped popping prescription pills, you learned that it takes time to heal naturally. You're learning to live holistically, and the learning takes time.

When you got off (or were forced off) the treadmill, you gave up the StairMaster. When you opted out of the rat race, you stopped training for the marathon. Hyperactive workouts, though better than nothing, were not the answer to a stress-filled but sedentary lifestyle.

You're in better shape now than you've ever been. You've integrated your workout routine into your life. If you haven't given up the lawn altogether, you've phased out your power mower. Now you use one of the high-tech, lightweight push mowers—as unlike grandpa's heavy metal monster as your IBM ThinkPad is from his old Underwood typewriter.

You wouldn't dream of spending money you can't afford on a rototiller for the garden. The physical work with the pitchfork and shovel builds bone and muscle; there is an innate satisfaction in the work itself, and a built-in reward at harvesttime.

You still use the gym in winter, in rainy weather, and for classes. You've given up cosmetic or single-focused workouts. You now train the three inner centers (physical, emotional, mental) at once. If you've worked hard enough at it, and in just the right way, you will be experiencing those moments of heightened self-awareness—altered states that make you realize that more is at stake than even health and fitness. You may suddenly know what that much-abused word *spiritual* means.

You've given up high- and low-impact, step and slide aerobics to become an "aerobic warrior"—doing an aerobic workout that teaches you self-defense techniques. Since you're putting in the physical effort anyhow, why not learn something with a practical application? As you and those like you put new lives together, the rest of America grows more violent than ever. In 1994, with 60 percent growth, martial-arts instruction was the second-fastest-growing business category in the country, according to American Business Information.

THE GREAT OUTDOORS

Though violence remains a fact of daily American life, and a massive, insoluble social problem, it has not generated the massive countertrend—the victim mentality—predicted by futurists.

People refused to live as hostages on their own turf. They were not bunkering down and holing up, hoping to stay out of trouble and/or escape life's harsh realities. Nor did the information superhighway generate the ballyhooed cybersociety—masses of people confined to their homes, satisfying their souls electronically. The contingent of recluse hackers has been insignificant.

Spending more time at home didn't mean spending more time in the house. Though individual motivations differed, large numbers of people rebelled against spending their lives cooped up indoors. In the mid-1990s, according to the Institute of Medicine, Americans were still spending 93 percent of their lives indoors.

▶ **TRENDPOST** *By January 1, 2000, the nationwide return to nature and the great outdoors, a trend that began in the seventies but was slow to mature, will take hold and catch fire. Businesses and services participating in this trend can expect strong growth throughout the twenty-first century.* ◀

America was blading, kayaking, fishing, hunting, canoeing, rowing, running, golfing, camping, hiking, and biking as never before.

The baby boomers, previewing their lives and proacting, were making more time "quality" time. They were living through a second adolescence—very different from and more satisfying than their first adolescence, which was spent mostly in front of the TV or just hanging out. Generation X (the 44 million born between 1965 and 1976) hit the blades, and they never did get off their bikes. They pushed the trend forward along with the boomers.

Staying healthy was not an extracurricular activity. Apart from hiking and biking vacations, millions of people were also integrating walking and bicycling into their lives to do things they normally did—shop, visit, and travel to work.

I LIKE BIKE

Throughout the eighties and nineties, the bicycling trend grew steadily. Still, it wasn't for everyone. Cyclists were only just behind possums and squirrels in the roadkill statistics. Attempts were made to cater to growing public demand. Old railroad lines were converted to hike-and-bike trails. A few cities set up designated bike lanes. But there was no widespread operating infrastructure to make life easy, or even safe, for bicyclists.

Although, according to a Harris poll, 60 percent of all Americans were telling Washington to devote more funds to making bicycling safer, no action was taken to implement this expressed public wish.

In 1995, the total federal budget was $1.5 trillion. It included $270.7 billion for defense, $100 billion for corporate welfare, $30 billion for the CIA and intelligence operations, $35 billion for the war on crime, $18 billion for foreign aid,

$13 billion for the war on drugs, and $18 million for the special climate-controlled commuter subway that whisked U.S. senators and representatives from their offices to the capitol in 1.7 minutes instead of making them walk a half a mile. But there was no money left for bicycle paths. There was no money left for anything the American people said they wanted that might enhance and enrich their lives. Overwhelming public opinion was simply ignored. Polls showed that 85 percent of Americans felt that protecting national parks was very important. Nevertheless, Washington was cutting the national parks budget ($1.4 billion in 1995, or less than $1/100$ of 1 percent of the total national budget). The government could find $60 billion for thirty new submarines at $2 billion apiece—each one costing more than the entire national parks budget—and could fund B-2 bombers at $1.5 billion apiece, but there was no money for parks.

Politicians had to pay back the sponsors who had financed their campaigns. Timber and mining companies were given carte blanche to continue ravaging and degrading what little wilderness remained.

Existing restrictions and safeguards were lifted. Public land was given away to corporate interests at ludicrous bargain rates—thus depriving taxpayers in the short term of large amounts of money that should have gone into public coffers. In the long term, it deprived them—and their children and grandchildren—of ever enjoying what was, after all, their birthright: public land.

**STOP THE GIVEAWAY: GET FAIR PRICE FOR
PUBLIC'S PROPERTY**

Your public land is rich in beauty and minerals. But your government . . . has been giving it away:

- 780 acres of coastal sand dunes in Oregon to a sand and gravel company for $1,950. Estimated value: $12 million.
- 1800 acres in Nevada to a Canadian goldmining company for $10,000. Estimated mineral wealth: $10 billion.
- 2000 acres in Montana to a platinum mining firm for $10,000. Estimated mineral wealth: $32 billion.

(Editorial, *USA Today*, 11/23/93)

For over a century, hundreds of billions of dollars in profits had been extracted from public lands, with virtually nothing going back into the Treasury. The wholesale plunder and destruction provided jobs for miners and loggers until the mines were depleted and the forests destroyed. Large mining and timber corporations—often foreign—cleaned up in profits but rarely cleaned up after themselves. Mining operations alone have left over ten thousand miles of rivers poisoned with metal residues and acids. Taxpayers face a cleanup bill estimated at $72 billion.

In 1993, feeble attempts to reform the antiquated 1872 General Mining Law, which had allowed and perpetuated the plunder, failed.

But by January 1, 2000, the public was beginning to effect change. Recognizing the American two-headed, one-body political system for what it was, people began acting in their own interests. Quality-of-life issues suddenly became real issues—sometimes life-and-death issues.

One of the first positive actions taken was the reclamation of the American outdoor heritage. As America worked its tortuous way out of the Industrial Age, the new consciousness was taking hold. The return to nature and the outdoors was common sense, but often it was even dollars and sense.

The public money that could not be found for bike paths or parks in 1995 began to materialize by 2000. It was one way to underwrite and promote a new worldwide trend.

▶ **TRENDPOST** *Ecotourism will be the fastest growing segment within the travel industry. Baby boomers, Generation Xers, and their children will power the trend.* ◀

Under straitened economic circumstances, and a devalued dollar, Americans traveled less abroad, but foreign tourists flocked here. Domestic ecotourism flourished. States vied with one another to accommodate a new breed of outdoor enthusiast.

Quick to spot future profits, the most advanced states developed networks of intrastate hiking/biking trails. Before long, contiguous states connected their systems. Early in the twenty-first century, the long-established interstate highway system was joined by a new interstate bikeway/hikeway system. Outdoors was in.

Exploring the great outdoors was one of the chief family activities of the new millennium—only the family was not what it used to be. Like so many other American institutions, the conventional American family was transforming itself into new and unfamiliar configurations.

FAMILY VALUES

In 2000, what people called family did not much look like what grandma and grandpa used to call family. The traditional, old-world extended family—two or three generations living together—was effectively history. The extended family fell victim to the prosperity and mobility that followed World War II.

By the 1950s, the family had fragmented into a modern standard of nuclear units. Modern moms and dads no longer lived where they had grown up. They separated themselves from grandparents, uncles, aunts, and cousins, thereby trading off the support structure of the traditional extended family for a newfound freedom from family supervision and intervention.

The system worked economically in the fifties and sixties. A single income—usually dad's—was enough to keep Middle America going and growing.

In the 1970s, the system began to falter. The cost of financing the Cold War and the Vietnam War was beginning to sap the economic vitality of the country. The last U.S. budget surplus was recorded in 1969. In that year, total federal spending was $183 billion. In 1996, it was $1.6 trillion. During that quarter century, the government also incurred a debt of more than $4 trillion (approximately $40,000 debt per U.S. household). The percentage of federal income taxes required to service the nation's interest bill rose from 16.6 percent in 1970 to 40 percent in 1996.

Profligate government spending provoked Richard Nixon to abandon the gold standard in 1971 for a floating dollar. Within a week, the dollar lost 17 percent of its value. Inflation would soar, interest rates would gyrate wildly, and the dollar would never regain its once-regal position.

From 1970 on, the overall American standard of living steadily declined, as the American family unwillingly sacrificed an ever-increasing percentage of its income to finance government spending.

Mothers could no longer afford to stay at home and raise children. Financial need drove women to work, whether or not they were "liberated." After adjusting for inflation, between 1973 and 1990 the median income of families with children headed by a parent under thirty dropped 32 percent. In 1960, 19 percent of married women with children under six were in the workforce. By 1995, the figure hovered around 65 percent. Economically, the one-income nuclear family could no longer function as the standard working model. It had ceased to function as the standard social model, as well. Family life in the United States had altered drastically.

More than half of all marriages ended in divorce. The

Parent-Teacher Association estimated that as many as 7 million latchkey children between the ages of five and thirteen cared for themselves after school till either mom or dad came home from work. Only half of the 66 million American children lived in traditional two-parent families. Unmarried mothers became heroines in TV sitcoms and soaps.

The splintering family, and, even more so, the change in attitudes that went with it, provoked marathon handwringing and lamenting from the lunatic middle. But their moral crusade to legislate lost family values back into mainstream America was as futile as legislation designed to bring back the horse and carriage would have been.

Busybodies believed, and politicians professed to believe, that by passing laws, people's beliefs, lifestyles, and emotional lives could be regulated. But just as Prohibition and the war on drugs and the war on crime had ended in abject defeat, exacerbating rather than remedying the respective problems, so the war on immorality accomplished nothing—beyond pouring fuel on the fire.

Overall, 77 percent of Americans polled agreed that the government had no business passing laws to regulate morality, or how people lived their private lives.

An ongoing campaign of private vigilante moral terrorism and politically sanctioned public meddling antagonized and polarized America. Ultimately, the grumbling and beleaguered majority of Americans would be driven to organized self-defense to protect themselves against roving gangs of moralizing muggers intent upon robbing them of their freedom—if need be, at gunpoint.

Apart from the forces assaulting the nuclear family, a new perception was gaining ground, hazily delineated at first but then acquiring sharper focus over time.

For five thousand years, the horse (with or without carriage) had been the best and fastest way to get from one place to another. As the world changed, it was no longer the best and fastest. So it was with the traditional family. It was no longer perceived as the one and only solution to the problem of men and women living together and raising children. It was just one solution, not necessarily the best.

OLD WHINES IN NEW BOTTLES

To the lunatic middle, the vision of the model twenty-first-century family was that of Ozzie and Harriet with laptops (with laws against cybersex, making it illegal to "get off" on-line).

However, to a growing number of nonlunatics, it was becoming increasingly clear that the familiar broadcast image of the family was an illusion. The solid, happy all-American family existed mainly in television sitcoms, on old *Saturday Evening Post* covers by Norman Rockwell, and in the disordered imaginations of politicians.

Misremembered as *Happy Days,* family values prevailed when dad went out to work, mom stayed home and cleaned the house, and the kids sat in front of the nonviolent, black and white TV, eating Oreo cookies, and drinking Bosco and milk. And there was plenty of money for all.

For those who admired Norman Rockwell, this was a reassuring picture. But only one element within that rosy, nostalgic fifties scenario was accurate: the money.

It was a time of unparalleled American prosperity for large numbers of people—even though more than 20 percent of the population did not share in the largesse and lived below the poverty line. Few noticed their existence. They constituted a special pariah caste within the American system: the unmentionables. For a majority, it was boom time. Economically, America was indeed the promised land—the land of (homogenized) milk and money.

But beyond the economic prosperity, for those who remembered accurately, it was not wall-to-wall Ozzie and Harriet at all. It was a time of racism, McCarthyism, and J. Edgar Hooverism. Women's rights, civil rights, and gay rights existed mainly in the dreams of visionaries. It was a time of hypocrisy, sexual, political, and social repression, and blind conformity.

And it was the living experience and accurate perception of that stifling era that finally provoked the rebellion of the sixties. Sudden easy access to drugs, the outrage over the Vietnam War, and the huge influx of an army of baby boomers swelling college campuses provided the fertile breeding ground for revolt.

If fifties family values had been real, there would have been no sixties revolution. It would have been impossible for a few unarmed and powerless malcontents to disrupt a basically harmonious society. Prosperity masked the malaise for two decades but could not cure it.

Ironically, it wasn't the hippies or the so-called radicals who were responsible for the breakup and breakdown of the American family; it was the spiritual elder brothers of the people whining today about the loss of family values.

PARANOIA IN HIGH PLACES

Those same spiritual elder brothers were the people who enthusiastically pushed America into financing a $12 trillion Cold War. They were the "experts," military and civilian, who dictated policy from on high. They looted the U.S. Treasury and plundered the mine.

In the days before CIA abuses, Pentagon cover-ups, and presidential lies became common knowledge, their fabrications were accepted at face value and reported as facts.

A trusting America believed that the Russian bear was a fearsome grizzly ready and able to move in, devour all our provisions, lay waste to the global campsite, and, worst of all, force everyone into espousing bearism as a political philosophy. Anyone daring to dissent was a Commie, a pinko, and un-American.

PATTERN OF DECEPTION IS SEEN AT PENTAGON

Federal investigators have determined that the Pentagon misled Congress about the costs and the necessity of many weapons built in the 1980s to counter the forces of the Soviet Union.

Eight reports from a three-year study by the General Accounting Office, an investigative arm of Congress, show a pattern of exaggeration and deception by military leaders. ". . . the Pentagon understated the cost of nuclear missiles, overstated the radar-evading ability of new nuclear bombers and exaggerated the threat posed by Soviet defenses."

The reports say military officers misled Congress to preserve unnecessary weapons programs during the biggest military buildup in the nation's history. (*NYT*, 6/28/93)

And there was no money for parks or bike paths.

When the Berlin Wall came down, that savage Soviet bear turned out to be so toothless, diseased, and flea-bitten, it barely had the energy to rifle the garbage cans, much less wreak worldwide havoc.

The Vietnam War added further trillions to the bill, but its hidden cost could not be calculated in dollars, only in pain. Countless families were destroyed, broken, splintered. In 1993, on any given night, 250,000 veterans, most from Vietnam, were homeless. At least 500,000 were homeless in the course of a year. The psychological horrors of Vietnam, as well as its corrosive and divisive aftermath, tore at the fabric of everything Americans believed in—including family values.

The trillions squandered on defense were irrecoverable. It was President Dwight D. Eisenhower, perhaps the most respected general of the twentieth century, who warned of the consequences that unchecked military spending would have on society. He said: "Every gun that is made, every warship launched, every rocket fired signifies in the final sense a theft from those who hunger and are not fed, those who are cold and not clothed. The world in arms is not spending money alone. It's spending the sweat of laborers, the genius of scientists, the hopes of its children."

The economic juggernaut of the fifties and sixties had been real enough. The lunatic middle derailed it in midcareer. And now it was trying to legislate the return to family values, bringing with it the old prosperity. And American life would be Bosco and milk in front of the violence-free TV all over again.

The high times would never come back, although another kind of prosperity would take hold in the global Renaissance of 2001. But a new philosophy would prevail. In it, traditional family values would play a very different role.

FICTION AS FACT

So-called family values had been a fiction for centuries. This is not to say that happy families did not exist. But in the real-life experience of most people, they were the exception, not the rule.

The vast body of Western literature, drama, and cinema exists as proof. For literature is to the psychological/emotional world what science is to the factual/physical world. It is an accurate description of its reality. Serious literature, drama, and cinema are real life heightened, ordered, and orchestrated, life distilled into its essence. The facts of a good novel may be fictional, but the panorama painted is more real than any collection of facts. The serious modern writer functions as a sensitive nerve end of society, expressing what many feel but cannot express.

Few works of serious literature, drama, or cinema have ever painted family life as anything other than dysfunctional, warring, and troubled.

To the lunatic middle, the 1950s family was a model designed by God, or at the very least a spin-off of ancient, time-honored tradition. By 2000, it was becoming generally recognized that this genealogy was suspect.

God's role was impossible to objectively confirm (or deny), and therefore it had to remain a matter of personal conviction. And "tradition" amounted to little more than obedience to a conventional code of morality that may or may not have made sense fifty, or a hundred, or a thousand years ago.

By the late 1960s, throughout the Western world, but especially in the United States, the accepted standard was suffering the psychological/emotional equivalent of metal fatigue. Large numbers of people decided en masse not to repeat the pattern of their own parents, and their parents before them . . . as far back as memory stretched. This is not to say that they found easy solutions to their problems, or any solution at all.

The widely publicized sexual revolution certainly brought down the overall (mostly unacknowledged) American frustration level. But it didn't make people happier. Anarchy and confusion replaced repression and hypocrisy.

On the broader sociological level, the changes were dramatic and irreversible and carried momentous consequences in their wake. Sprung from the prison of an outmoded code of morality, vast numbers of people suddenly decided *not* to do what mom and dad had done: stay married through thick and thin, till death did them part, even after they had long since stopped enjoying each other's company.

In response to the reduced social stigma attached to divorce, laws changed, and divorce rates tripled, from 16 percent in 1960 to 50 percent in the late 1970s, never to return.

Still, for all the moralizing and moaning, 50 percent of marriages did *not* end in divorce. In 1991, 33.4 million children still lived in families with both biological parents and brothers and sisters. The nuclear family could hardly be called an endangered social species.

But for better or for worse, formal marriage was no longer the unquestioned norm—or even the ideal for numbers of people. Cohabitation was an increasingly popular choice for many couples. Nearly 50 percent of couples under forty were cohabiting in 1994. Single-parent families became commonplace. In 1993, 27 percent of children under age eighteen lived with one parent, up from 12 percent in 1970. Between 1960 and 1995, the percentage of children born outside of marriage sextupled from 5 percent to 30 percent.

In 1995, according to the Census Bureau, one in four Americans over eighteen (about 44 million) had never married, up from one in six in 1970. At any given time, about half the adult Americans were not married. In 1993, 23.6 million adults lived alone, up 15 percent since 1985. Gay rights brought homosexuals and lesbians out of the closet, with widely varying degrees of social acceptance.

As the new millennium dawned, increasing numbers of people were experimenting with new community models, and rethinking every aspect of the traditional male/female roles. They were looking outside the concept of family values for their answers.

17

FORWARD
TO THE PAST

COWBOYS AND INDIANS

A trend blueprint drawn in the seventies was acted upon in the nineties. A radical reassessment of the lifestyles of traditional tribal societies stirred the public imagination.

In the eighties, a parallel trend was also set in motion. An equally radical reinterpretation of the sophisticated thinking, philosophy, religion, and science of the vanished civilizations of Egypt, China, and India was widely publicized and enthusiastically received.

As entrenched American sociopolitical institutions continued to disintegrate, people began to look afresh at both the vanished high cultures of the distant past and into what remained of the world's so-called primitive societies.

A serious search began for possible answers to the psychological, social, and emotional turbulence and chaos that filled the vacuum left by the vanished values of a dying age, family values high on the list.

The search for new values began at home. By digging through the recent past in America's own front yard, the cultures of this country's indigenous peoples came under a totally new and sympathetic scrutiny.

For two centuries, the American Indian had been depicted as a bloodthirsty, treacherous barbarian or a dumb, greedy primitive. In the Declaration of Independence, the Native Americans were called "merciless Indian Savages." Two hundred years later, America's favorite cowboy (and Ronald Reagan's favorite philosopher), John Wayne, was still echoing that sentiment: "I don't feel we did wrong in taking this great country away from them. There were great numbers of people who needed new land and the Indians were selfishly trying to keep it for themselves."

By 1980, more objective scholarly studies were portraying the Native American rather differently.

The treachery was mostly the responsibility of the U.S. government, which did not honor treaties signed with the Indians. The charge of greed hardly seemed appropriate when directed at people fighting for their own homeland.

The term *primitivism* applied only if technology and modern science were the sole valid criteria used for judging development. When considerations of quality of life and inner satisfaction entered the equation, the lifestyle of the Indians appeared sophisticated in its own right.

The 1980s and 1990s fostered a new appreciation for the unique gifts, knowledge, and rituals of Native Americans. Particularly attractive to a new generation of environmentally conscious Americans was the indigenous people's respect and reverence for the earth and all living things.

Native tribal and family practices also took on a new relevance. The Indian focus on the welfare of the tribe over the egotistic concerns of the individual served as a model for the new sense of community spirit developing all over America.

THE NEW PATRIOTISM

The trend that took the cutting-edge segment of America forward into the past put a new spin on a very old and over-worked word: *patriotism.*

By 2000, *patriotism* no longer meant "our country right or wrong." It no longer implied the knee-jerk endorsement of government policy. The trend toward distrust in government that was building throughout the nineties led people to look beyond the dictates of the two-headed, one-party system.

Old-style flag waving still went on, but it was out of style. The new majority did not equate the word *patriotism* with the conviction that the government had the moral right, even obligation, to silence dissent at home and enforce compliance abroad. The inalienable rights of "life, liberty, and the pursuit of happiness" articulated by the Founding Fathers were redefined.

The new patriotism espoused many of the beliefs and values of the American Indians. Primary among them was an abiding love and respect for the homeland—which was not Washington. It transcended the government's narrow definition of national interest, which had come to mean sending young Americans to fight and die in order to preserve the interests of special interests.

To the patriot of the new millennium, "a devotion to the welfare of one's country" (*Webster's Unabridged*) came to mean a respect for the balance of nature and people's individual and national responsibilities in defending that balance. In Native American tradition, human beings are endowed by the Creator with moral duties and obligations to all living things.

MULTIPLE CHOICE

Though American Indian lore captured the lion's share of America's attention, there was also a new interest in the beliefs, knowledge, and lifestyles of other traditional societies, as well: Australian Aborigines, African bushmen, Eskimos, desert nomads, and many others.

This was not merely nostalgia and romanticism—an attempt by bewildered people to escape modern complexities. Such interest had a valid foundation even within the established ground rules of contemporary science and scholarship. For two generations, scholars, including Joseph Campbell, Mircea Eliade, and Giorgio de Santillana, had been finding evidence of profound psychological insight along with surprisingly advanced astronomy and mathematics encoded within native legends and lore.

Movies such as *The Gods Must Be Crazy* and *Dances with Wolves* reversed standard stereotypes: the Westerner was cast in the role of savage or stooge; the Indian or African became the hero. Disney's smash hit animated film *Pocahontas* took the trend to America's children, and made millions of dollars in the process. The best-selling books of Carlos Castaneda portray a simple, unassuming Yaqui shaman and sorcerer as sage and mentor. The staggering success of *The Celestine Prophecy* was based upon (supposed) spiritual revelations written in an ancient manuscript.

Now, without the familiar family model to serve as a universal social ideal or as the one and only viable economic unit, a period of experimentation began, with people often looking to the distant past or into the cultures of the American Plains, or the Australian outback, or the mountains, the jungles, and the desert sands for counsel.

Each of these highly individualized societies has its own way of dealing with families, marriages, rites of passage, child rearing, sexual relationships, and death and dying.

A reappraisal of the past did not mean nostalgia for pharaoh worship, or acceptance of human sacrifice, or female circumcision. It meant a new anthropological and archaeological perspective that did not regard anything old and non-Western as automatically outmoded and irrelevant, or undeveloped and uncivilized.

While no single system promised instant paradise, some looked promising as potential new models, especially in areas of child rearing, caring for elders, and shared tribal/community responsibilities. As with new millennium medicine and the new millennium morality, the new millennium family had the opportunity to choose from the best of the new and the best of the old.

The demographics were unmistakable and irreversible. The breakup of the family, the aging of the population, the steady decline in overall average real wages, rising crime, the crisis in education and health care, the degradation of the environment and the corresponding assault upon health, and the abdication of public responsibility by an overwhelmed, unresponsive, autocratic government—these were powerful, negative, fully mature trends. Operating in concert, they were mutually reinforcing and unstoppable. Blame was irrelevant. Opinions hardly mattered. The material facts were undeniable.

Mobilizing in the face of this formidable arsenal of overt and obvious destructive hardware, there was a subtle and elusive counterattack. Global Age software of tentative new solutions, new attitudes, and new strategies for personal and communal survival was being installed into the nation's downsized, upgraded mainframe.

The news sped along the Internet. It was spread by word of mouth. Sometimes it showed up in the lifestyle sections of newspapers, in non–prime time shows on cable television, and in depth in alternative magazines (*Utne Reader, In Context, Mother Earth News, Atlantis Rising, New Age Journal, Natural Healing, In These Times, Covert Action, Perceptions, The Sun, Quest,* and *New Frontiers,* among others).

A new philosophy of life took root and flourished wherever and whenever it fell on fertile ground. The recognition of the need to safeguard personal health, the new community spirit, the new respect for the planet and all living things, and the renewed spiritually based philosophy combined to provide new approaches to family values.

Family roles, relationships, and arrangements adjusted to accommodate the changed conditions and attitudes. Driven initially by economic necessity, the traditional one-income family—where dad worked and mom stayed home with the kids—became an exception (approximately 20 percent of households in 1994). By 1995, working women were bringing in half or more of their households' income while still being responsible for family care.

A new understanding of responsibility developed.

THE REEXTENDED FAMILY

A number of creative (and sometimes desperate) solutions were found for a wide spectrum of new situations. The meaning of the word *family* broadened beyond that of blood relationships. It came to mean groups of interdependent individuals with shared values, goals, and responsibilities and a long-term commitment to one another and the community.

Aging, often ailing, unable to care for themselves, and unable to afford quality care, large numbers of retirees were moving back in with their adult children, married or unmarried, with or without children of their own. According to a report from the Healthy People 2000 Program in the *Journal of the American Medical Association,* the average person in a seventy-six-year life span can expect to have about twelve unhealthy years, most of them toward the end of life.

Another common scenario saw perfectly healthy but widowed and divorced parents setting up house with their own single or married children—ideally with separate entrances, separate kitchens, separate lives.

► **TRENDPOST** *The need to care for elders will generate a lively business in building additions and freestanding cottages— including modular structures and mobile homes. Properties with expansion capabilities will have premium market value. The trend's buzzwords will be:* granny flats, ECHO housing *(Elder Cottage Housing Opportunities),* maintenance-free, one-level, *and* easy access. ◄

The rationale for sharing was often as much social as economic.

INTERACTION ENCOURAGES LONGER LIVES

There's more evidence that human interaction is good for you.

Isolated people have nearly twice the risk of early death as others and not because they're sicker or anti-social, says a study in September's *Epidemiology*.

"In general more social involvement reduces risk," says researcher George Kaplan, California Department of Health Services, Berkeley. (*USA Today*, 8/30/94)

Lonely people hardly need statistics to tell them that loneliness is unhealthy.

FROM BOARDINGHOUSE TO COHOUSING

The boardinghouse returned, but in an upgraded version designed to meet the needs of vast numbers of lower- and lower-middle-income single people. Disposable incomes continued to fall, the job market tightened, and workers at every age were unable to afford the rent of even a studio apartment. By the year 2010, 31 million people would be living alone.

Two could live cheaper than one, but ten could live substantially cheaper than two. Successful new millennium boardinghouses became social oases in an impersonal world. Ways were found to minimize the unavoidable lack of privacy and the inevitable friction while providing home-cooked communal meals and a congenial family-like atmosphere.

▶ **TRENDPOST** *The renewed demand for boardinghouses and other forms of shared housing will make multi-family dwellings excellent investment opportunities, particularly in gentrified urban areas, stable suburbs, and new exurban population centers.* ◀

The boardinghouse was an effective defensive tactic. The new cohousing trend was a constructive, offensive long-term strategy.

First developed in Denmark in 1976 and then spreading throughout northern Europe, cohousing arrived in the United States in the early nineties. Cohousing provided condo-style comfort and privacy with commune-style shared responsibilities and shared amenities.

The complexes began as cooperatives, usually involving a dozen or more individual families. They were built from scratch, or existing structures were retrofitted to incorporate advanced architectural design, environmentally safe materials, and high-tech facilities. Individual units came in at prices comparable to normal costs for new housing.

The concept of cohousing solved a number of pressing socioeconomic and family-related problems simultaneously, while minimizing the drawbacks inherent in the commune or tribal society.

The main difference between cohousing and the standard apartment complex or development was the sharing, which was tailored to suit the needs of individual complexes. Most time-consuming, labor-intensive family duties, including meals, child care, elder care, and, in some cases, even education, were handled communally to some extent.

The result was a very considerable savings in time and effort, along with pleasant and productive socializing—at least when the personality mix was right. For example, a typical communal dinner arrangement would find participants cooking and serving about once every two weeks, in exchange for the remaining thirteen dinners cooked and served to them.

Apply the principle conscientiously and intelligently to child care, elder care, education, and even to landscaping, gardening, laundry, and dog walking, throw in barter of goods and services, and a wholly new lifestyle emerges. Amenities and equipment unaffordable on an individual basis became accessible to the complex: hot tub, sailboat, power and home-office equipment, even darkrooms and studios. By 1996 there were twenty operating cohousing communities and over 150 in development.

The advantages of cohousing, and often the necessity to share responsibilities, were not confined to the educated or the upscale. Vast numbers of retirees, forced to make do with a fraction of the income they were used to, turned to cohousing to make ends meet in sociable surroundings. Once financing institutions understood the viability of the concept, it would effectively function at every socioeconomic level, including the inner city and moribund former industrial towns. The principal was universally applicable. But the further down the economic/educational scale, the more difficult it became to apply.

RE-'X'-TENSION

Whether or not they preferred it that way, more and more people were being compelled to live together. Ultimately, it boiled down to two choices. Either it worked or it didn't work. The choice was up to you.

Here's your situation. You're twenty-six years old, a Generation Xer. You're a graduate of a good state university, and you've got your MBA, one of almost 100,000 in the class of 1998. You were hoping for an entry-level job starting at a salary somewhere between forty thousand and sixty thousand dollars. But with all the downsizing, more people are getting fired than hired. Now you're thinking of going back to school to get a Ph.D., because the sales job you finally found doesn't leave you enough to pay back your student loans. The trouble is that your friends with Ph.D.'s are in the same boat. The advanced degree improved your chances; it guaranteed nothing.

As a group, the high-techies are doing fine (demand for computer professionals rose 45 percent between 1993 and 1994 and kept on rising). You know a couple of people on Wall Street and in industry who are already upscale and forging ahead. The young doctors are okay, but the lawyers are hurting—paralegals, clerks, and outsourced professionals are doing the entry-level work. A couple of your friends are working for their fathers. Overall, your generation makes 20 percent less in real income than your father's generation. In 1973, 23 percent of household heads under twenty-five owned their own homes; in 1990, only 15 percent did.

People with just bachelor's degrees are in even worse shape. They're underemployed—in telemarketing, retail sales, data entry, and temp jobs. In the first half of the nineties, the temporary-help industry soared 50 percent. Some are driving taxis, cleaning offices, painting houses, or waiting on tables—at the country club they always thought they'd be a member of. Some aren't doing anything at all.

Photo by Kathy McLaughlin © 1995

GRADUATES LEARN DIPLOMAS AREN'T
TICKETS TO SUCCESS

According to the U.S. Bureau of Labor Statistics, nearly 18 million college graduates are expected to join the labor force between 1992 and 2005, but only 14 million jobs requiring college experience are expected to open up during that period. . . . And the same data show that in 1992, about 20% of all those with bachelor's degrees earned less than the median salary for all high school graduates. (WSJ, 10/10/94)

The outlook is bleakest of all for the 75 percent of young adults who did not graduate from college. The real income of this group, adjusted for inflation, fell 30 percent between 1979 and 1994. For them, it is not a question of a good job; it is a question of any job at all. The official unemployment statistics, citing low figures "below the natural rate of unemployment," were misleading.

This is a phoney measurement. If a private research firm were to go there and find how many people have stopped looking for jobs, and how many people are in temporary employment and don't want to be, how many recent college graduates with wonderful degrees and computer skills and all that can't find a decent job . . . if you measured unemployment in a more complete manner you'd see that unemployment is a lot worse than that. (Preston Martin, former vice chairman of the Federal Reserve Board during the Reagan administration, *Marketplace*, American Public Radio, 1/31/95)

Twenty-six! Time to have your own place, but you're back at home. You've made the choice. You could leave and just scrape by in a hole somewhere. Home is the preferred solution, even without the space and the privacy. You're not alone or unusual in that respect. In the mid-1990s, 45 percent of unmarried men in their twenties went back to live with parents; 35 percent of women also did.

It wasn't easy going back home after those years of freedom. Your friends have similar problems: The house rules are not your rules. At first, it was a disaster; you never thought it could work. But now it seems to be working.

The big change began when the folks came back from the longevity center—and didn't yell at you when the place looked like a set for *Animal House*. That was the first surprise. Then there was the attitude change—no more orders and ultimatums (which you never obeyed anyway), but defined responsibilities that you had to fulfill or else leave the house. It involved more than just pulling your own weight with the work around the house; it was the responsibility for finding out who you were and your place in the family and on the planet.

At first, you didn't know what they were talking about. As a loyal Generation Xer, you knew very well that you weren't responsible—for the family's problems or the world's problems. You were born into them. It wasn't your fault. You didn't wreck the economy. You didn't ruin the environment. It was the boomers, not you, who had squandered the nation's riches.

Your folks disagreed about who had wrecked what but agreed on one point: It wasn't your fault. But it *was* your responsibility. And it was their idea for you to spend the summer working at one of the "intentional communities" (the Omega Institute, New York; Hollyhock Farm, British Columbia; and Brighton Bush, Oregon, among others) that they'd learned about at the longevity center.

INTENTIONAL COMMUNITIES

At fifty dollars a week, plus room and board, your friends thought you needed your head examined. But it took just one summer. You learned more there in eight weeks than you learned in four years of college—about things they never taught or talked about in college. Most of what you learned at school was career- or job-oriented, or was learned in humanities courses that, in some undefinable way, were supposed to be essential if you were to emerge a "well-rounded" individual. No one ever talked about the meaning or purpose of your life; no one mentioned "right livelihood."

The teachers you met there were a very different breed from the ones you knew at school. This was a revolving door of writers, artists, scholars, doctors, psychologists, dance and martial-arts instructors—some of them masters, most of them accomplished, a few just spouting New Age hot air. Some were famous, and some were known only within their special fields: Bernie Siegel, Deepak Chopra, Rupert Sheldrake, John Perkins, Fritjof Capra, Thich Nhat Hanh, Roger Woolger, Marie-Pierre Astier, Tsultrim Allione, Chief William Cammanda, Susun Weed, Marion Woodman.

These were not soldiers in the academic army who taught you in school—the adjuncts, the associates, and the tenured professors. They were guerillas of the global Renaissance.

You ate with them, studied with them, worked out with them, sang with them, and laughed with them; you even cried with them. And you came home changed. The message—whether it was from meditation, martial arts, or creative writing—was that *you* had to do it . . . *you* had to change.

Reading about the new consciousness, or just listening to lectures, took you to the starting line. That was as far as it took you. Real change called for more than an attitude adjustment.

Then the work began. And you found the inner work was harder than any outer work you'd ever done. Meditating?

Just sitting still for half an hour? What was the big deal? Not so easy once you've tried it. The sitting still part was hard enough; the ability to still the senses, to get quiet within, to suspend confused mental activity, to get your mind to obey your will seemed impossible at first. You never would have believed it. This was hard work!

And so was everything else. The martial arts you learned weren't the ones you saw in the movies. You could relate to the physical workouts easily enough. But how to stay loose in a close-combat situation? Easily said . . . but done only after years of unremitting dedication.

You suddenly realized that what you thought you knew— about life and about yourself—was not much. Concepts and beliefs that you had been taught were sacrosanct and self-evident turned out to be neither. Authority had to be questioned.

► **TRENDPOST** *Once looked upon as camps for aging hippies, intentional communities and Renaissance learning centers will appeal to a growing segment of aging baby boomers and maturing Generation Xers. The trend will grow steadily for at least the next fifteen years as more and more people seek stability and inner peace.* ◄

GENERATION BLENDING

You changed. Your folks changed. It wasn't ideal, but you were making it work.

Some of your friends had bigger problems. With prices rising, medical care curtailed, and pensions stretched beyond the limit, grandparents moved back in and the family extended to three generations, usually in cramped quarters. Sometimes there were four generations when married or unmarried Xers moved back home with young kids.

Healthy grandparents pulled their weight as baby-sitters. The trend was already strong in the mid-1990s. In 1994,

44 percent of grandparents were spending on average 650 hours a year (82 eight-hour days) taking care of grandchildren, according to the National Institute on Aging.

But more than baby-sitters, grandparents also functioned as home educators. The tribal elder, valued and revered for wisdom and experience in traditional hunter-gatherer societies, returned in a new guise.

The reextended family provided valuable insights into the nature of the famed generation gap.

In the nineties, books, media, and marketers hyped Generation X as a unique demographic entity. Supersavvy, superhip, Generation Xers were supposed to be as different from their baby-boom parents as boomers were from their parents, who were born in the 1920s and 1930s.

As the trend toward the reextended family threw the generations together, the similarities and differences became clear.

Between boomers and their parents, the generation gap was a psychological chasm: Perry Como, the Andrews Sisters, and Lawrence Welk versus Bob Dylan, Janis Joplin, and the Stones; "He's your President, right or wrong" versus "Hell no, I won't go"; gray flannel suits versus jeans and sandals; Burns and Allen versus Cheech and Chong; shotgun weddings versus legal abortions.

But between boomers and Xers, the gap was more age than mind-set. Music and entertainment tastes differed, but there was common ground. Both felt betrayed by the government and other institutions. Xers had been brought up without faith in the corporate world; downsized and underemployed boomers had the faith beaten out of them. Both were environmentally conscious. Both recognized the need for change. Despite differences, a spiritual kinship bonded Generation X to the baby boomers. They blended together into a 123 million–strong X-boom population supersegment.

► TRENDPOST *New, lucrative mass-marketing possibilities will present themselves as the X-boom supersegment acquires its own distinct personality. Marketers whose goods and services are not generation-specific will do well to stress commonalities rather than differences between boomers and Xers.* ◄

What your folks learned at the longevity center and what you learned at the intentional community put you at the leading edge of the X-boom supersegment.

The family was a unit again, though that unit took many untraditional forms. The new family's survival meant coping successfully with a set of untraditional problems—among them, education.

18

INTERACTIVE U.

A NATION AT RISK

The alarm went off in 1983. America was declared "A Nation at Risk."

This landmark report, by the National Commission on Excellence in Education, detailed the condition of the nation's educational system. "If an unfriendly foreign power had attempted to impose on America the mediocre educational performance that exists today we might have viewed it as an act of war," the report declared.

In graphic detail, it spelled out a crisis situation. The same dire story was retold in reports from other prestigious and unimpeachable sources.

American students could not compete intellectually with students from other industrialized countries. About 30 percent of children were dropping out of high school; in urban areas, the figure rose to between 50 and 60 percent. Illiteracy rates were soaring. Twenty-seven million Americans over the age of seventeen were illiterate. Another 45 million were barely competent in basic skills. The Institute for the

Study of Adult Literacy at Penn State calculated that illiteracy was costing the United States $225 billion a year in welfare, crime, prison expenses and lost productivity.

Deficiencies in learning were mirrored by deficiencies in teaching. The Carnegie Foundation for the Advancement of Teaching warned that "the severe crisis in teaching relates directly to the fact that the best and the brightest are not choosing teaching anymore." Albert Shanker, president of the American Federation of Teachers, said, "You are getting illiterate, incompetent people who cannot get into any other field."

Washington responded by trying to do away with the Department of Education altogether, and by stepping up defense spending to an annual level of $300 billion a year. "I tried to convince the President and his people of the bonds that tie together education, the economy, and military strength," wrote Secretary of Education Terrel Bell after resigning. "But notwithstanding the fact that I had been a teacher for much of my adult life, I never succeeded in getting this lesson across to them."

Actually, the lesson did not go entirely unheard. "A Nation at Risk" called for top-to-bottom reform. Instead, Washington hired an education czar (intriguing choice of title to bestow upon an official charged with initiating change). Reform-of-the-Month programs were set up, and high school graduation standards were raised—with mixed results. Ten years later, a report by the International Center for Leadership in Education found graduates less prepared than any other group in U.S. history. Other studies came to similar conclusions. By 1994, SAT scores were well below 1969 levels.

U.S. STUDENTS ARE FOUND GAINING ONLY IN SCIENCE

American students have gained almost a full grade level in science proficiency since the 1983 report "A Nation at

Risk" described a crisis in American schools. But there have been no gains in reading and writing skills and overall achievement levels are far below national goals, the Department of Education said today. (*NYT*, 8/15/94)

Limited and disappointing improvements were restricted to more affluent and rural districts. Studies showed that reform bypassed the cities almost entirely, though 13.5 percent of the nation's students were enrolled in city schools.

Ten years after the first seminal report on the state of education, it was not just "A Nation at Risk"; the students and teachers were at risk—physical risk—as crime moved off the streets and into the classroom.

VIOLENCE UP IN 38% OF SCHOOLS announced one headline. "School violence is more than a big city problem, a new survey finds, with one in four schools reporting deaths or serious injuries last year."

Schools were passing students through metal detectors in order to discover knives and guns—15 percent of high school students were packing weapons, according to a 1993 Harris poll. Heroin, crack, and high-potency designer drugs were readily available, and powerful peer pressure was exerted to make use of them.

Teenage crime raged at an epidemic level. This was a brand-new and intractable problem, in a nation already beset by rising, rampant crime. Children, mostly from underprivileged and broken families, had easy access to both deadly weapons and drugs. Much too young to have developed powers of discrimination, teens were killing one another and anyone else who got in the way.

Even without the violence, education was in crisis. Add in the crime and the situation became irreparable.

The official debate was mostly over money. A 1989 report by the Education Writers Association estimated that antiquated U.S. schools (31 percent built before World War II,

43 percent during the 1950s and 1960s) would need $125 billion in repairs and construction for their failing facilities.

But in the big picture, money wasn't even the most important issue. No amount of money poured into education was going to resolve nationwide economic fallback, splintered families, latchkey children, new floods of immigrants, and growing unemployment and underemployment for the young. "Schools have been responding diligently over the last ten years. But the results have been disappointing. The problems have been deeper and tougher than we thought. And they go beyond the school doors," said former Secretary of Education Terrel Bell in 1993.

The system had been designed for other times. Modern education was an invention of the Industrial Age, retooled, after World War II, to service the corporate age. It taught people how to read, write, do some math, follow instructions, and become good employees. It didn't teach them to think, ask questions, analyze problems, or find solutions. Creativity and individuality were discouraged or suppressed.

In the post–World War II heyday, it was an article of faith that there were jobs waiting for high school graduates, better jobs waiting for college graduates, and everyone was upwardly mobile in an upwardly mobile world.

By the eighties, education was confronted by complex and powerful global socioeconomic forces of change. It could not prepare masses of young people to cope with the new conditions; nor could it reform itself to meet them. America's corporate/Industrial Age educational system fell headlong into progressive obsolescence, sped on its way by a handful of wild-card trends.

RESPONSIBILITY TAX

History reveals that tax issues have often been a catalyst for reform movements and revolutions.

An antitax movement had been building throughout the eighties. Taxpayers were chafing at inequities in the tax system. Beyond the big tax bite, they resented paying taxes for services they did not use. A trend, identified by the Trends Research Institute as one of the top ten trends of 1995, was set in motion that would culminate in a responsibility tax. This was an extension of the familiar user-tax principle: those who benefit from a public service have the primary responsibility to pay for it (gasoline taxes, highway tolls, fishing, hunting, boating, and driver licenses, and so on).

By 2000, the principle was broadened and applied to formerly protected areas. Welfare reforms produced a viable workfare; businesses, profit and nonprofit, accustomed to receiving special tax breaks, subsidies, and grants, were taken off the corporate welfare rolls. The responsibility tax was also applied to education.

Changing demographics plus economic fallback forced a rethinking of who paid for education.

There were significant increases in single adults, childless families, retirees with grown children, and in families with children in private or parochial schools.

These groups were putting vast sums of money into the system to educate other people's children. In prosperous times, with the educational system working reasonably well, it seemed a sound investment. Taxpayer money went in and national prosperity came out. But with the economy in shambles and the educational system in free fall, this enormous composite taxpayer segment began to rethink its financial responsibility.

The trend began at the grass-roots level and then picked up momentum. By 1993, taxpayers were toppling one in four school budgets. With less money at their disposal, the already-overburdened, inefficient school systems further curtailed services.

As standards declined and violence increased, parents

with school-age children looked for other ways to educate them. So desperate had the situation become that public school teachers were leading the charge, taking their own children out of the schools they taught in.

> Urban public school teachers often send their own children to private schools. . . . education analyst Denis P. Doyle says that in about one third of the nation's one hundred biggest cities, public-school teachers are more than 1.5 times as likely as others to send their children to private school. 44.6% of Boston's public-school teachers enroll their children in private schools compared with 28.9% of all families. (*USA Today,* 5/6/95)

By 2000, major school tax reform legislation was enacted. A powerful majority coalition opposed to the school tax formed; it consisted of childless taxpayers and taxpayers who had taken their children out of the public education system. These people were joined by parents opting to withdraw their kids from the public system because of religious reasons. Though parochial school enrollment had been declining steeply since the seventies, enrollment rebounded as the public school system degenerated.

An opposite set of religious reasons motivated another group opposing the school tax. In 1995, a Supreme Court ruling blurred the distinction between church and state, opening the door to religious activities in publicly funded schools. Throughout the nineties, in certain areas, local school boards were falling under the control of religious factions. The Supreme Court ruling was interpreted by these boards as a license to enact religious agendas. Separation between church and state was also blurred by "voucher" programs, in which school tax dollars could be funneled into parochial schools. People who did not want to pay for private religious education, and/or did not want somebody else's religion (or any religion at all) imposed upon their children, also opted out of the public system.

The privatization of formerly public schools exerted still further pressure on the system as a whole. An HMO-style "solution" was applied to education. Looking for survival strategies, beleaguered, overburdened school boards (Massachusetts, Maryland, Connecticut, Minnesota, Michigan, and others) tried contracting management of their schools out to private firms. Taxpayers, especially the childless, strongly objected to public tax money going to support private enterprise.

The new responsibility taxes put the burden of payment on the backs of the users. School taxes were no longer shared equally across the board by homeowners, single or married, childless or with children, irrespective of numbers or whether or not the children attended public schools. By the early nineties, there were more households of childless couples and people living alone than households consisting of married parents living with children. The new taxes were structured so that those with the most children in public school paid the most taxes. The reformulated school tax would serve as the taxation model for a broad range of twenty-first-century responsibility taxes.

But responsibility taxes drastically altered the character of the American public school system: Public education became like public health. It was there for everyone, but it was used mainly by those who had no other options.

WHATSAMATTA U.?

The education crisis at the college level was less dramatic, violent, and headline-worthy, but scarcely less foreboding for the future. Colleges were pricing themselves out of range of the middle class, which was itself declining in numbers. A college degree no longer guaranteed a good job.

The student body of traditional eighteen- to twenty-four-year-olds was shrinking. Their enrollment fell from 30 million in 1980 to 26.8 million in 1990. State and federal aid was drying up, resulting in fewer and less generous scholarships and research money. Tuition was rising. Once again, college was becoming inaccessible to those who were not well-off.

As with corporate America, universities were downsizing, eliminating jobs, curtailing services, and imposing heavier workloads on their professors. While assessments of education quality on the grade school and high school levels were unanimously negative, on the college level, reviews were mixed.

Foreign students placed a high value on the American university system. Enrollment rose steadily, according to the Institute of National Education. Since most foreign students were paying their own way, an American university was their education of choice, and therefore a testimonial to the value placed upon an American degree abroad.

But the report card at home was less favorable. Studies carried out by a variety of watchdog organizations deplored falling standards for higher education.

REPORT SAYS COLLEGES ARE FAILING TO EDUCATE

Blaming higher education for a failure to produce highly skilled workers, a report by a group of sixteen leading educators, business leaders, foundation executives and others says that undergraduate education in the United States is too often "little more than secondary school material— warmed over and reoffered at much higher expense." (*NYT*, 12/5/93)

STUDY FINDS GAPS IN ABILITIES OF MANY COLLEGE GRADUATES

Graduates of four-year and two-year institutions "are certainly more literate on average than those that did not go to college or did not graduate," the report said. "But their levels of literacy ranged from a lot less than impressive to mediocre to near alarming." (AP, 12/10/94)

Though subject to widespread intellectual criticism, the college crisis was nevertheless more a question of cost than quality. By 1995, a four-year education at Harvard, Yale, MIT, Stanford, and other top-of-the-line colleges and universities had passed the $100,000 mark. The average cost for a residential student at a private institution was $75,000, and $36,000 at a public college.

Costs spiraled upward at double the national overall inflation rate, while at the same time real income decreased for 80 percent of American households. Colleges (apart from a handful of the most prestigious and richly endowed) found themselves unable to attract enough full-time paying students to cover costs, and were forced to dip into discretionary funds set up to finance worthy but financially needy students. In 1994, less than half of all college students were paying full tuition. The crunch was felt even at the Ivy League level.

INTERACTIVE U.

Universities, looking to attract full paying students, tried applying sophisticated corporate marketing expertise. They experimented with bold and ingenious discount schemes and incentive plans, thereby hoping to increase "market share."

Unable to recognize that education was subject to the same complex of forces that produced trends in other areas, educators and politicians did not see that higher education, Western-style, was a trend in its own right. It was long past its prime, ailing, and infirm. The institutions designed to further it and instill it were obsolete, physically damaged, and increasingly irrelevant to the new Global Age. Nevertheless, education as a *process* was given a huge, unexpected, exhilarating shot in the arm even as educational institutions found themselves increasingly besieged.

Cavalry bugles sounded loud and clear—not out in the educational field itself but along the information superhighway. By the mid-1990s, computer literacy at the college level was near universal. With the interactive facilities of the Internet, CD-ROMs, and other technological innovations sweeping the country, most elements within the standard university education were just becoming available at home.

Interactive TV, beamed by satellite, had already been drafted into limited educational service, transmitting credit courses and postgraduate degrees to special classrooms set up by corporations and communities.

NEW TECHNOLOGIES ON CAMPUS

Five thousand students will attend Virginia's Old Dominion University this fall without ever setting foot on campus. They are earning degrees through "distance learning" courses taught via live TV. . . . The Norfolk, Va., college beams classes to 16 community colleges across the state, offering undergraduate degrees in 10 fields including nursing, counseling and criminal justice. (AP, 7/23/95)

In its maiden "Internet Directory" (6/29/95), a monthly special section, the *Wall Street Journal* listed over one hundred advertisers. While most of these were related to business and finance, a handful advertised accredited university courses.

The University of Phoenix offered "online classes leading to degrees in business, management, and information systems." At-home study was also offered by Purdue University and by the American University of Paris, among others. (Hooray! No need to go to Paris to get your diploma!) Response to this first directory was so heavy, the *Wall Street Journal* said, that many Web sites couldn't handle the traffic.

The message was already clear. It was no longer necessary to attend a university in person to get a degree. In 1996, Brown University and the University of Pennsylvania were offering graduate courses over the Internet. The trend was in its early infancy.

▶ **TRENDPOST** *Interactive, on-line learning will revolutionize education. Demand for "distance learning" software, hardware, and services will generate a mighty new component within the telecommunications and publishing industries. Especially in its early stages of development, distance learning will provide rich opportunities for small entrepreneurs, scholars, artists, educators, and inventors, as well as for established communications giants.* ◀

The education revolution will have as profound and as far-reaching an effect upon the world as the invention of printing. Not only will it affect where we learn; it also will influence how we learn and what we learn. Within decades, it will make a near totality of the world's resource libraries available to students without them ever leaving their homes. A whole new interactive multimedia life that did not exist just a decade earlier will be summoned up at the tap of a key.

Throughout the nineties, colleges, aware of the power of computer and communications technology, were integrating it into their curriculums. But even these on-trend institutions did not realize that the physical university itself was an artifact. The virtual interactive university on the Internet could provide the same or even higher levels of learning than the colleges. Undergraduates did not have to sit in a crowded lecture hall with three hundred other students and listen to an overworked, uninspired professor drone on and on.

Just as the Internet could provide access to the world's best knowledge, so it could provide access to the best teachers. Competing universities and independent, unaffiliated programs will feature the superstars from every field of study.

This ability to access the best in any given field will be a unique historical development. Throughout history, only a handful of lucky disciples had personal access to Pythagoras, Plato, Jesus, Buddha, Muhammad, Galileo, Einstein, or any other great leader or thinker. As the new millennium gets under way, everyone with the hardware and a thirst for knowledge can acquire the software. Actually, television had held out that promise from its earliest days. But, ruled and monopolized by commercial interests, it never delivered.

Many inherent Interactive U. problems such as monitoring exams and providing science and engineering labs and field trips would be solved through common testing centers and outsourced facilities.

As with all new technologies, the first forays into distance learning were tentative and expensive. But since Interactive U. was essentially a software phenomenon, it was intrinsically inexpensive. The price of a fully accredited college education dropped precipitously over the first decades of the twenty-first century, thus providing affordable equal education opportunities to almost everyone, even at the inner-city level.

There were many other advantages to Interactive U. Students could learn at their own individual pace and level. No longer bound by restrictive curricula, students could choose the courses they wanted from a vast intellectual repertory. More important than where you learned was what you learned and whom you learned it from.

The academic Iron Curtain had been lifted. It was no longer possible for credentialed commissars to impose their intellectual and artistic party dogmas upon their students. The new freedom to choose inspired a renaissance of individuality, creativity, independent thinking . . . and dissent.

In the tumultuous wake of this tremendous revolution, the whole educational system was fighting for survival. This did not mean that the entire traditional university system suddenly collapsed. There were still plenty of parents who could afford to send their kids to college, and plenty of kids who still wanted to go away for the learning experience. Not all the campus ivy withered and died.

With modifications, the richest and most prestigious schools carried on. Tradition had its own power, perks, and glamour. You couldn't be a member of the Harvard Club unless you graduated from Harvard.

For others, the survival involved more dramatic action. They pruned back, grafted on new stock, fertilized, and cultivated their gardens. Taking a cue from longevity centers, colleges integrated alternative thought and values into their programs, thereby attracting some of the brightest and most original minds.

Outside of the formal university framework, individuals were customizing their own courseware to suit their personalities, needs, and dreams. With all-star teams of teachers accessible to all, there were now viable and accepted alternatives to the official diploma that in the past had so often determined a student's future career possibilities.

NET NERDS OF THE WORLD UNITE!

Widespread enrollment in Interactive U. had important sociological consequences. A substantial percentage of college students were now living and learning at home. Now every town was a college town, thus altering the community personality. Like their parents, often working at home and involving themselves in community affairs, students also became activists.

The advantages of Interactive U. were many, but enrollment had its downside. There was no campus, and therefore no campus life. For the sect of devoted Net nerds busily exploring cyberspace, this was no problem. But for the others, a virtual life of cybersex, stimulated by cyberdrugs at cyberparties, gyrating to the beat of cyberrock was hardly life at all. In a new era of unshackled creativity and originality, students generously applied these faculties to finding ingenious solutions to the social dilemma.

Home learning removed the element of peer pressure from study, but this also had its downside. Personal motivation, a serious problem under normal college circumstances, was still more difficult to generate when working at home alone. Like-minded students formed ad hoc study and discussion groups. Connected via videophone to other groups and to instructors affiliated with their interactive programs, students were able to re-create the intensive and fruitful seminar atmosphere of college life at its best.

By 2020, higher education had so transformed itself that students of that progressive era wondered how, without interactive capabilities, their parents and grandparents had ever learned anything at all. It was like trying to imagine a world without automobiles, or computers, or Saran Wrap.

LEADING EDGE-UCATION

The principles working so successfully at Interactive U. were applied in modified form to the very different but graver problems facing elementary and high schools.

A home schooling trend was already under way in the

nineties. Though legal nationwide, it was not encouraged. But as dissatisfaction with public education grew, parents began teaching their children at home.

The majority of early home schoolers had religious agendas, but they were soon joined by a larger wave of parents taking their kids out because the schools were deficient and/or dangerous. In 1996, an estimated 1.2 million children, or 2 percent of the student population, were being taught at home. The figure was growing at 15 percent a year. With the public education system deteriorating, the pace accelerated.

The one big obstacle to home schooling had always been that it was a labor-intensive one-on-one procedure, a labor of love for a small minority of devoted parents. By 2000, the homing trend would be joined to the power of interactive technology, and this obstacle would be overcome, opening the floodgates to a tidal wave of home education.

A bonanza of user-friendly educational software would accommodate every level of learning, and every group with particular needs—from the learning disabled to those in the inner-city ghettos. Everyone with access to a computer and multimedia technology could plug into the appropriate programs. By the first decade of the new millennium, this trend would reach the adolescent stage of its growth cycle.

► **TRENDPOST** *The growth of the home ed and Interactive U. trends will accelerate rapidly once tele-videophony or other comparable multimedia-interface technologies become available and affordable.* ◄

Of course, young students could not be expected to monitor and control themselves, and to learn unassisted. Now, however, thanks to the homing trend, there was a vast pool of skilled, semiskilled, or just willing volunteer help to draw from: grandparents, retired neighbors, parents working part-time, unemployed and underemployed young adults, and others.

Home ed, perceived as something brand-new, was again something very old in reincarnated form. The reextended family fostered a new form of the old apprenticeship system. Children going through school at home could tap into the skills and experience of multiple generations.

These benefits and possibilities did not apply universally. Thirty percent of children were being raised by single parents. Two-income families with both wage earners working away from home still made up a substantial demographic segment. Other parents did not have the time, skills, or inclination to school their children. Those in the inner city and the working poor usually lacked the family support, the education, and the money to access the new technology.

For these groups as well, there will be interactive learning options. Primary and secondary education will be turned into community or quasi-community activities. Parents will band together to share the workload. Professional teachers downsized out of jobs or dissatisfied with the bureaucratic policies and restraints of the public system will be hired full-time or part-time for their professional expertise.

In the nineties, enterprising teachers were already setting up private modern versions of the nineteenth-century one-room little red schoolhouse. From the South Bronx to Le Sueur, Minnesota, teachers were enrolling groups of students in small classes and giving them extensive individual attention.

By 2020, home ed and interactive schooling will eclipse private and parochial schools as the preferred alternatives to the public educational system.

▶ **TRENDPOST** *Austerity budgets coinciding with economic fallback and burgeoning interactive educational technolo-*

gies will disrupt all levels of the teaching profession. But despite layoffs and cutbacks, on-trend teachers and educators will find new professional opportunities opening up on the interactive home schooling network. ◄

Private schools, interactive tutoring, consulting, and counseling, the development, marketing, and distribution of learning software, and a wide variety of community-focused educational programs will provide full- and part-time employment.

In 1994, total public and private education expenditures were estimated at approximately $500 billion. As the home education/interactive education trend gathers strength, there will be extensive school and college failures and closures, cutbacks, layoffs, downsizing, and distribution shake-ups in the way these enormous sums of school money are spent. But the end result will be more jobs, rather than fewer, and more money spent on schooling overall—something akin to the way the automobile quickly put horse breeders and carriage makers out of business but generated a much larger industry to supplant them.

AKIO

Interactive educational facilities revolutionized the way students learned and set the stage for the greater revolution: *what* they learned. They paved the way for new schools of highest education, called AKIO (advanced knowledge interactive organization).

Over the course of the first decade of the new millennium, education shifted its focus altogether, from the preschool level on up. The objective had changed. The aim of education was now to enhance the unique talents that every individual is born with and blessed with. Education was no longer an intellectual assembly line turning out a trained, smoothly functioning but standardized human product.

On grade school and high school levels, history was now taught as an exciting conflict of ideas, not just as an incomprehensible clash of armies and a list of dates learned by rote. The arts were no longer afterthoughts to the curriculum; they were integral to it, a vital part of everyday living. Mathematics—geometry in particular—was taught as a potential key to understanding universal processes, not as a cerebral exercise in manipulating numbers.

On the college level, an Interactive U. diploma included courses in lost civilizations, sacred geometry, alchemy, reincarnation, psychic phenomena, ancient prophecies, extraterrestrial life-forms, alternative medicine and healing, esoteric philosophy and metaphysics, and other subjects formerly taboo at the university level.

But even at its most radical and imaginative, the new university education was directed mainly at the intellectual center: It was "head" learning. It had an emotional impact, but it did not train the heart or the soul . . . or the body. It was unbalanced.

The Global Age called for a Globalnomic approach to life. The entire system had to be connected and integrated. It was at this point that the information superhighway came to a dead end. Technology could facilitate access to information with breathtaking ease. It could not, in and of itself, convert information into understanding. This involved a private, inner, emotional process.

At AKIO, mind, heart, body, and soul *all* were trained—to produce a functioning "educated" individual. Understanding could not be conveyed by machine, or at a distance, or in any other way than hands-on.

Education at an AKIO center—like medicine, the family, and the home—blended the old with the new. It took its form and much of its subject matter from the new intentional communities and longevity centers. Yet it would have looked strikingly familiar to Plato, with his gymnasium, or educational training center.

Initially operating at a postgraduate level, AKIO took young people and trained their intellectual, emotional, and physical centers simultaneously. Students worked the land, grew their own produce, raised their own livestock, cooked their own food, and landscaped and built buildings with their own hands. They practiced (not just learned about) the arts—music, painting, sculpture, architecture. They worked at martial arts, sacred dance, and other consciousness-raising physical disciplines. They studied the ancient sciences as well as breakthrough contemporary science. Above all, they studied themselves.

Those who graduated after four or more years were potentially balanced individuals. They had gone far enough along the path to developed consciousness to know where it could eventually lead.

Personal experience taught them that their existence had a meaning, individually and collectively. They were prepared to take responsibility for their own lives and their own destinies. They were capable of functioning in the new Global Age and of furthering its ideals. They had a big job ahead of them.

AKIO would eventually serve as both educational and lifestyle model for the global Renaissance. But AKIO was not reserved just for young adults. The integrated and intensive teaching you got at AKIO attracted a mature set of students looking for wisdom that was unavailable elsewhere. Along with longevity centers AKIO became a place where working professionals spent long sabbaticals getting their hands dirty and their minds tuned. The seeds of AKIO had been sown over the course of the last half of the twentieth century. A few AKIO-style initiatic communities were taking root as the century ended. They would weather the troubled times ahead, and emerge healthy and sound into the new millennium and flourish and prevail.

book
three

19

UNCIVIL WAR

SPONTANEOUS COMBUSTION

They flooded the streets. Day and night, they marched. They yelled, they screamed, they chanted, they danced, and they prayed.

No one saw them coming, and they came from everywhere. The country had never seen such massive demonstrations. At first, "the experts" compared it to the sixties, when draft-age dissenters, women's libbers, and civil rights advocates took to the streets in protest. But this was no sixties sound. This time, there were millions on the streets.

It began as just another student protest—not so different from the one in New York back in 1995, when thousands of City College students, mostly ethnic minorities, marched on City Hall. They were incensed by rising tuition and cuts in aid, loans, and scholarships—economic measures that would force them out of school.

Mounted police dispersed them with crowd-control sprays and nightsticks. The episode barely made the national news and drew little notice in New York. But it was a harbinger.

The big trouble began in the year 2000, when the latest in a long series of city, state, and federal cutbacks and simultaneous tuition hikes was announced. The effect of the legislation was to make college diplomas available only to those who could afford them. It was a return to the pre-World War II era. Back then, it was accepted that higher education was a prerogative of the wealthy.

That perception changed over the second half of the twentieth century. It had become a universal American belief that a college education at some level should be available to any bright and willing student, regardless of income.

Before World War II, a college degree was a huge career advantage, but it was not the only ticket to success. In 2000, while the degree did not guarantee a good job, without it there was little hope for success. To legislators, depriving students of a degree was a cost-cutting move; to students, it was a career death sentence. They rose in protest.

America was not supposed to be a country where the rich grew richer and everyone else grew poorer. Finally, the well-publicized income disparity between the rich and the shrinking middle class and growing underclass served as the predicted flashpoint.

"Almost all the increase in average family income (since 1978) . . . has gone to the top fifth," of U.S. population, Labor Secretary Robert Reich asserted.

". . . the bottom twenty percent lost fifteen percent of real family income."

The resulting disparity, he said, poses "an enormous problem for this country. . . . If unaddressed this can rip our country apart." (AP, 4/21/95)

Three months after Secretary Reich's speech, Washington addressed the "enormous problem." President Clinton signed legislation cutting $16 billion in education, job training, and other programs from the 1996 budget.

Equally short-sighted and insensitive legislation continued throughout the remainder of the decade—until New York's students again took to the streets.

This time, the news was posted on the StudentNet. Sympathy protests simultaneously combusted on college campuses and in cities around the nation. As the demonstration mobilized and gained momentum, the students were joined by their uncollegiate peers—the unemployed, the underemployed, the unemployable, the short-fused . . . and the armed.

Afterward, there were conflicting reports. No one was sure what had turned the protesters into marchers, or what had pointed them in the direction of Wall Street. All that was known for sure was that a mob of adrenaline-pumped young people funneled into the narrow streets of the Financial District, taking everyone in their path along with them.

Intending to block their further progress before they reached the New York Stock Exchange and the Federal Reserve, riot police set up barricades. But the front ranks of the marchers, pushed by the masses of people behind, were forced forward through the barriers. Outnumbered and overwhelmed, the police turned to their standard riot-control equipment. When the tear gas was unleashed, the armed element within the protest movement answered back with bullets. The police returned the fire.

They said it was Kent State all over again, but it was bigger, much bigger, and very different. And this time you didn't have to wait to see it on the cover of *Newsweek*. It was seen by millions watching live television coverage.

It hardly mattered who had fired first.

MILLENNIUM MARCHERS

The violence ended with the Wall Street Massacre, but the demonstrations didn't. In Boston, Chicago, Atlanta, Miami, Austin, Los Angeles, Baltimore, Peoria, Portland, Bismarck, Honolulu, Anchorage, in every Middletown and Centerville, a stunned nation took to the streets and wouldn't leave.

What began as a student protest against education cutbacks escalated into a broad-based people's protest. Unlike the sixties, this protest was not confined to the young, but, like the sixties, it *was* about the war . . . eventually.

Government efforts to dismiss the rebellion as a "radical fringe movement" were dismissed in turn. And this wasn't one of those typically futile rallies with fleets of chartered buses converging on the Washington Mall for a Sunday afternoon to listen to blowhard activists.

With children in hand, graying boomers of protests past joined the vigil in the streets.

Grievances had been building for years. They had been dutifully reported and officially ignored. What was surprising was the surprise expressed by the lunatic middle, who could find no rhyme or reason for the fury.

The tens of millions in the streets were recruited from significant established majorities: the 80 percent of Americans who for a decade had been telling pollsters they did not feel "our government can generally be trusted to look after our interests," the 91 percent who "had little or no confidence in Washington," the 80 percent who felt "the government favored the rich and powerful," the 73 percent who did not want to see environmental regulations rolled back, the 80 percent who were opposed to the Mexican bailout. There were jobless Generation Xers, tax protesters, retirees with devalued pensions, the underemployed, the working poor, the downsized and out, the aware, and the unbuffaloed from every strata of society. It should have come as no surprise when the 90 percent of the nation who said they wanted change demanded change.

Clumsy attempts to disperse the crowds were ineffective and only intensified resistance. No one dared give the order to open fire. It was made clear that without provocation from the crowds, National Guard troops and the police would not use their weapons. This was the United States, not Tiananmen Square, and American troops were not going to fire on their brothers and sisters.

It was this kind of nonviolent, unbudging mass protest that in 1989–1990 had brought down the Communist tyrannies of Eastern Europe—millions of people in the streets who refused to leave, government brought to its knees, business at a standstill. The difference was that this was not a move to overthrow the government.

Over the course of several tumultuous unplanned days, the vast movement began to acquire a focus. Only gradually did the mutually supportive multigenerational crowd realize that it was on the verge of acquiring its birthright: democracy.

It was in a position to tell the government to do what the government was supposed to do: carry out the will of the people. With Wall Street, Main Street, and Pennsylvania Avenue closed down, the government listened.

The first thing the people told the government was that they wanted affordable education; they wanted their scholarships, grants, and loans restored. The second thing they told the government was that they wanted corporate welfare stopped. They wanted an end to policies that allowed two-thirds of the nation's wealth to accumulate in 1 percent of U.S. households. They wanted tax money presently squandered on defense, boondoggles, and pork-barrel projects to be spent on the people, not just a few people. The third thing they told the government was to stop the war.

THE WAR

By 2000, the United States was under attack. The enemy was invading from all sides, and from within. No *Star Wars* shield could stop it from coming in. The Atlantic and Pacific fleets were helpless; stealth bombers could not zero in their targets; tanks, artillery, and missiles were useless. The A-bomb, nerve gas, bacteriological weapons, and Agent Orange would have just added to the problem. Defenseless, U.S. troops could only watch.

The government said it was doing what it could to stop the assault. But a Maginot Line of talk, threats, boycotts, and unenforced regulations could never bring this war to a stop.

Radioactive poison from nuclear meltdowns and nuclear terrorism rained in. Radiation levels rose, and so did the cancer rates. The protective ozone shield, already damaged, was under new assault and near destruction. Malignant melanoma rates were soaring.

The blitzkrieg went on. Yet the Envirowar, what would become the Great War of the twenty-first century, had never been officially declared.

Industrial pollution from Asia, Africa, South America, and Eastern Europe was pouring into the atmosphere in unprecedented quantities and being carried to the United States. Respiratory illnesses were epidemic; forests and woodlands were dying. Sewage, pesticides, and toxic chemical wastes were poisoning the seas and fouling the shores.

Who was responsible? No country was entirely without blame, but some were more guilty than others.

On the home front, the war on the environment was being waged and won by our own two-headed, one-party system.

The chemical, nuclear, and automotive industries, the artificial food–processing industry, agribusiness, mining and logging interests, and utilities lobbied to roll back or circumvent any regulation that placed a higher value on public and planetary health than upon corporate health.

Abroad, in the Third World theater, economic "development" went on amok, without concern for man or beast. Formerly agrarian societies jumped into the twentieth century overnight, with no thought for the twenty-first. These "emerging markets" were destroying in two decades what had taken the industrialized West two centuries to ruin, and now they resented being told not to do it by the countries that had taught them how.

Millions were being killed—slowly, but as surely and as painfully as if they had been shot or bombed. By 2000, death by environment was no longer regarded as a local or internal issue. Now the millions in the streets wanted a stop to the slaughter.

SHELL-SHOCKED

The first shell of the international counterattack was fired in Europe in 1995, but few recognized its significance. Britain had approved plans to allow the Royal Dutch/Shell Group to dump a massive oil platform 150 miles off the Scottish coast. The aging *Brent Spar* allegedly contained 130 tons of heavy metals, radioactive waste, and other pollutants.

Greenpeace commandos stormed and occupied the rig as it was being towed to its dumping site, defying Shell to sink it with them on it. Germany, the Netherlands, Belgium, Denmark, and Switzerland condemned the planned sinking. A successful European consumer boycott of Shell ensued. Unable to withstand the 30 percent drop in its business, Shell abandoned the plan.

This marked an escalation of the environmental small-arms fire of whaling moratoriums, fishing treaties, and logging quotas. The historical significance of the *Brent Spar* episode demonstrated the economic and political power of a people-generated protest. This time, the people directed the government rather than the government dictating its decisions to the people. A multigovernment/citizen coalition had compelled another sovereign country and a major multinational corporation to retreat on an environmental issue.

▶ **TRENDPOST** *Environmental desecration that crosses national boundaries will increasingly serve as a justification for war. Affected countries will declare such ecological violations enemy invasions. Equating environmental violations to international aggression will become a major foreign policy issue in the twenty-first century. Violators will be tried as the war criminals of the new millennium. Governments will use other nations' environmental violations as both grounds and pretexts for imposing tariffs and trade embargoes.* ◀

THEO-ECONOMY

The message to stop the war was written on a million posters and written into a million faces; this was a demand of unprecedented magnitude.

Restoring grants and scholarships and lowering tuition could be initiated with the stroke of a pen. Rescinding corporate welfare, cutting back on defense spending, and eliminating pork-barrel projects would be complex but legislatively attainable.

Stopping the war meant unconditional surrender. It meant abandoning the doctrine that had become the world religion—Theo-economy. Under this doctrine the economy is God, and finance its philosophy. Though the religious foundation of the doctrine was not usually acknowledged by the faithful, its true nature had been experienced and preached by its mystics and apostles. It was Calvin Coolidge who said: "The man who builds a factory builds a temple. And the man who works there worships there. . . . The business of America is business."

Theo-economy had taken root in the industrialized West. Its missionaries, as zealous as their earlier counterparts, had proselytized it universally.

Photo by Michael Pugh

THEO-ECONOMIC BAPTISM OF NEW COCA-COLA PLANT IN RUSSIA

By 1995, with the end of the Cold War, the entire world had embraced the faith. Political beliefs and foreign policy agendas that had once dictated national policies and initiated wars gave way to pure Theo-economic considerations.

FOREIGN RELATIONS: MONEY TALKS, POLICY WALKS

"Everyone's been saying for a long time that foreign policy is becoming economic, but like everything it's taken a while for the message to sink in around here," the former Treasury Secretary, Lloyd Bentsen, said just before he left town [Washington] last month. (*NYT*, 1/15/95)

After Treasury Secretary Bentsen left town, his replacement, Robert Rubin, drove the message home: "The future prosperity and security of the United States requires that our nation remain engaged and lead globally in opening markets, in promoting development, in assisting economies in transition and in dealing with global financial problems."

TRADE'S BOTTOM LINE: BUSINESS OVER POLITICS

For the first time in this century, the government has regularly put promotion of business interests at the top of its foreign policy agenda.

"Everyone acknowledges that economics now plays a central role in foreign policy—that battle is over," one of Mr. Clinton's top economic advisors said the other day. "What no one has really grappled with is what happens when commercial concerns push out other interests." (*NYT*, 7/30/95)

Actually, "what happens when commercial interests push out other interests" *had* been "grappled with" in the past. Abraham Lincoln said: "The money power preys upon the nation in times of peace and conspires against it in times of adversity. It is more despotic than monarchy. More insolent than autocracy. More selfish than bureaucracy. I see in the near future, a crisis approaching that unnerves me and causes me to tremble for the safety of my country. Corporations have been enthroned. An era of corruption will follow and the money power of the country will endeavor to prolong its reign by working upon the prejudices of the people until the wealth is aggregated in a few hands and the republic is destroyed."

The "era of corruption" took longer to establish than Lincoln envisaged. But he had accurately predicted the results of Theo-economic rule. Human rights, political liberties, social justice, and individual freedoms became closet issues. What Lincoln could not foresee was the Rain of Terror—the Theo-economic holy war waged on the environment.

The millions massed in the streets at the millennium were calling for an end to the Envirowar.

The march ended. The vigil was over. The message was clear.

Not many realized that peace—a return to planetary health—meant abandoning the articles of the religious faith that had won the unshakable allegiance of virtually every government on Earth. This was not to be accomplished with a pen stroke, not even through top-to-bottom reengineering of government policy.

But people were changing their ideas. When ideas change, everything changes. The articles for a new faith had been drawn.

► **TRENDPOST** *The successful businesses of the Global Age will practice a compassionate capitalism. Money will be made by individuals and firms capable of producing and marketing products and services that satisfy a world with changed values. Products that address real physical, emotional, and artistic (quality-of-life) needs and do not destroy the earth in the process will be in demand.* ◄

But it would take tumultuous and troubled decades before the embracing ideals of the new patriotism superseded and supplanted the Theo-economic priesthood and its metafinanciers.

20

THE STORM BEFORE
THE LULL

COMMUNIST REFORMATION

The fall of communism had opened up a vast new Disney World of McPossibilities. When the Cold War ended, Western missionaries descended upon the former Communist empire to spread the gospel of Theo-economy.

Not all the natives, however, were prepared for conversion. Salvation through "open market" was a difficult theological concept to convey to dozens of nations and billions of people shackled for decades to a different and opposing faith.

By the mid-1990s, disenchantment with Western-style capitalism was rife. A high-profile elite of successful nouveau Yuppies within the former Communist states applauded the new order. But virtually all others—peasants, workers, army, intelligentsia, national and religious minorities—were convinced they had been swindled by profiteers and carpetbaggers, foreign and domestic, who had privatized their countries under fire-sale conditions. In 1996, 60 percent of Russians said, "The West is pursuing the goal of weakening Russia with its economic advice." Eighty percent of those polled said their lives had grown worse.

Hyperinflation, acute and chronic unemployment, skyrocketing crime, plummeting life-expectancy levels, and increasing poverty would lead to uprisings, coups d'états, and civil wars.

Broken and disillusioned, masses of people reevaluated their Communist past. Faced with a Hobson's choice between open-market anarchy and a life devoid of freedom but with guarantees of cradle-to-grave sustenance, many will opt for a re-revolution, back to some form of communism.

The Communist Reformation of the twenty-first century will be a different shade of red: less dogmatic than the earlier model, allowing varying degrees of social justice, individual freedoms, private property, and business rights. But they will still have strong centralized governments and profess to be anticapitalist. These reform Communists will be called "enemies of democracy" by the United States and its allies. A Cold Peace of closed or controlled markets will replace the Cold War.

This medley of fractious republics, wildcat dictatorships, neo-Communists, and ethnic and religious fiefdoms will create a state of ongoing disunity. Instability and war—a Yugoslaviazation of the twelve thousand miles stretching from the Balkans to the Pacific—will prevail.

This "Eurasian Volcano Belt" will be one of the insurmountable obstacles to the establishment of the global Theo-economic religion. The new Crusades will be another.

CRUSADES 2000

The seeds of the new Crusades were sown in areas of Africa, the Middle East, Eastern Europe, and Asia. Throughout the Muslim world, devout masses, politically repressed and impoverished, were rising up against their endemically corrupt and inefficient secular governments with their pro-Western alliances. Imperialism, directly or indirectly, took the blame for the poverty, the lack of opportunity, and the social and moral decay.

Disenfranchised, desperate, politically powerless, Muslims in many countries looked to charismatic clerics to change their destiny.

Like the original Crusades—fought by Christians with papal sanction between the eleventh and thirteenth centuries to recover the Holy Land from the Muslims—the new Crusades will be fought in the name of God. But this time, the God of record will be called Allah, and the sanction will come from Islamic clerics.

Already in the 1990s, the Crusades were erupting with varying degrees of intensity and magnitude in Egypt, Algeria, Sudan, Somalia, Turkey, Chechnya, Yemen, Jordan, Bosnia, Azerbaijan, Tajikistan, India, Indonesia, the Philippines, Albania. . . .

With no central organization, but united in the name of the jihad, Crusaders of the Crescent took the battle to wherever the faithful were opposed—by secular Muslims within Islam, by hostile religious majorities outside Islam, and by Western imperialists everywhere.

The formal battle lines for the new Crusades had been drawn when Israel was created in 1948. But Israel, however complex politically and militarily, was no more than the latest episode in a conflict going back more than a thousand years.

Underlying it, in the Western world, there is and was a deep-seated, organic anti-Islam, anti-Eastern bias. In 1995, this was illustrated dramatically by the notorious Oklahoma City bombing.

> Hours after the bomb went off, CBS Evening News [4/19/95]
> featured Steven Emerson, a ubiquitous "terrorism expert"
> who eagerly presented his biases as objective analyses: "This
> was done with the intent to inflict as many casualties as pos-
> sible. That is a Middle Eastern trait." (Fair, 4/95)

This openly racist last sentence, if directed at Jews, blacks, Hispanics, or any other substantial ethnic minority within the United States, would have been answered by outraged protests, television coverage, and lead editorials.

Instead, for two full days following the bombing, a wide variety of "experts," without a single piece of evidence, blamed Middle Eastern extremists for the attack. Their views were accepted by the media and reflected by public opinion. "A poll of 1004 Americans begun April 19th, the day of the bombing . . . showed that 45% agreed with the statement: 'Muslims tend to be religious fanatics.' "

Extending back to the rise of Islam in the seventh century, then crystalizing during the original Crusades, this pervasive prejudice has percolated down through the centuries. Even our Western account of history and the rise of civilization has been skewed to exclude or distort the contributions of Egyptians, Asiatics, Semites, and Africans.

The history we're taught in school tells us that every significant ancient advance in science and philosophy was produced by the Greeks, with little or no input from other ancient cultures. Yet the proud, nationalistic Greeks themselves (Homer, Plato, Thales, and Aristotle, among others) were not ashamed to acknowledge that virtually everything considered Greek had its genesis elsewhere.

But to modern Western scholars and historians, civilization in any meaningful sense could only be European and Caucasian. The inability of Westerners (diplomats, politicians, and academics, along with the general populace) to recognize this "genetic" prejudice poisoned any possibility of mutual understanding between East and West.

Crusades 2000 will be another violent episode in the on-going world theater. The drama will pit Eastern frustration and fervor against Western obduracy and insensitivity.

The Crusaders' stated mission will be the overthrow of governments opposed to traditional Islamic rule, or the establishment of separatist Islamic states in countries with sizable Muslim minorities.

Though intense, bloody, and destructive, many of these conflicts could be contained within national or ethnic boundaries. However, when Western nations perceive them as threats to their own national interests, they will intervene—with economic sanctions and/or military might. The corresponding violent retaliation by the Crusaders will be labeled "terrorism."

By 2000, terrorism will be pandemic.

TERRORISM: THE GENIE UNCORKED

Terrorism became the retribution of choice for any nation, group, or individual—political, environmental, ethnic, secular, or religious—believing its life to be threatened by government policies.

What was being deplored as terrorism and denounced as cowardly and immoral by the affected nations was just called war by the perpetrators. Hamas said the Jerusalem bus bombing in which five died is part of "a systematic military campaign."

Governments have always been quick to moralize about the rules of engagement in war. In 1930, the U.S. Senate passed a resolution in response to Japan's war with China, denouncing the "inhumane bombing of civilian populations." The State Department condemned the attacks as violations of international law. President Franklin D. Roosevelt asked all nations to pledge they would never engage in such "inhumane barbarism."

But once the battle begins, it is assumed that war is morally justifiable.

"No. 1, there is no morality in warfare—forget it. No. 2, when you're fighting a war to win, you use every means at your disposal to do it," said Paul W. Tibbetts, pilot of the *Enola Gay*, the B-29 that dropped the atomic bomb on Hiroshima.

"War and individual ruin are synonymous terms," declared William Tecumseh Sherman after his renowned march to the sea.

In world wars, civil wars, holy wars, "just cause" wars—official or unofficial—the end result is the same: People get killed. The weapon does not matter—atom bomb, firebomb, car bomb, napalm; all are acts of war.

Without the weaponry or organization needed to fight a war in the field, terrorism became the only effective strategy available for sustaining the battle—short of surrender. And no country was safe.

In an August 29, 1990, news statement, the Trends Research Institute warned of impending terrorist strikes on the United States. But to most Americans, until 1993 terrorism was still something that happened abroad. The World Trade Center bombing in New York City jolted the country into the reality of terrorist violence. The 1995 Oklahoma City bombing drove home its potential magnitude. This was the beginning.

The Oklahoma bombing was a strike to America's heartland. Following it, seven out of ten Americans believed that terrorism would strike again. Capitalizing upon that legitimate fear, the government pushed through the FBI's preexistent plan to deprive citizens of individual constitutional rights in return for a promised war on terrorism. Two weeks *before* the bombing, President Clinton was already pushing the Omnibus Counterterrorism Act of 1995.

TERRORISM BILL HURTS RIGHTS

. . . The bill expands executive powers at the expense of both citizens and aliens.

The President alone could designate groups "detrimental to the interests of the United States." With that declaration, non-citizens who belong to or contribute to those groups could be deported. U.S. citizens doing likewise could face prison or fines or both.

. . . As we learned with Central America during the Reagan Administration, one man's "terrorist" may be another man's "freedom fighter."

Not surprisingly, the bill's godfather, the FBI, also would reap new power . . . that means your phone could be tapped if the FBI thought any suspect might use it. So much for Fourth Amendment protection. (Editorial, *USA Today*, 4/10/95)

In the wake of the Oklahoma horror, opposition to the bill was overpowered by the emotional state of the nation and it sailed through the Senate. "So much for Fourth Amendment protection."

But, like the other Washington-declared wars (on drugs, on crime, and so on), this war would not be won by hiring more police, building more prisons, broadening the enforcement powers of government agencies, or depriving citizens of their constitutional rights.

As with crime and drugs, the war on terrorism would provoke impassioned rhetoric, cost billions, claim countless casualties, and do little or nothing to prevent the trend from escalating.

Terrorism no longer meant the lone anarchist with his homemade bomb. International terror had developed into a sophisticated form of guerilla warfare. And it worked.

For decades, governments had huffed, puffed, and

bluffed, claiming they would never accede to demands made by terrorists. In fact, actions spoke louder than words. When American hostages were taken in Iran, Washington cut a deal to cut them loose. The bombing of the Marine compound in Lebanon was followed by a U.S. withdrawal. Even the lone Unabomber had his way when the *New York Times* and the *Washington Post* published his manifesto.

However, these sporadic tactical victories were treated as isolated events. Following the World Trade Center blast, FBI Director William Sessions told Congress that the bombing should not be seen as the start of a wave of terrorism in the United States.

The official response to any terrorist act was predictable: The perpetrators would be swiftly apprehended and brought to stern justice as a warning to those contemplating similar heinous deeds; new laws and tighter surveillance were needed to prevent further attacks; and future terrorists' demands would never be negotiated.

World governments would not publicly acknowledge that trillions spent on defense could not defend against either high-tech or low-tech terrorism. Nor would they acknowledge officially that terrorism would alter the intrinsic nature of twenty-first-century warfare—though that was the conclusion reached by the highest official there was.

"Our enemy today is not international communism. . . . It is international terror," said former President George Bush in April 1995.

With or without official endorsement, the new rules of war went into de facto operation in the summer of 1995.

Russia's brutal and bloody suppression of the Chechen rebellion laid waste to the predominantly Muslim republic. Though beaten, Chechen leader Dzhokar Dudayev promised retaliation by terror.

In the summer of 1995, Shamil Basayev, a Chechen

commander, made good the threat, launching a guerilla raid against the Russian city of Budyonnovsk and taking thousands of hostages.

Russian officials said they "wouldn't bend to terrorism" and countered with a series of bungled commando raids, killing hostages the Chechens used as human shields. The drama was played out live on Russian television for the entire nation to see. Unable to free the hostages and forced to negotiate, an embarrassed and helpless Russian government caved in. Basayev insisted upon a cease-fire, the withdrawal of Russian troops from Chechnya, and immediate peace negotiations. The cease-fire ensued; peace talks began. A daring, wily leader with a little band of a hundred guerillas had forced Russia to genuflect at the altar of terrorism.

Sophisticated weaponry was meaningless; the air force and army were helpless; stockpiles of nuclear weapons served no purpose. Tough talk, antiterrorism legislation, and threats of reprisal were equally futile.

In the United States, with the media transfixed on every intimate detail of the oral sex misadventures of actor Hugh Grant, there was little time left to report on Shamil Basayev, the man who had changed history. "I have opened the bottle and let the genie out. People now know what to do—even without me," Basayev declared.

The "genie" was a tested and proven model for twenty-first-century warfare. It would provide determined people with a means of retaliation against superior forces. And as technology became increasingly sophisticated, "micro" dominated and inexpensive, it would augment the terrorists' retaliation arsenal. Terrorism would be the response whenever a breakaway nation, a disaffected political or religious group, or an individual with a private ax to grind was threatened or imagined a threat to its existence.

On the domestic level (the World Trade Center and Oklahoma City bombings, the Unabomber), there was virtually no defense against terrorism. But on the broad-scale international level, there was a remedy.

Whenever the government of one nation took sides in another nation's conflict, it would automatically be regarded as the enemy by the side it opposed. The standard and predictable response would be terrorist retaliation.

To eliminate or at least drastically curtail international terrorism, governments had to stop meddling in the affairs of other countries. It was not a lesson easily learned.

In 1995, with the war in the Balkans intensifying, Washington wore a public cloak of neutrality, but behind closed doors it cross-dressed in partisan combat gear.

CROAT SAYS U.S. GAVE GREEN LIGHT

The United States gave Croatia very strong advice on how to conduct its massive assault on rebel Serbs and tacit approval for the operation, Croatian Foreign Minister Mate Granic indicated in an interview Saturday. (AP, 8/5/95)

CROAT LEADER: U.S. ADVISED US

The American influence on Croatia has grown steadily and last November the United States signed a military cooperation agreement with the Croatian Defense Ministry.

Around the same time an American company, Military Professional Resources, Inc., signed a long term contract with Croatia to help "democratize" its armed forces and reorganize its officer corps. (AP, 8/5/95)

MPRI was under contract with the Pentagon, and it was headed by several retired U.S. generals and the former head of the Defense Intelligence Agency. The company said it was "capitalizing on the experience and skills of America's best combat-seasoned professionals." But the use of corporate language did little to disguise MPRI's true identity. They were soldiers of the Fortune 500.

Following the Croat victory, and the displacement of 200,000 Serbs from territory they had occupied for three centuries, a demonstration of 20,000 Serbs massed in Belgrade, vowing vengeance on the United States for its role in the Croat offensive. Another enemy had been made.

Until the United States gives up taking sides in foreign internal conflicts, policing the world, and using its power to "spread democracy" and "open markets" and to protect special interests in the name of national interests, the terrorism trend will continue.

UNDESIRABLE ALIENS

In 1994, according to the Worldwatch Institute, thirty-four wars were raging throughout the world, twice as many as during the 1960s.

Driven by bloodshed, famine, poverty, and persecution, the world's refugee population swelled to an all-time high of 23 million people—all of whom were searching the globe in vain for a spot to settle. Another 26 million were displaced within their own countries.

This was an international problem on an unprecedented scale. While immigrants and refugees had never been welcomed with open arms, and had sometimes been repulsed by local populations, there had always been physical room somewhere in the world to accommodate masses of newcomers: those fleeing the potato famine in Ireland, the pogroms in Russia, the poverty in Italy, and war everywhere.

Even after the frontiers vanished, refugees were able to find homes for themselves. As recently as the 1980s, prosperous industrialized nations around the world were inviting an influx of cheap immigrant labor to build their economies and take the menial, low-wage jobs.

But by 1990, refugees were no longer needed or wanted. Most of Europe was in recession, and looking for ways to get rid of their Turks, Kurds, Algerians, Tunisians, Moroccans, Indians, Pakistanis, Sri Lankans, Bengalees, Nigerians, Jamaicans, Indonesians, and others who were swelling welfare rolls and producing broods of new children much faster than the nationals.

The United States and Canada faced similar problems with Mexicans, Haitians, Latin Americans, Eastern Europeans, and Asians. Measures were being taken everywhere to prevent still further floods of immigrants from entering.

In the United States, nearly 9 million legal immigrants arrived during the 1980s. Estimates ranged that from 5 to 10 million illegal aliens were living in this country in 1994, with millions more arriving every year.

Seventy-seven percent of the people surveyed in a 1994 *Time*/CNN poll felt the government was not doing enough to keep out illegal immigrants. Anti-immigrant sentiment grew intense and became a campaign issue. California's Proposition 187 cut off public schooling, welfare, and non-emergency health care to the state's 1.6 million illegals.

MIGRATION THREAT TO GLOBAL STABILITY

Migration is a greater threat to global stability than has been recognized. The sheer press of numbers of the very poor made aware, by radio and television, of living conditions a boat ride away . . . is likely to become a steadily more destructive political force for Western democracies. (Jessica Matthews, Senior Fellow at the Council on Foreign Relations, *Poughkeepsie Journal*, 12/27/94)

Millions of people facing starvation, poverty, repression, disease, or warfare at home looked for refuge in countries that did not want them, would not allow them in, and regarded them as threats. Unable to enter legally, masses continued to find ways to enter illegally—by boat, by plane, by land.

Without resources, skills, or a knowledge of the native language, they took up anonymous lives in the impoverished inner-city ghettos, looking for any kind of work that might pay a subsistence wage or for some way to get public assistance.

Ugly clashes between the immigrants and the unemployed and the disenfranchised native underclasses were commonplace in Italy, France, Germany, Portugal, and England. Fascists and racist rabble-rousers grew increasingly powerful at the polls. The refugees of the world grew increasingly unwelcome as they grew more desperate and numerous.

Immigration, with its own self-sustaining heating system and an endless supply of fuel, was a hot issue. In recessionary times, even menial jobs are prized, and immigrant labor drives wages down still further. A University of California study showed that roughly one-fifth of the growth in the wage gap between the skilled and the unskilled since the mid-1970s was linked to the growing supply of unskilled immigration labor. Illegal immigration was costing the chiefly affected states (New York, Florida, Texas, Illinois, and California) an estimated $8 billion a year in services. Money spent on illegal immigrants was money *not* spent on needy citizens.

Racism took on a variety of new forms. Within the inner cities, proximity bred new ethnic hatreds and a brushfire explosion of anti-immigrant factions. Throughout the United States, immigrants were regarded as an unaffordable socioeconomic burden by the people and as a hot-button issue by politicians.

Data from the 1990 census already showed that the poverty rate of post-1970 immigrants was 42 percent higher than that of native-born Americans. As anti-immigrant sentiment developed into rage, legislation was passed that made welfare and jobs still more difficult to get.

By 2000, war, famine, and plagues in Africa; poverty, crimes, and civil war throughout the former Soviet bloc; worker uprisings and bloody battles in China among a new class of economic warlords jockeying for power; population explosions in underdeveloped and developing nations of South America, Asia, and the Middle East; and major nuclear accidents and incidents resulted in a global immigrant crisis.

With no jobs available, no aid, no access to education, and because, unlike McDonald's, Pillsbury, Campbell Soup, and other needy huge corporations, immigrants were ineligible for subsidies, loan guarantees, grants, tax breaks, and bailouts, the route to survival for many immigrants was crime. In decaying urban areas around the world, crime was already entrenched. Russian mafioskis, Chinese gangs, and Latino drug rings staked out claims in homegrown organized-crime territory.

CRIMINAL ELEMENTS

Largely due to the cinema, the United States had acquired an international reputation as the crime capital of the world. Its cities were synonymous with mobsters, street gangs, and muggers, and its open spaces with gunslingers and desperadoes. Though overstated and oversimplified, America's frontier mentality and traditional easy access to weaponry justified the reputation—symbolically if not statistically. In the 1970s, 1980s, and 1990s, the numbers caught up with the symbols.

RANDOM KILLINGS HIT A HIGH

. . . gang-related killings have soared 371 percent since 1980. Small towns suffered the highest percentage increase in murder rates during the first six months of this year.

"Every American now has a realistic chance" of being murdered because of "the random nature the crime has assumed," says the FBI's Uniform Crime Report for 1993.
    There were 24,526 murders in 1993, up 3.2 percent from 1992. (*USA Today*, 12/5/94)

Violent crime rose 5.6 percent in 1993, continuing a seven-year upward trend, a 1994 Justice Department study showed. The teenage homicide toll rose 165 percent from 1983 to 1993. Between 1973 and 1993, criminals injured 37 million people.

BANK ROBBERIES SOARING DESPITE THE RISKS
(*NYT*, 3/28/95)

U.S. INCARCERATION RATE SOARS

The number of men and women in the nation's prisons and jails climbed to nearly 1.6 million last year, culminating a decade in which the U.S. rate of incarceration nearly doubled, the Justice Department reported. (AP, 8/19/96)

In 1995, apart from inmates, there were also 4 million people on parole or on probation. The breakdown of the nuclear family, the fragmentation of the educational system, dramatic increases in the American underclass and immigrant populations, chronic and acute inner-city unemployment, drugs, homelessness, and the increasing popularity of teenage gangs all contributed to skyrocketing figures.

By 1995, several studies were showing that overall crime rates were declining, but the statistics were suspect and disputed. One private study estimated the number of rapes in the United States at 683,000. An official government estimate put the number at 170,000, then revised it to 310,000 after the survey questions were rephrased. In any event, the long-term crime trend line was upward. A temporary spike or dip in a trend is a statistical commonplace. Crime had persisted at intolerably high levels for over twenty years.

Some criminologists attributed the decline in the 1995 figures to demographics. Proportionately, more crimes are committed by fourteen- to twenty-four-year-olds than by any other age group. The criminal element within the large, aging boomer population was less inclined to violence than it had been in its youth. In 1994, the group of fourteen- to twenty-four-year-olds was smaller and therefore incorporated fewer violent criminals.

But proponents of get-tough, "three strikes and you're out," "lock 'em up and throw away the key" laws were quick to attribute the decline to Congress's policies of lengthening prison sentences and building more prisons.

"If you can get these violent criminals to serve more time, you will inevitably reduce the violent crime rate. Anyone who is locked up will not commit a crime," said Congressman Bill McCollum, chairman of the House Subcommittee on Crime.

Though compelling, Congressman McCollum's logic applied only to violent criminals caught and in jail. It did not apply to the unapprehended majority. (According to FBI statistics, only 18 percent of crimes are actually resolved.) Nor did it apply to the much larger group of preteenage criminal apprentices waiting in the wings in the inner-city breeding grounds. By 2005, the 40 million preteenagers (the largest such group in decades) would reach their crime-prone peak teens and early twenties.

POLL: PRISONS AREN'T SOLUTION

Three out of four Americans believe a combination of prevention, punishment and treatment stands a better chance of reducing crime than prisons alone, according to a poll commissioned by an organization of prison officials.

"These results show that the public's mood may not be so punitive as some politicians would have us believe," said Bobbie L. Huskey [American Correctional Association president]. "Some would have us believe that punishment and incarceration alone are the single most effective strategies at reducing crime, but as corrections professionals we know that prevention and treatment will reduce crime in the long run." (AP, 6/14/95)

Ignoring the advice of the professionals and the opinions of the public, Washington opted for a "punishment and incarceration alone" approach. "Nothing is going to stop violent crime except tough sentencing," said Senator Orrin Hatch.

"Sometimes I wonder if the world is run by smart people who are putting us on, or imbeciles who really mean it," Mark Twain once said.

Punishment-only policies were not designed to address the causes of crime: poverty, dysfunctional family life, lack of education, lack of opportunity.

"[T]he percentage of Americans going in and out of jails is phenomenal . . . as you go down the socioeconomic scale, the percentage gets much higher," said Jerome G. Miller of the National Center on Institutions and Alternatives.

Economic fallback pushed more people under the poverty line. New legislation deprived millions of the already poor and the destitute of the support of the social safety net.

By 2000, the combination of poverty, demographics, and punitive policies turned the crime wave of the eighties and nineties into the crime tsunami of the new millennium.

THE CRIMINAL-INDUSTRIAL COMPLEX

Politicians played upon the fears of the public, transforming real and perceived problems into campaign platforms.

The war on crime was waged with the passion and the procedures earlier applied to the Cold War. Criminals (and, by extension, the poor) had become the new Communists—an evil empire within that had to be defeated at all costs. Anyone questioning policy and/or unwilling to support the war was castigated as soft on crime.

> "Tougher isn't always smarter," says former deputy attorney general, Philip Heymann, who resigned last week. But "it's almost politically suicidal for people to stand up and demand common sense in dealing with crime."
> Says Frank Cullen, president of the Academy of Criminal Justice Sciences: "We're pursuing policies in criminal justice that have no scientific support whatsoever." (*USA Today*, 2/7/94)

The United States was spending $31 billion on prisons in 1992, an 800 percent increase from 1975, according to the Census Bureau. In 1994, Congress passed a new $32 billion anticrime package. According to Senator Kent Conrad, this "would say to those who commit violent crime, 'The jig is up.' "

The prison population was showing a net gain of sixteen hundred inmates per week. It cost seventy thousand dollars to build each new cell and twenty thousand to house a criminal for a year. Correction spending by states and local governments grew by 232 percent between 1970 and 1990. The Federal Bureau of Prisons' budget increased by 475 percent since 1981; the Justice Department's budget increased more than 350 percent.

Defense industry leaders such as General Electric, Westinghouse, General Dynamics, Minnesota Mining & Manufacturing, Alliant Techsystems, Inc., and Motorola now played roles in a new criminal-industrial complex. "The future of it is phenomenal. It's now an industry in and of it-self," said Jerome G. Miller. "Corrections today is a gigantic cash machine," said Alvin J. Bronstein, director of the Prison Project of the American Civil Liberties Union.

With the military mind-set applied to the "criminal problem" old military bases were being recycled as prisons. Juvenile offenders were dealt with like adults and drafted into "boot camps." Army-style discipline was designed to "turn boys into men." The program was popular with politicians of all persuasions—both those believing in discipline as rehabilitation and those believing in discipline as punishment.

But boot camps produced a 10 to 12 percent *increase* in repeat offenders, according to the Center for Crime and Justice Policy at Vanderbilt University. The boot camps took in young offenders, taught them to be "all that they could be," and graduated classes of mature, efficient, hardened criminals.

Gun control was another popular, hotly contested issue. But with over 200 million firearms already in circulation, the problem did not lend itself to a legislative solution.

And, short of turning the nation into a police state, putting more cops on the beat could at best put a dent in the statistics. The U.S. Justice Department had been told that it would take 5 million new cops to bring the cop-to-crime ratio back to 1960s levels. (In 1994, there were 554,000 public police officers in the United States.)

▶ **TRENDPOST** *Like the Cold War before it, the war on crime will be lavishly funded by taxpayers. Businesses, manufacturers, entrepreneurs, anybody providing services relevant to the surveillance, arrest, and incarceration of criminals will find roles to play in a major growth industry. The trend began in the mid-1980s and will see steady growth through 2010.* ◀

HYPERSAFETY

In 1994, a *Los Angeles Times* poll showed that 43 percent of Americans rated crime as the nation's most pressing problem. Other polls put crime at the top of a list that included health care, the economy, the deficit, foreign policy, and drugs.

Crime was real and pervasive, the perception of it scarier still. Hypersafety was the reaction to both perceived and real dangers. People were taking whatever measures they thought would work in order to stay alive and to secure their property.

▶ **TRENDPOST** *Security- and safety-oriented businesses and services will boom in the next two decades. The $70 billion hypersafety industry (1995) will continue to grow at 9 percent per year through the turn of the century.* ◀

In 1994, private police officers outnumbered public police by three to one. Two hundred thousand new jobs for security guards were projected between 1995 and 2005. Computer security was a booming high-tech manifestation of the trend (growing 22 percent annually since 1990), along with sophisticated personal alarms, home alarms, car alarms, and other security technology. People were taking self-defense courses in record numbers. Handgun sales, especially to women, were up sharply, along with pepper sprays, tasers, and other deadly or disabling weapons and devices.

In 1995, after a series of threats, drive-by shootings, and the Oklahoma City bombing, President Clinton permanently closed Pennsylvania Avenue in front of the White House, an act of immense symbolic significance. The state of siege, though undeclared, was official.

UNSAFE HAVEN

Early in the new millennium, the United States lost its movie image as the criminal capital of the world. By 2000, other nations were vying for top criminal honors.

In the Communist bloc, organized crime had always been a government monopoly. When the government fell, crime was democritized—more successfully than any other aspect of Russian society—and without any input from Western "experts."

By 1995, bank executives, successful businessmen, politicians, and media critics were common top-level assassination and kidnapping victims. Hit men were rarely caught.

Organized mafioski controlled 45,000 private businesses. Crime reports confirmed that 80 percent of all businesses were paying heavy tribute to organized crime. Open-market anarchy created a huge network of business gangsters fighting for market-share control. Protected by private armies, the Russian crime lords also had access to the arsenal of sophisticated weaponry left behind by the Soviet army. They were capable of operating on every level of warfare, from individual assassination to nuclear annihilation.

China's conversion to Theo-economic principles produced its own form of open-market anarchy, and its own inscrutable criminal class. Brazil, Mexico, Argentina, Romania, Ukraine, and many other emerging-market countries each produced an appropriately ethnic gangster class—within and outside their governments. By comparison, the United States looked safe.

The same applied to most of the other intractable problems besetting America as the twentieth century ended. Each country had its own mix. Some (Mexico, Egypt, India) had worse pollution, some (Israel, Algeria, Sri Lanka) bloodier terrorism, some (England, Japan, Mexico) worse recessions, some (Germany, France, Italy) more racism and fascism, some (Egypt, Indonesia, India, Vietnam) worse overpopulation; some were fighting border scrimmages, civil wars, or each other (Ecuador, Peru, Chad, Libya, Somalia, Sudan, Angola, the Philippines).

Most had worse and even less responsive governments than the United States. All had fewer opportunities and possibilities.

21

RENAISSANCE 2001

REDISCOVERY OF AMERICA

While not a utopia, the United States with its wide-open spaces, lower population density, comparatively stable government, and less rigid lifestyle looked like the promised land to tens of millions of refugees.

To would-be immigrants, even crime and mugging seemed a low-risk long shot compared to starvation, mortars, and machine guns.

By 2000, the Immigration and Naturalization Service could not cope with mounting immigrant pressure on America's five thousand miles of coastline and five thousand miles of national boundary. Confronted by citizen pressure within to seal the borders, the federal government deployed the armed forces.

For the first time in fifty years, the United States was using the trillions of dollars spent on defense for the actual defense of the nation.

A series of immigration laws, starting with the 1882 Asian Exclusion Acts, had set restrictions (based mainly on race, "desirability," and perceived economic impact) on new arrivals to the United States. Historically an emotionally charged issue, immigration had become less racist by 2000, but also less democratic than ever. With its own massive underclass population, the United States did not need or want more uneducated, impoverished, unemployed, unemployable, and often unhealthy people.

But this time, unlike earlier great waves of immigration, it was not only the impoverished, the disadvantaged, and the persecuted who sought refuge. As recessions became depressions, as civil wars proliferated and crossed borders, as radiation and pollution rendered vast tracts of continents uninhabitable, the educated, the wealthy, the powerful, and the talented wanted in as well.

Legislation that would favor these groups over others set off intense debates and accusations of discrimination and elitism. A consensus developed that building a twenty-first-century America meant assuming the responsibility emphasized by John F. Kennedy: "Ask not what your country can do for you: Ask what you can do for your country."

For America to prosper, it had to take care of its own; its huge and growing underclass had to be nurtured and educated, not enlarged. Only those immigrants who would contribute to the country's immediate health and well-being were welcome.

They would jump into the melting pot and help in the building of a new and very different America, which in turn would eventually serve as a model for the global Renaissance.

THE BRAIN GAIN

By nature and by training more sensitive to shifts in the tempo of the times than others, the artists of the world (writers, filmmakers, musicians, painters, actors) rode the first waves in. Early in the new millennium, the United States would be recognized as the world's artistic leader, generating art styles and trends that became universal.

A new genre of millennium music emerged. Rock and roll, like swing and ragtime before it, was replaced by a new American beat that resonated globally. The anger, anguish, and despair that late-twentieth-century cutting-edge rock expressed gave way to the upbeat exhilaration of the global Renaissance. The new millennium music had a mass-appeal sound and style, bridging generations and ethnic sensibilities.

Art invariably mirrors the spirit of its age. Of all the arts, architecture returns the truest image. The dehumanized consciousness of the Industrial Age and post–World War II era was expressed unmistakably in the architecture of its factories, industrial parks, cookie-cutter tract housing, low-income developments, urban renewal projects, shopping malls, power centers, and skyscrapers.

New-millennium architecture rehumanized the home, the office, the workplace. As with health, education, and the family, the new forms applied the technology of the new to the principles and values of the old. A brilliant synthesis prevailed—harmoniously proportioned, imbued with spirit, highly efficient, durable, environmentally safe, and easy to maintain.

The plastic arts of painting and sculpture were revolutionized as artists learned to integrate computer power and versatility and virtual reality capacities into their individual visions.

The influx of international talent created new cultural centers, revitalized old and dying ones, and reinforced those already flourishing. The American map was dotted with vibrant versions of 1920s Paris—with its rich polyglot mix of expatriate and émigré artists and writers.

▶ **TRENDPOST** *The United States will be the epicenter of the global Renaissance. Its cultural life will have the richness and diversity of the Italian Renaissance, but in an appropriately high-tech format.* ◀

As a new consciousness gradually supplanted the debased values of the dying Industrial Age, art—in all its forms and manifestations—regained the place of honor it once held in society.

The distinctions between art and entertainment blurred. As in fifteenth-century Florence, the best and most profound works were often emotionally accessible to the public at large—not just to a sophisticated elite. All Florence wept when Jacopo Bellini died. The masters and masterpieces of the global Renaissance enjoyed a mass-market appreciation.

However, America's cultural influence was far wider reaching than Paris's or Florence's ever was. Following World War II, English became the world's second language. For several centuries, French had occupied that position; before that, at least in the Western world, it was Latin. But by 2000, English was the unchallenged world lingua franca. If an educated Zimbabwean wanted to talk to an educated Chinese, or a Brazilian to a Pole, the language was English.

The new literature, thought, philosophy, spirituality, and science of the new millennium was expressed primarily, read primarily, and understood primarily throughout the world in English. This language monopoly bestowed upon the United States an incalculable but subtle power: the power to transform ideas, and therefore lives, and therefore societies, and therefore the world.

WINDOWS OF THE WORLD

Apart from the literary primacy of English, it had been, from the beginning, the dominant language of databases and on the Internet. It also served as the motivation for the new, universal technological, scientific, and commercial cyberlanguage of the millennium.

Already by 1995, 40 percent of American households had personal computers, double the percentage of Taiwan and South Korea and five times that of Europe. Because of their complex script, the Japanese could not fully exploit the computer. The average Japanese office had ten PCs per one hundred employees, while the average U.S. office had forty-two per one hundred people, according to IDC Japan.

► **TRENDPOST** *The United States will continue to reign as world leader in hardware and software development beyond the foreseeable future. This dominance will oblige the rest of the world to communicate in cyber-English.* ◄

By 2010, for the first time since the fall of the legendary tower of Babel ("and the whole earth was of one language and of one speech"—Genesis), a single universal language would exist on Earth. A new generation of computer-literate people could communicate instantly with one another on equal footing.

Though developed to meet the needs of a computerized age, the new icon-based cyberlanguage was reminiscent of hieroglyphic languages of the past. A single picture might carry several simultaneous meanings. For example, in ancient Egyptian, the glyph for a bird could mean an actual physical bird. But it could also mean flight, and that which has the power to fly; or the principle of the volatile, to vaporize in thin air. Ultimately, metaphysically, the bird could mean that which is not bound to earth—the immaterial, or spirit.

Unlike the babel of scientific, commercial, artistic, religious, professional, and even sports and street jargons that confused and compartmentalized the world in the past, the rich cyberlanguage unified and clarified. It was not literary and discursive; it did not explain. Rather, it communicated directly across cultures and language barriers via symbols—to all those initiated in its secrets: the worldwide fraternity of the computer literate.

CREATIVE CAPITALISM

The world's technological and scientific elite, along with rich and educated Europeans, Arab sheiks, and well-to-do Asians with nothing left but their money soon followed the artists to America. All would contribute to making the United States the scientific, technological, intellectual, and cultural world capital.

Imported genius did not show up in the balance-of-trade figures. But immigrant talent and expertise helped cement America's dominance in commercial fields and in applications that could not be reproduced abroad by cheap labor.

The overriding chief feature of the technorevolution of the global Renaissance, its one constant, was change. Change was by definition impossible to monopolize. In the last two decades of the twentieth century, the rate of change was accelerating exponentially.

The computer was the most familiar case in point. It took seventy years just to apply electricity to the manual typewriter. In two short decades, the computer repeatedly evolved into unrecognizable higher transformations of its earlier self—and changed society in the process.

Post–World War II manufacturing strategy was characterized by the principle of planned obsolescence. Goods once considered durable were deliberately designed to wear out quickly, forcing consumers to buy replacements. The objective was to sell more products, not necessarily to produce better ones. Change and quality were by-products, not motives.

But in the change-oriented twenty-first century, staying competitive required *constant* innovation, ingenuity, and the will, expertise, and infrastructure to apply it. Savvy corporations could facilitate change by systematically monitoring and managing trends. But they couldn't monopolize change. Neither could nations. Genius did not necessarily go to the highest bidder; it went to where it was given the most encouragement and freedom. Throughout the opening decades of the global Renaissance, that meant the United States.

New products' "time to market" was measured in months, not years. But now *new* meant better, faster, more powerful, and it carried with it a social accountability. A combination of economic necessity and awakened personal and planetary conscience was making "junk" manufacturing as obsolete as built-in obsolescence. Cradle-to-grave manufacturing responsibility was written into law throughout the capital-developed nations.

► **TRENDPOST** *By 2000, a trend toward manufacturing products that satisfy and address real physical, emotional, and artistic (quality-of-life) needs will enter into the growth stage of its life cycle. An enlightened consumer society driven by back-to-basics values will replace the society manipulated by Madison Avenue's "Hidden Persuaders."* ◄

OUT OF FASHION

In Florence in 1390, there was no prevailing style of dress; everyone dressed as they pleased. This did not mean that people individually were not fashion-conscious; it meant that people did not take fashion orders from self-elected, self-promoted fashion dictators.

The return of individuality in the new global Renaissance effectively spelled an end to the multibillion-dollar fashion industry, itself a twentieth-century development.

In the business world, by the early 1990s, baby boomers were moving into CEO positions throughout the United States. They took with them the casual dress codes of their own formative years in the sixties and seventies. A trend toward casual moved into the workplace.

When staid corporate-culture leaders such as IBM and Ford lifted formal dress codes for management in 1995, the trend was legitimized.

The millions swelling the growing at-home workforce did not need nods from on high to jump out of their office uniforms: power ties, panty hose, power suits, and high heels.

By 2005, traditional business, "formal" and "fashion" attire was used only on special ceremonial occasions by the general public and the business community. As work-day dress, it was worn only by a handful of specialized professions or groups: undertakers, diplomats, lawyers and judges, ultraconservative religious factions, and others.

During the global Renaissance, the bulk of the day-to-day apparel consisted of inexpensive, durable, mass-produced casual wear. This was a kind of return to the ethnic folk costumes of old, but on a global scale; dress was traditional yet not conformist.

But where appearance mattered (either for professional reasons or personal self-esteem), individualized "smartwear" took fashion out of the hands of a clique of big-name designers.

▶ **TRENDPOST** *Smartwear will bridge the gap between casual and formal. It will be appearance-enhancing but personalized and comfortable (what's smart for me). Computerization plus declining wage scales will bring custom tailoring back into an affordable price range. The creative will design their own smartwear; millions of others will consult or collaborate with a new corps of personal dressmakers and tailors.* ◀

Teenagers were the last to embrace the individualized smartwear concept. Uncertain of themselves, lacking developed identities of their own, twentieth-century youth still needed role models. The ancient archetypes of hero and king/queen continued to exercise their influence in degenerate disguise. Jocks were mock heroes and celebrities were quasi-kings and queens. They set the styles—from athletic shoes to hair styles to breast implants.

Teenagers were brought up in a culture devoid of rites of passage and initiation ceremonies—practices that in ancient and traditional societies brought the young safely through adolescence into adulthood as individuals. Their youthful need to conform, belong, and identify kept the fashion industry alive beyond 2000. But as the individualism of Renaissance ideas percolated down into all levels of society, a new crop of rebellious teenagers became the nouveau hippies of the new millennium. Conformity went out of fashion.

Just as art, architecture, music, and literature are products of the age that produced them, so it is with fashion.

The tight corporate/cultural conformity of Industrial Age fashion gave way to the casual, functional, and, above all, individualized fashion of the global Renaissance. Apart from the financial repercussions, the decline and demise of fashion as we knew it had a deeper symbolic significance. It reflected the greater spirit of a new age.

NEW CORPORATE CULTURE

The new spirit expressed itself in all human activities but most dramatically in the new impetus and importance of the arts. The scientific rationalism of the Industrial Age had reduced the arts to frivolities or luxuries; something you did when you had nothing more important to do. (The section of the *New York Sunday Times* devoted to the arts is called "Arts and Leisure.") New millennium art (literature, cinema, television, and drama) reacquired the status it had enjoyed in the first Renaissance, and in every healthy civilization throughout history: art satisfies vital emotional and spiritual needs as much as the sciences satisfy intellectual and material needs.

"Corporate Culture" in the global Renaissance will take on a meaning beyond "what life is like inside a corporation." Business leaders in the Renaissance will become champions of the arts in much the same way that princes, churchmen, and nobles were in the last Renaissance. They will associate themselves and their companies with new millennium creativity. This will not mean simply acquiring expensive, already acknowledged masterpieces, or sponsoring the occasional musical event or museum endowment.

The new visionary corporate leaders will champion independent thought and have the insight to distinguish superior quality from fake originality. They will look to art to uncover the true source of the human spirit.

▶ **TRENDPOST** *Corporations that become sincere and adventurous patrons of the arts will not only play an important role in enriching society's emotional and spiritual life, but will also see their support and sincerity favorably reflected in their balance sheets. A grateful public will be quick to show its appreciation with its own form of support.* ◀

INFINITE ENERGY

Although the corporation would not take on its art patron role until early in the new millennium, already by the 1980s, forward-looking corporations were forming alliances to promote social responsibility in business. The idea that profit was not the sole aim of corporate existence amounted to a breach of Theo-economic faith. By early in the new millennium, this heresy had undermined the religion of the Industrial Revolution.

According to Theo-economic dogma, the economy was

God and finance its philosophy—but it was fossil fuel that energized the movement. To drive the Industrial Age machinery, mountains of coal, oceans of oil, and tons of uranium were needed. But in the undogmatic Global Age, God was God and higher consciousness its philosophy—and the fuel that energized the movement was . . . water . . . and air . . . and sun. . . .

The energy sources for the global Renaissance were renewable, free or almost free, and nonpolluting. To tap into energy in the new millennium did not require huge utilities to provide it or a complex infrastructure to mine, drill, refine, process, deliver, and store it.

The promise of "free" energy, held out by visionaries over the last decades of the twentieth century, was made good in the first decades of the twenty-first.

Alternative energy had been a buzzword since the OPEC oil embargo of 1973. But a variety of factors, mainly connected to funding, kept the most obvious alternatives (wind, solar energy, geothermal energy) from becoming economically viable and universally applicable. In 1981, only $155 million a year went into solar research and development. A single B-1 bomber cost $250 million. Nevertheless, despite underfunding, significant progress was made that would make solar power economically more viable.

Eventually, the search for alternative sources turned up leads that in the twenty-first century would deliver endless supplies of clean, cheap, environmentally safe energy.

The most promising of these was cold fusion, or new hydrogen energy, discovered in 1989. It was a relatively simple process, but it had scientists baffled.

The process involved applying a small amount of energy to a cell (containing deuterium, or heavy water, a hydrogen isotope). Early experiments produced undependable, irregular results, but when successful, cold fusion reactions produced as much as ten times *more* energy than went in.

Even cold fusion's discoverers were confounded. There was nothing in known science to account for the phenomenon. It was as though three hundred years of rational science suddenly had to deal with an alchemist's dream come true. Unable to explain the process, and unwilling to face its implications, scientists attacked and dismissed cold fusion—even as actual commercial heating units were being produced in Eastern Europe by using a process clearly related to the original discovery.

From Galileo to the Wright Brothers to Wegener and his theory of continental drift, the history of science is an unbroken sequence of breakthrough discoveries automatically dismissed and derided by the establishment of the day. Major newspapers ignored the historic Wright brothers flight of 1903—mainly because *Scientific American* claimed it was a hoax. For the next five years—with the Wright brothers routinely flying test flights around the field at Kitty Hawk—experts continued to argue that heavier-than-air machines were scientifically impossible.

Scientific and industrial opposition might slow the energy revolution; it could not stop it. The Industrial Age was dying. The fossil fuels that drove it were no longer required. Global energy sources would include cold fusion, solar energy, geothermal energy, and even wind—along with others that could not be predicted specifically but that were bound to be discovered, given the rate of new discovery and the thrust of scientific research at the millennium's end. New energy sources transformed the Global Age world more radically than the jet plane transformed travel.

It was a revolution on the order of the discovery of fire.

▶ **TRENDPOST** *The energy revolution will be the single-biggest investment opportunity of the twenty-first century. Its ramifications will extend to practically every aspect of human and planetary life. To profit from the trend, potential investors should*

begin familiarizing themselves with the field thoroughly and imme-
diately, and keep abreast of developments before they become of-
ficial. (Recommended reading: *Infinite Energy* magazine, PO Box
2816, Concord, NH 03302. Tel: 603-228-4516.) ◀

The energy revolution of the twenty-first century
changed the way life was lived.

The technology was in place and spreading quickly.
Within a generation, there were no gas bills, no oil bills, no
wood bills, no coal bills, no electric bills, no gasoline bills,
and no polluting coal- or oil-fired power plants or furnaces,
no gasoline engines, no nuclear plants generating still more
radioactive waste. In one blow, industries and households
were relieved of a significant percentage of their expenses.

The energy revolution made it possible for large numbers
of people to live the alternative lifestyles they believed in.

It freed people in direct and in subtle ways from reliance
upon established institutions and infrastructures. Practically, access to free energy made a life of voluntary simplicity, self-sufficiency, and technotribalism feasible without
hardship. Freed from the energy grid, people could build
houses anywhere that suited them. A permanent free supply of energy also meant that new buildings did not have to
use toxic or environmentally destructive building and insu-
lating materials just to conserve energy.

Psychologically, it re-created in technological format
something akin to the sense of inner freedom enjoyed by
Australian Aborigines and American Indians and other pre-
technological and nomadic societies.

Globally, unlimited energy threw a wild card into the
doomed hand being played out by the world's nuclear industries. If clean, free energy sources could be implemented quickly enough to shut down the world's ailing
nuclear power plants, looming disaster might be avoided.
New processes also held out the promise of neutralizing the
radioactive wastes of the world.

NATIONS IN TURMOIL

Oil-producing nations had their revenues decimated. Countries whose economies depended wholly or substantially upon oil exports sank into depression, recession, or chaos. Developed nations convulsed from within as their energy infrastructures disappeared. For developing nations, the effects were almost entirely beneficial. Unlimited nearly free energy meant that vast sums of scarce hard currency no longer had to be spent on energy.

For a transitional couple of decades, products relying upon petrochemicals for their manufacture would sustain a diminished oil industry. Japan, other oil-poor nations, and much of Europe would continue to import. But the United States had an ample domestic supply to satisfy its needs. Eventually, petrochemicals would be profitably synthesized from hydrogen and carbon.

By the middle of the twenty-first century, the oil industry would be as dead as the whale oil industry.

▶**TRENDPOST** *The chain of ancillary industries, products, and services that depend on or sustain the fossil fuel and nuclear energy industries will go down with them—mining, drilling, refining, processing, delivering, storage, equipment. Public utilities will cease to exist. On-trend investors with money in these industries should monitor events closely to safeguard their holdings. Threatened industries should reinvent their mission statements.* ◀

The oil-rich Muslim countries, deprived of revenue, seethed with rebellion. Religious reformers had little trouble convincing the impoverished masses that secular governments allied with Western interests were responsible and the jihad was the solution. The chaos in non-Muslim oil-producing nations would be equally extreme but not religiously based.

Politically, the energy revolution and the demise of the Industrial Age's single most important industry affected foreign policy and the world balance of power. Sensitive strategic alliances were rethought. America's "national interests" no longer meant oil interests; it meant the nation's interests.

America was looking within. And the world was looking at America.

THE RENAISSANCE

No longer obliged to put huge sums of money into paying for energy, the United States directed its energies toward reenergizing itself.

Applying the principles of technotribalism, practical and enlightened programs were begun to transform decaying, crime-ridden, and crowded Industrial Age cities into Global Age urban communities.

Save the Children campaigns turned around a generation of kids who ten years earlier would have been lost to drugs and crime by the time they hit puberty. Class warfare, ethnic divisiveness, the intolerable disparity between the few rich and the many poor had to be intelligently and effectively addressed before Renaissance values could take root.

Advanced technologies, access to free energy, and the will to make it happen produced mass-transportation systems that finally made the modern city life-enhancing. This was part of a larger trend toward fast and efficient mass rail transport and a breakaway from the road mentality that strangled the cities and stifled the suburbs. Within two decades, Mag-Lev (magnetic levitation) and other high-speed rail systems and "people movers" took the pressure off of roads and highways. Advanced ground transport replaced the plane for short- and medium-range travel.

Thanks in large part to the information superhighway and the energy revolution, freedom had been reacquired: external freedom. But to solve the problems of America, individuals first had to solve their own.

Only internal freedom, on a meaningful social scale, could generate a renaissance.

A new consciousness was sweeping America, a new spirituality, which was not based upon traditional religion and yet was religious.

Unlike secular humanism and the materialism of Theoeconomy, the new spiritual quest was *not* in fundamental opposition to traditional organized religion. This new religiosity opposed only the doctrinaire, dogmatic, and authoritarian nature of religions as *institutions*.

In 1994, a Roper poll revealed that 69 percent of Americans felt that "religion as a whole was losing its influence on U.S. life." This sentiment was reflected in steadily declining figures for attendance at religious services—despite repeated predictions by church leaders of an impending upsurge in religious observance. In 1996, 37 percent of Americans were attending weekly religious services, down from 49 percent in 1991.

In the new world of creative capitalism, only those corporations capable of reengineering themselves to meet the new global needs and demands would survive. So it was with organized religion. Only those religious institutions capable of reengineering themselves and returning to their spiritual source thrived.

Renaissance spirituality was directed toward the attainment of a higher (or divine) state of consciousness. This was originally the basis of all traditional religions and shamanistic societies. Throughout history, human beings had understood that life had a meaning, collectively and individually. Over the course of the Industrial Age, this understanding had been lost, blurred, or conquered by belief in Theo-economy.

The reestablishment of that understanding—that life had a meaning—made the global Renaissance possible. When the movement reached critical mass, it meant the establishment of a civilization that encouraged and furthered the quest for consciousness among its individuals. The circle was complete. The individual will and the collective will coincided. It was an era of intense individuality, directed toward a common good.

People reclaimed their lives, and regained their dignity. It was as simple as that—and as complex: a society in which the majority had the opportunity to express their own inner creativity through the practice of "right livelihood."

Right livelihood means earning a living doing something that provides inner joy and that in some way, big or small, helps others. It is right livelihood that gives real and lasting satisfaction and that nourishes the soul.

People, many people, were creating new inner worlds for themselves. With the world inside changing for the better, the outer world changed with it.

And, like the Renaissance in Europe of the fourteenth through seventeenth centuries, the global Renaissance became an era of rich intellectual, artistic, philosophical, and scientific achievement—a period of genius in the world's history.

In 1995, leading-edge scientists of the Society for Scientific Exploration were proving that mind and will can influence matter. In controlled laboratory experiments conducted at the Princeton Engineering Anomalies Research Laboratory, subjects were producing nonrandom results in random processes, just by thinking. In layman's language, by thinking "tails" it was possible to influence the toss of a coin.

The implications of these experiments are staggering. If

mind can affect matter, it means that what human beings think and feel matters. Not only the individual human life, but by extension the life of all society—and even the planet itself—must respond to thoughts, will, and emotion.

Think hate, fear, power, control, and a society based on hate, fear, power, and control will surely be the result. Think love, freedom, peace, and contact with the gods, and a society that reflects those thoughts will surely be the result. But the process is not automatic. Without action it doesn't happen. The most important resource we have is the power of the mind . . . and the ability to manifest that power through action. "Seize the moment. Whatever you can do, or dream you can, begin it. Boldness has genius, power, and magic in it," said Goethe.

America was re-creating itself in an image closer to the vision of the Founding Fathers than the America the Founding Fathers had created.

On January 1, 2000, it was not yet apparent to everyone that light was being woven into the dark and violent backdrop of destructive and devolutionary trends. Yet it would not be so very long before the golden threads of Renaissance thought, emotion, and values took command of the new millennium tapestry.

Ideas had changed. People changed. Everything changed. The Global Age was born.

NOTES

CHAPTER 2

THE MEANING OF THE MILLENNIUM

PAGE 9—The Century is dead . . . *New York Times,* January 1, 1901.

PAGE 13—There is a certain . . . Georgio de Santillana and Hertha von Dechend, *Hamlet's Mill,* David Godine; Graham Hancock, *Fingerprints of the Gods,* Crown; Rand and Rose Flem-Ath, *When the Sky Fell,* St. Martin's Press; Robert Bauval, *The Orion Mystery,* Crown.

CHAPTER 3

SEEING INTO THE FUTURE

PAGE 21—"If we're successful . . ." *USA Today,* April 13, 1995.

CHAPTER 4

THE MORNING AFTER

PAGE 28—One in three said . . . Northwestern National Life Insurance Poll, *Focus* magazine, May 1, 1995.

PAGE 28—"Stress related problems . . ." *USA Today,* February 28, 1994.

PAGE 28—Fifty-two percent of Americans . . . Harris Research, November 14, 1994.

PAGE 29—High-tech corporations . . . Associated Press, September 15, 1994.

PAGE 30—In one week of January 1995 . . . Tyndall Report, January 27, 1995.

PAGE 31—Rather scolded news media . . . Radio and Television News Directors Association, September 29, 1993.

PAGE 31—Even as people submitted . . . *Wall Street Journal,* December 14, 1994.

PAGE 33—But if it's obvious why . . . *USA Today,* April 1, 1993.

CHAPTER 5

QUACKENOMICS

PAGE 35—Between 1990 and 1992 . . . *Wall Street Journal,* January 25, 1995.

PAGE 35—Real wages for 75 percent . . . *Extra,* January/February, 1995.

PAGE 36—Between 1989 and 1993 . . . Associated Press, November 17, 1994.

PAGE 36—Department of Labor reports showed . . . *New York Times,* August 16, 1994.

PAGE 36—The Commerce Department reported . . . U.S. Department of Commerce, December 1995.

PAGE 37—According to studies . . . *New York Times,* June 4, 1995.

PAGE 39—The *Wall Street Journal* crooned . . . *Wall Street Journal,* March 31, 1994.

PAGE 39—"Since we believe . . ." *Wall Street Journal,* March 31, 1994.

PAGE 39—Two days later . . . *Poughkeepsie Journal,* April 8, 1994.

PAGE 39—William Dunkelburg . . . Associated Press, May 24, 1994.

PAGE 41—The net result . . . Associated Press, February 29, 1996.

PAGE 42—"A Gannett News Service . . ." Gannett News Service, February 22, 1994.

PAGE 43—Professor Rudi Dornbusch . . . *Wall Street Journal,* January 6, 1995.

PAGE 44—Mexico had been called . . . Associated Press, January 22, 1995.

PAGE 44—"A 'catalytic impact . . .' " *New York Times,* January 26, 1995.

PAGE 44—According to . . . *New York Times,* January 12, 1996, p. A21.

PAGE 45—" 'Once the financial crises . . .' " Associated Press, January 22, 1995.

PAGE 45—" 'I know no one . . .' " *New York Times,* January 27, 1995.

PAGE 46—"So we have done . . ." *New York Times,* February 22, 1995.

PAGE 47—" 'With the signing of this agreement . . .' " *New York Times,* February 22, 1995.

PAGE 48—By 1995, over a trillion dollars . . . Associated Press, April 24, 1995.

PAGE 51—According to a 1993 study . . . *Poughkeepsie Journal,* March 23, 1993.

CHAPTER 6

BACK IN THE USSR

PAGE 54—" 'I think Yeltsin . . .' " Associated Press, January 21, 1994.

PAGE 55—"Russia is still . . ." *New York Times,* December 11, 1994.

PAGE 55—"As Russia's only . . ." *The Trends Journal,* Spring 1993.

PAGE 55—"Our aim has been . . ." *USA Today,* January 3, 1995.

PAGE 55—Russian newspapers compared . . . *USA Today,* January 3, 1995.

PAGE 56—Bob Dole said . . . *Face the Nation,* January 1, 1995.

PAGE 61—"Dressed in combat fatigues . . ." *New York Times,* January 21, 1995.

PAGE 62—"We are ready to fight . . ." *USA Today,* January 4, 1995.

CHAPTER 7

FROM MELTDOWN TO MAYHEM

PAGE 65—Whether it's Ford . . . *New York Times,* April 26, 1996.

PAGE 65—. . . or Intel manufacturing . . . *Wall Street Journal,* April 13, 1995.

PAGE 65—In 1995 there were 432 . . . *Wall Street Journal,* April 27, 1995.

PAGE 74—A 1994 Harris Poll . . . Louis Harris and Associates, Inc. 1994.

PAGE 74—Victims of the experiments . . . *New York Times,* July 13, 1995.

CHAPTER 8

THE FALLOUT FROM FALLOUT

PAGE 79—The cancer rate had been soaring . . . *USA Today,* September 30, 1994/Associated Press, September 29, 1994.

PAGE 81—"Americans did not fight . . ." *New York Times,* January 4, 1991.

PAGE 82—"In 1996, Congress . . ." "Where Your Income Tax Money Really Goes," War Resistance League, No. 714, 1996.

PAGE 83—A February 1995 poll showed . . . *USA Today,* April 13, 1995.

PAGE 84—Just as environmental protection . . . *In These Times,* February 6, 1995.

PAGE 84—" 'It's clear from . . .' " Associated Press, January 25, 1995.

PAGE 85—Ninety-one percent said . . . *Poughkeepsie Journal,* August 21, 1994.

PAGE 88—(Ironically, these special-interest groups . . . Associated Press, April 13, 1995.

CHAPTER 9

SURVIVAL KIT FOR THE MILLENNIUM

PAGE 90—But with 71 percent of Americans . . . *Poughkeepsie Journal,* February 27, 1995.

PAGE 90—But however real the trend . . . *USA Today,* August 10, 1993.

PAGE 90—Millions in the eighties . . . *USA Today,* August 10, 1993.

PAGE 91—"It's a myth . . ." *New York Times,* February 3, 1993.

PAGE 91—Actually, the percentage of people . . . Associated Press, December 8, 1994.

PAGE 91—The wealthy and educated . . . *USA Today,* July 8, 1993.

PAGE 91—The majority actually lost . . . *New York Times,* November 11, 1994.

PAGE 91—Even American kids . . . Associated Press, November 10, 1994.

PAGE 92—Former Surgeon General C. Everett Koop . . . Gannett News Service, February 6, 1995.

PAGE 92—Even as they became more conscious . . . Associated Press, January 11, 1995.

PAGE 93—In 1993, American industries . . . Associated Press, March 28, 1993.

PAGE 102—Also responding to the study's . . . *USA Today,* October 19, 1994.

PAGE 102—In the U.S. . . . Beverage Marketing Corp., *Bottled Water in the U.S.,* 1996 edition.

PAGE 103—The world will spend . . . Associated Press, August 6, 1995.

PAGE 103—"A new Finnish study . . ." Associated Press, August 21, 1994.

CHAPTER 10

NEW MILLENNIUM MEDICINE

PAGE 112—Thirty-seven percent of people . . . Public Citizens, "Worst Pills, Best Pills," 1994.

PAGE 114—Even so, only a small percentage . . . John Robbins, *Diet for a New America,* William Morrow.

PAGE 115—By 1995, one-third . . . *New York Times,* February 7, 1996.

PAGE 115—It allocated $2 million . . . *New York Times,* March 16, 1993.

PAGE 115—"You heard of the tail . . ." *New York Times,* March 16, 1993.

PAGE 118—In 1994, the five leading insurers . . . *New York Times,* April 2, 1996.

PAGE 118—Financially, this standardized . . . *New York Times,* April 11, 1995.

CHAPTER 11

LIVING LONGEVITY

PAGE 126—In 1995, vitamins/supplements constituted a . . . *Vitamin Retailer Magazine,* 1995.

PAGE 126—. . . which was growing . . . *New York Times,* June 17, 1996.

PAGE 128—KELLOGG'S INTRODUCES NEW CEREAL . . . Associated Press, November 11, 1994.

PAGE 128—In 1995, four percent . . . Organic Food Production Association.

PAGE 128—Between 1980 and 1992 . . . Associated Press, April 16, 1994.

PAGE 129—Seventy percent of winter fruits . . . *Wall Street Journal*, May 22, 1995.

PAGE 129—More than twenty thousand chemicals . . . *Poughkeepsie Journal*, July 25, 1985.

PAGE 130—Every year in the U.S. there are . . . *USA Weekend*, January 7, 1996/*Mother Jones*.

PAGE 130—Over two billion pounds . . . *USA Today*, June 24, 1993.

PAGE 130—Altogether, four hundred types . . . *New York Times*, October 10, 1993.

PAGE 130—"PESTICIDES FAR MORE HARMFUL . . ." Associated Press, June 7, 1996.

PAGE 131—While only 1.5 percent . . . *USA Today*, July 1, 1993.

PAGE 131—"They are one of the few . . ." *Wall Street Journal*, July 8, 1994.

PAGE 132—Organically grown fruits . . . *New Age Journal*, March/April 1994.

PAGE 132—Here, new markets . . . *USA Today*, May 2, 1995.

PAGE 133—The average American child . . . *New York Times*, December 15, 1994.

PAGE 133—For the 1.6 million children . . . *USA Today*, May 20, 1994.

PAGE 133—Nearly 15 percent of the meals . . . Trends Research Institute.

PAGE 134—Two million acres per year . . . Gannett News Service, July 13, 1993.

PAGE 134—In 1994, the U.S. Census Bureau . . . *Poughkeepsie Journal*, October 9, 1993.

PAGE 137—Children have a higher . . . *New York Times*, October 10, 1993.

PAGE 138—Less than one percent of all produce . . . *USA Today*, June 24, 1993.

PAGE 138—" 'The EPA already . . .' " *USA Today*, June 24, 1996.

PAGE 138—A story headlined "THE FOOD FIGHT . . ." *USA Today*, June 24, 1993.

PAGE 138—"Most people don't have time . . ." *USA Today*, June 24, 1993.

PAGE 140—With three teaspoons of sugar . . . *USA Today*, August 17, 1994.

CHAPTER 12

TECHNOTRIBALISM

PAGE 148—In his 1995 book, *In Retrospect: The Tragedy and Lessons of Vietnam . . . USA Today,* April 10, 1995.

PAGE 149—In April 1995, President Clinton . . . *Time,* May 15, 1995.

PAGE 151—"The American political system . . ." *Chicago Tribune,* May 15, 1995.

PAGE 152—"The Cato Institute calculates . . ." *New York Times,* April 5, 1995.

PAGE 152—Asked if these . . . *Poughkeepsie Journal,* September 20, 1995.

PAGE 156—In 1988, according to . . . *American Demographics,* December 1988.

PAGE 156—By 1995, this figure had swelled . . . *Poughkeepsie Journal,* April 30, 1995/Link Resources, 1996.

PAGE 157—A mighty $25 billion dollar . . . *Wall Street Journal,* May 9, 1994.

PAGE 157—By 1995, 10 million employees . . . *Wall Street Journal,* June 19, 1995.

PAGE 158—In 1995, Link Resources Corp . . . *Poughkeepsie Journal,* Sunday, April 30, 1996.

PAGE 159—More than 3 million . . . *USA Today,* March 22, 1994.

PAGE 159—(A small but positive . . . *Wall Street Journal,* December 29, 1993.

CHAPTER 13

INVOLUNTARY VOLUNTARY SIMPLICITY

PAGE 162—" 'Everyone has a sense . . .' " *New York Times,* May 1, 1994.

PAGE 164—To put the matter into . . . Graef Crystal, University of California, HAAS School of Business.

PAGE 164—In 1993, IBM laid off . . . *USA Today,* July 27, 1993.

PAGE 164—Despite the most extensive . . . Gannett News Service, May 16, 1995.

PAGE 165—Those who lost jobs . . . U.S. Department of Labor, 1995.

PAGE 167—By 1995, 25 million . . . *USA Today,* April 29, 1996.

PAGE 172—In 1996, 12 percent of downsized . . . *USA Today,* April 29, 1996.

P_AGE 174—To maintain a fifty-thousand-dollar . . . *Bloomberg Business News,* May 22, 1995.

P_AGE 174—According to a 1993 . . . Associated Press, May 15, 1995.

P_AGE 174—Two-thirds of the . . . Kate Blackwell and Karen Fergusun, *Pensions in Crises,* Arcade.

CHAPTER 14

REENGINEERING THE HOME

P_AGE 178—Home garden-oriented . . . *Fortune,* May 29, 1995.

P_AGE 179—The conversion of millions . . . *Time,* January 7, 1994.

P_AGE 179—The seventy million pounds . . . Gannett News Service, May 15, 1994.

P_AGE 179—A modest twenty-by-thirty foot . . . *The Complete Book of Edible Landscaping,* Rosalind Creasy, Sierra Club Books.

P_AGE 183—By 1995, the gross . . . *Wall Street Journal,* February 13, 1995.

P_AGE 183—"There is practically nothing . . ." *Wall Street Journal,* February 13, 1995.

P_AGE 185—In 1994, home health aides . . . Staffing Industry Report, May 15, 1995.

P_AGE 186—Home improvement and remodeling . . . Associated Press, May 16, 1995.

P_AGE 188—An estimated twenty-five million . . . Gannett News Service, April 30, 1995.

P_AGE 189—Not all of the newly discovered . . . Associated Press, June 6, 1995.

P_AGE 191—In 1995, recyclers paid . . . *USA Today,* April 17, 1996.

P_AGE 191— . . . old newspaper was selling . . . *USA Today,* August 18, 1995.

CHAPTER 15

COMMUNITY SPIRIT

P_AGE 196—In 1980, there were . . . *USA Today,* June 9, 1995.

P_AGE 196—Microbakeries grinding their own . . . *USA Today,* June 9, 1995.

P_AGE 196—Great Harvest, a franchise . . . *USA Today,* June 9, 1995.

P_AGE 197—So great was . . . *Wall Street Journal,* August 8, 1996.

P_AGE 199—Between 1993 and 1995 . . . *USA Today,* June 13, 1995.

CHAPTER 16

FAMILY VALUES

PAGE 207—In the mid-1990s, according to . . . Associated Press, May 28, 1993.

PAGE 208—Although, according to . . . *USA Today,* August 8, 1996.

PAGE 208—Generation X . . . *USA Today,* September 23, 1993.

PAGE 208—In 1995, the total federal budget . . . *New York Times,* March 26, 1994.

PAGE 209— . . . U.S. Senators . . . *USA Today,* May 18, 1994.

PAGE 209—Polls showed . . . Associated Press, May 23, 1995.

PAGE 209—Nevertheless, Washington . . . Associated Press, March 7, 1995.

PAGE 210—Mining operations alone . . . *New York Times,* April 27, 1993.

PAGE 210—Taxpayers face . . . *USA Today,* November 23, 1993.

PAGE 212—The last U.S. budget . . . *USA Today,* February 8, 1994.

PAGE 212—The percentage of Federal . . . *USA Today,* April 15, 1996.

PAGE 212—Profligate government spending . . . Joel Kurtzman, *The Death of Money,* Little, Brown & Co.

PAGE 212—After adjusting for inflation . . . Joel Kurtzman, *The Death of Money,* Little, Brown & Co.

PAGE 212—In 1960, 19 percent . . . *USA Today,* September 2, 1993.

PAGE 212—More than half of all marriages . . . *New Age Journal,* September/October, 1994.

PAGE 212—The Parent Teacher Association . . . *New York Times,* May 9, 1988.

PAGE 213—Only half of the 66 million . . . *New York Times,* August 30, 1994/*USA Weekend,* April 26–28, 1996.

PAGE 213—Overall, 77 percent . . . *Wall Street Journal,* June 11, 1993.

PAGE 214—It was a time of unparalleled . . . *New York Times,* October 5, 1993.

PAGE 216—Countless families . . . *USA Today,* November 10, 1993.

PAGE 217—He said: "Every gun that is made . . ." From a speech before the American Society of Editors, April 16, 1953.

PAGE 218—In response to . . . *Wall Street Journal,* March 17, 1993.

PAGE 219—In 1991, 33.4 million . . . *New York Times,* August 30, 1994.

PAGE 219—Nearly 50 percent of couples . . . *New York Times,* July 6, 1995.

PAGE 219—In 1993, 27 percent . . . Associated Press, July 20, 1995.

PAGE 219—Between 1960 and 1995 . . . *Wall Street Journal,* March 17, 1993.

PAGE 219—In 1995, according to . . . *USA Today,* March 13, 1996.
PAGE 219—In 1993, 23.6 million . . . *Wall Street Journal,* July 6, 1995.

CHAPTER 17

FORWARD TO THE PAST

PAGE 226—Driven initially by . . . *Wall Street Journal,* May 12, 1993.
PAGE 226—By 1995, working women . . . *Poughkeepsie Journal,* May 14, 1995.
PAGE 226—According to a report . . . *USA Today,* April 12, 1995.
PAGE 227—By the year 2010 . . . U.S. Census Bureau, April 1996.
PAGE 228—First developed in Denmark . . . *New York Times,* February 25, 1993.
PAGE 229—By 1996 there were . . . *Wall Street Journal,* February 26, 1996.
PAGE 230—As a group, the high-techies . . . *Wall Street Journal,* February 21, 1995.
PAGE 230—Overall, your generation . . . *New York Times,* September 26, 1993.
PAGE 230—In 1973, 23 percent . . . *New York Times,* September 26, 1993.
PAGE 230—In the first half . . . Associated Press, July 7, 1995.
PAGE 232—The outlook is bleakest . . . *USA Today,* February 15, 1994.
PAGE 232—In the mid-1990s, 45 percent . . . *USA Today,* February 12, 1993.
PAGE 235—In 1994, 44 percent . . . *Wall Street Journal,* March 7, 1994.

CHAPTER 18

INTERACTIVE U.

PAGE 239—About 30 percent . . . *New York Times,* February 16, 1988.
PAGE 239—Twenty-seven million . . . *New York Times,* February 20, 1988.
PAGE 239—The Institute for . . . *New York Times,* February 20, 1988.
PAGE 240—The Carnegie Foundation for . . . *Poughkeepsie Journal,* August 24, 1983.
PAGE 240—Albert Shanker . . . *New York Times,* August 13, 1983.
PAGE 240—Washington responded . . . *Poughkeepsie Journal,* April 24, 1988.
PAGE 240—"I tried to convince the President . . ." *Poughkeepsie Journal,* April 24, 1988.
PAGE 240—Ten years later . . . *Wall Street Journal,* October 16, 1994.

PAGE 241—A 1989 report . . . *USA Today,* July 19, 1994.

PAGE 242—"Schools have been . . ." *New York Times,* April 28, 1993.

PAGE 243—By 1993, taxpayers . . . *Poughkeepsie Journal,* May 27, 1993.

PAGE 244—Though Parochial School . . . *USA Today,* May 7, 1993.

PAGE 245—Their enrollment fell . . . *USA Today,* February 28, 1994.

PAGE 246—Enrollment rose steadily . . . *USA Today,* December 7, 1993.

PAGE 247—By 1995, a four-year education . . . *New York Times,* December 25, 1994.

PAGE 247—In 1994, less than half . . . *New York Times,* December 25, 1995.

PAGE 253—In 1996, an estimated . . . *USA Today,* January 9, 1996.

PAGE 255—In 1994, total public . . . *USA Today,* September 3, 1993.

CHAPTER 19

UNCIVIL WAR

PAGE 263—President Clinton signed . . . *Wall Street Journal,* July 24, 1995.

PAGE 264— . . . the 91 percent . . . *USA Today*/CNN/Gallup Poll, February 17, 1994.

PAGE 267—The first shell . . . *The Trends Journal,* Summer 1995.

PAGE 267—Greenpeace Commandos . . . *The Trends Journal,* Summer 1995.

PAGE 270—"The future prosperity . . ." Associated Press, June 6, 1995.

CHAPTER 20

THE STORM BEFORE THE LULL

PAGE 273—In 1996, sixty percent . . . *USA Today,* May 14, 1996.

PAGE 273—Eighty percent said . . . *La Stampa,* 1995.

PAGE 276—"A poll of 1004 . . ." *Quill,* July/August, 1995.

PAGE 277—"Hamas said . . ." *New York Times,* August 22, 1995.

PAGE 277—Governments have always . . . *New York Times,* August 6, 1995.

PAGE 278—"No. 1, there is no morality . . ." *New York Times,* August 6, 1995.

PAGE 278—"War and individual ruin . . ." Michael Fellman, *The Life of William Tecumseh Sherman,* Random House.

PAGE 280—"Our enemy today . . ." Associated Press, April 29, 1995.

PAGE 281—"I have opened the bottle . . ." Associated Press, June 26, 1995.

PAGE 283—In 1994, according to . . . Associated Press, June 10, 1995.

PAGE 283—Driven by bloodshed . . . *New York Times,* March 5, 1995.

PAGE 284—In the United States . . . *Poughkeepsie Journal,* March 13, 1995.

PAGE 284—Seventy-seven percent . . . *Time,* October 3, 1994.

PAGE 284—California's Proposition 187 . . . *USA Today,* November 7, 1994.

PAGE 285—A University of California . . . *New York Times,* September 6, 1994.

PAGE 285—Illegal immigration . . . Gannett News Service, September 15, 1994/*USA Today,* December 6, 1994/*New York Times,* June 9, 1994.

PAGE 285—Data from the 1990 . . . *New York Times,* January 26, 1994.

PAGE 287—Violent crime rose . . . *Poughkeepsie Journal,* October 3, 1994.

PAGE 286—The teenage homicide . . . *USA Today,* April 11, 1995.

PAGE 287—Between 1973 and 1993 . . . *USA Today,* November 22, 1993.

PAGE 287—In 1995, apart from . . . Associated Press, August 25, 1995.

PAGE 287—One private study . . . Associated Press, August 17, 1995.

PAGE 288—Proportionately, more crimes . . . Associated Press, February 17, 1995.

PAGE 288—"If you can get . . ." *New York Times,* August 10, 1995.

PAGE 288—(According to FBI . . . *EXTRA,* June 1994.

PAGE 288—By 2005, the forty million . . . Associated Press, February 17, 1995.

PAGE 289—"Nothing is going to stop . . ." *USA Today,* January 25, 1995.

PAGE 289—The percentage of . . . *New York Times,* August 10, 1995.

PAGE 290—The United States . . . *USA Today,* August 10, 1995.

PAGE 290—It cost seventy thousand . . . *USA Today,* February 7, 1994.

PAGE 291—Corrections today is a gigantic . . . *New York Times,* November 6, 1994.

PAGE 291—But boot camps produced . . . *USA Today,* September 28, 1994.

PAGE 291—Gun control was another . . . *New York Times,* March 19, 1994.

PAGE 291—The U.S. Justice Department . . . *The Trends Journal,* Summer 1995.

PAGE 291—In 1994, a *Los Angeles Times* . . . February 13, 1994.

PAGE 292—In 1994, private police . . . *The Trends Journal,* Summer 1995.

PAGE 292—The $70 billion . . . Trends Research Institute, 1995.

PAGE 292—Computer security . . . *USA Today,* March 6, 1995.

PAGE 293—Organized Mafioski . . . *New York Times,* February 20, 1994.

CHAPTER 21

RENAISSANCE 2001

PAGE 299—Already by 1995 . . . Associated Press, February 24, 1995.

PAGE 304—In 1981, only 155 million . . . *New York Times,* March 7, 1989.

PAGE 310—In 1994, a Roper poll . . . *Wall Street Journal,* December 2, 1994.

PAGE 310—In 1996, 37 percent . . . *USA Today,* April 4, 1996.

INDEX

THE TRENDS JOURNAL
YOUR PASSPORT TO THE FUTURE

Whatever you do, whatever your interests, *The Trends Journal* will help you do it better by preparing you to anticipate and profit from change.

The Trends Journal distills the voluminous ongoing research of the Trends Research Institute into concise, readily accessible form. By tracking 300 separately defined domestic and international trend categories including: business, economics, politics, social developments, education, health, science, technology, philosophy, the arts, entertainment, and fashion, *The Trends Journal* establishes the connections that others fail to see or misinterpret. Its Globalnomic® method cuts through the confusion of information overload and zeroes in on the trends that will shape the future.

■ Allows you to anticipate, recognize, and preempt significant changes in virtually every field of modern life.

■ Alerts you to the trends that motivate or that result from change and that will in turn shape the future.

■ Identifies short- and long-term strategies for profiting from trends.

Individual readers from every walk of life, along with small businesses, corporations, industries, trades, professions, educational and religious institutions . . . all can put *The Trends Journal*'s trend forecasts and trend analyses to practical use.

OTHER INSTITUTE SERVICES

The Trends Research Institute specializes in custom designing detailed trend forecasts tailored to the specific needs and goals of individual businesses, industries, and professional organizations. It is also the world's only organization that develops in-house trend-tracking systems for businesses and teaches trend tracking to clients. Institute Director Gerald Celente regularly delivers keynote addresses and seminar presentations to professional and academic conferences worldwide.

For information about the Institute, its services, and *The Trends Journal*, call 1-888-ON-TREND; e-mail: 73441.3516@compuserve.com; or write to the Trends Research Institute at: Salisbury Turnpike, Rhinebeck, NY 12572.